To Bobby

GOD BLESS THE U.S.A.

Biography of a Song

Lee Greenwood
and Gwen McLin

PELICAN PUBLISHING COMPANY
Gretna 1993

*The word "Pelican" and the depiction of a pelican are trademarks of
Pelican Publishing Company, Inc., and are registered in the
U.S. Patent and Trademark Office.*

Library of Congress Cataloging-in-Publication Data

Greenwood, Lee.
    God bless the U.S.A. : biography of a song / Lee Greenwood
and Gwen McLin.
        p. cm.
    ISBN 0-88289-905-8
    1. Greenwood, Lee. 2. Country musicians—United States—
Biography. I. McLin, Gwen. II. Title. III. Title: God bless the
USA.
ML420.G857A3   1993
782.42'16421599—dc20   92-39496
                                                        CIP
                                                        MN

Manufactured in the United States of America
Published by Pelican Publishing Company, Inc.
1101 Monroe Street, Gretna, Louisiana 70053

To all the patriots who have struggled throughout America's history to win and preserve our many freedoms, especially the countless numbers who have sacrificed their lives. These brave, dedicated men and women have left to us their legacy of liberty. They are the ones who have given us the right to say, "I'm proud to be an American."

PREFACE

Long after it was named Song of the Year by the Country Music Association, "God Bless the U.S.A." continued to move into the mainstream of American music. It was played at military and sports events, academic meetings, and scouting activities. It was being chosen by radio stations for their sign-off selection and it was even being used to conclude American naturalization services and other patriotic occasions. Finally, during Operation Desert Storm, radio and TV news reporters said that "God Bless the U.S.A." was the number-one requested song for our forces stationed in the Persian Gulf.

Often I was asked, "Why did you write 'God Bless the U.S.A.'?" When I decided to try to answer that simple question with a book, I thought about other songs I had written. Those lyrics, too, are expressive of my inner feelings, so they should be included.

"God Bless the U.S.A." started with an idea that evolved from my childhood days growing up on a farm, experimenting with my first faltering notes on the piano. It also stemmed from the respect, honesty, and patriotism that my mother and grandparents taught me. This was the beginning.

In this book, I was determined to give a taste of our country's own life story and the accomplishments of the many Americans who have helped to make the United States a world-respected haven of freedom.

7

So this is the story of the song "God Bless the U.S.A.," how its seeds were first planted, and where it has traveled since those earliest days in Nashville when it was struggling up the charts, on its way to becoming an American classic.

ACKNOWLEDGMENTS

Quite a few family members and close friends have taken the time to share their memories for this book about the song "God Bless the U.S.A." I wish to express my gratitude to my mother, Mrs. Bliss D'Antonoli, and her husband, Lewis, my sisters, Pat and Julie, and daughter, Kelly Greenwood Morris. For their invaluable help, I also thank Dan Bradley, Larry Lee McFaden, Ray Pillow, Jerry Bentley, and Kip Ingle.

Providing insight into the experiences of America's military sacrifices were Marine Terry Wildman, the parents of Vietnam MIA John Consolvo, Jr., Martha and John Consolvo, and Army Sergeant Allan Baker of the 101st Aviation Brigade, to which POW Major Rhonda Cornum was assigned during Operation Desert Storm.

A large measure of appreciation goes to many others for their advice and encouragement. But above all, I wish to thank my cowriter, Mrs. Gwen McLin, whose diligence and untiring efforts kept me motivated to complete this project.

Finally, I am especially indebted to Charlotte Sheedy for her early enthusiasm and to Dr. Milburn Calhoun and the staff of Pelican Publishing, whose belief in the viability of a "biography of a song" has made it a reality.

GOD BLESS THE U.S.A.
Biography of a Song

CHAPTER I

THROUGHOUT THE DARK AUGUST NIGHT, steel-clad "chariots of the desert" were on the move. Clouds of dust billowed up as the monstrous tanks lumbered across the sand, headed for a tiny, vulnerable nation.

Kuwait fell almost instantly. Rumors about the use of chemical weapons and lethal gas drifted along the airwaves as our listening world learned of Iraq's invasion. The news was ominous. But threats of nuclear warfare caused the most alarm for United Nations officials as they debated their response. Then the elite Iraqi Republican Guard and its army of over a million men turned toward Saudi Arabia, the next stepping-stone in Saddam Hussein's bid for control of the oil-rich Persian Gulf region. America's president called it "naked aggression." Solemnly declaring, "A line has been drawn in the sand," he gave orders for Operation Desert Shield, a massive mobilization of over 500,000 troops. Finally when Saddam ignored the mid-January UN deadline to leave Kuwait, Iraq felt the full power of our armed forces, along with military units of our French, British, Saudi, and other UN allies as they moved into Operation Desert Storm. It was a lightning-fast war. And the troops who had waited in readiness, then plunged into action, came home saying that the sound track of the Persian Gulf War was a song called "God Bless the U.S.A."

The 1991 rescue of Kuwait seemed like history being repeated, because during the year before I was born, the U.S. was drawn into a war in defense of liberty that totally changed the lives of millions of Americans. That conflict separated my parents and finally tore apart the Greenwood family.

Early on the morning of December 7, 1941, the first report rang out: "AIR RAID ON PEARL HARBOR. THIS IS NO DRILL." Suddenly the shocking news hit the airwaves that Japan had attacked Pearl Harbor. Only a few hours later, it was over. Nineteen ships in our Pacific Fleet lay shattered, or had been completely sunk, and the twisted remains of U.S. planes were scattered across Hickam Field. But most tragic of all, thousands of Americans had been killed.

We had been trying to stay out of the struggle. Japan had a strong ally, Germany. And during the past two years, Hitler's army had taken over Austria, Czechoslovakia, and Poland while other nations looked on, completely stunned. Then Norway and Denmark had been invaded by land, air, and sea. They survived only a few weeks. Holland and Belgium were next to fall. Soon France was forced to surrender, leaving British soldiers and pilots alone in defense of Europe. Now Japan's raid on Pearl Harbor had forced us into another global conflict, and the United States wholeheartedly took up the cause.

Helping to ease growing tensions on America's bases, Bob Hope had already begun his tours to lift the morale of our military personnel. While German planes and submarines were sinking Allied ships in the Arctic, Hope's talented singers, dancers, and comedians began venturing closer to the combat zones.

So I was born into a world at war, to a Navy family. My parents, Eugene and Bliss Greenwood, already had a little daughter, Patricia. But they wanted a son, and in 1942 they got one: Melvin Lee Greenwood, arriving on October 27 in South Gate, California.

My father was stationed aboard the *Trenton* and then on Adm. Thomas Hart's flagship, the *Marblehead,* where his favorite duty was playing sax in the band. Dad's shipmates started and ended their workdays to the sound of "Taps" from his bugle, so it seems natural that he married a girl with musical talent. She was a tiny, hazel-eyed beauty, an accomplished pianist. It was an ability that had come instinctively to Bliss as a child. Her only lessons had been on mandolin, but she could play the banjo and guitar, too. Early in their marriage, Bliss with her guitar and Eugene on his saxophone entertained in a local nightclub.

But Japanese naval forces were still capturing islands in the Pacific after his Navy tours were over, so Dad decided to join the Merchant Marines. That left my Mom with all the family responsibilities, waiting out the crisis of the war, and before long she found herself a job as a pianist with a small band. By daring to go out for late-night performances, my mother was flaunting tradition. In those days, that kind of woman was considered risqué. But rules for socially acceptable behavior could never hold Bliss back from playing music.

Mom was a fireball who stood up for her independence long before anyone ever heard of "women's liberation." She was beautifully petite, with sparkling dark eyes and flaming auburn hair. Although she was in love with her husband, life was pulling them slowly apart. Before long, as happens to many war-torn families, the separation became permanent.

My sister, Pat, and I found ourselves with our mother, who worked full time as a musician while still caring for her two little children. So when her parents in Sacramento phoned and said, "Bliss, you and the kids can come live with us," it seemed the only solution. And this is why Pat and Melvin, as I was called then, grew up as farm kids, working in the orchard and the fields, going to church, and having a routine that was scrutinized carefully by our grandparents, Edna and Thomas Jackson, with constant input from our mother.

In Sacramento, Mom had three jobs. It was a crushing schedule, but that affinity for hard work was an integral part of my mother's character. As a single parent, she was loving, but always corrective. She would command, "Melvin, comb your hair," or, "tuck your shirt in." Those words shot through the air like the orders of an overzealous Army sergeant.

But then she would give me a hug, look right into my eyes, and say, "Melvin, you look handsome!" And I'd be in tune with her again, hoping there might be a chance that this daz-zling extrovert would take me along when she went out, al-ways dressed in a gorgeous outfit and looking like a movie star. That would be a special treat for a small boy who idol-ized his flashy, almost recklessly attractive mother, who was by nature an unending seeker of perfection.

I was planted in California,
In the southern part of the state.
Before I was three, my mother took me
Just north of the Golden Gate.

Scenes of my childhood are hazy to me now. I only remem-ber the special occasions, and everything seems "larger than life." In reaching for the past, my mind flashes back to that Sacramento farmhouse and the family group that originally gave direction to my life.

In the eyes of this small newcomer, my grandparents' few acres seemed like an enormous spread of land. A long road looped through the heavily shaded front yard to the wooden, asphalt-shingled house. Right behind it was a small handy-man's dwelling, a windmill to draw water, and two high-ceilinged barns, with a grain harvester inside. There were a few pigs, three black and white milk cows, and a flock of chickens. The guard dogs were chained, one to each barn. Trixie was a little charcoal and brown fox terrier, and Turtle was surprisingly short for a black labrador retriever. They never bit anyone, but they would put up an earsplitting racket whenever a stranger strayed near the menagerie they pro-tected. What a funny-looking pair on guard duty! I can still hear the sound of those two barking like crazy.

At the same time that I was entering this new life in North-ern California, the U.S. was doing some pioneering of its own. Our engineers had been working on breaking the sound barrier since before I was born. No one was quite sure what would happen to a human being who was inside an air-craft traveling faster than the speed of sound. At an altitude of 40,000 feet, the pilot would have to withstand speeds of 660 miles per hour, as the shock waves crashed violently against his plane. Could a man endure such extreme pressure and survive? Chuck Yeager, an Air Corps jet pilot who had pitted his Mustang in dogfights against German fighters during World War II, was hot to try it. He had already felt the "pull of G's" during power dives, while maneuvering his small plane in a lot of sparring matches. Back in those days, Yeager's Mustang had vibrated, almost shaking apart, and he had to force the controls with all his strength to finally pull out of a dive.

Would a plane be crushed or disintegrate as it smashed through that invisible barrier? Here was a gutsy pilot hell-bent on finding out, and while I was about to embark on the untried ordeal of grade school, Chuck Yeager became the first man to travel faster than the speed of sound. When his Bell X-1 rocket plane hit the air at over six hundred miles an hour, America became the first nation to produce a piloted aircraft that could fly at Mach 1.

When I entered first grade at the age of five, there was a hollow feeling in the pit of my stomach. To tell the truth, being so young, I was a little bit lonely and scared. In Hagginwood Elementary School, a lot of times the city kids got their kicks from teasing all of us who came from the nearby farms. Even when I reached the fourth grade, I was still quite shorter than my schoolmates, and being labeled a farm boy made me feel very insecure. The quarter that my grandmother sent as lunch money was my ticket to pseudo-acceptance.

"You can't sit with us unless you give us your quarter," some of the school kids from the "in" group would taunt.

I would usually hand them my twenty-five cents just so they would let me hang out with them. It was worth it to me not to eat lunch, just to feel like part of their crowd.

How belittling that was! How demoralizing, and how destructive of self-esteem! It wasn't necessary. But I didn't find that out until years later.

As I was battling for a place in the isolated world of grade school, the larger world outside was getting into a much more serious fight. North Korea's forces started pushing down into

South Korea, and the United Nations sent troops to stop them. Although I was still too young to realize that American soldiers were being sent to that far-off area of turmoil, I was growing up with a fierce independent streak. By the age of eight, I was sure that I didn't want the name Melvin. A strong-willed little boy, I was determined not to be called Melvin for the rest of my life. Fortunately my mother, who by that time had remarried and then had gone through a second divorce, was the one I could turn to who would understand.

"What name would you like to have then, Melvin?" she asked.

"How about my middle name, Lee?" I smiled up, hopefully. Then, after a tentative pause, came the firm statement of a decision that had been hovering in my mind for many months: "I want to be called 'Lee'!"

The request seemed reasonable to her, and realizing that this was a serious matter in the mind of her young son, my mother took me down to the county courthouse, where she had my name officially changed from "Melvin Lee Greenwood" to "Lee Melvin Greenwood." As we were walking back through the high courtroom doorway, I can remember Mom looking down at me and softly saying, "It always was your dad's idea, anyway."

From then on I was called "Lee," although my grandparents never did get used to the change.

"Melvin," my sturdy little grandmother would call out, wiping her hands across the skirt of her oversized blue apron, "have you fed the cows yet, and watered my fruit trees? And don't forget Trixie and Turtle. They're depending on you. It's your responsibility. Then wash up for supper."

"Okay, Grandma," I would reply.

"Put your hands in your back pockets and pull your shoulders back," she'd continue, slapping me firmly below my thin shoulder blades. "Stand up straight!"

Brushing back her red hair, she'd turn and disappear again into the kitchen, my eyes following this older image of my mother. Mom was just like her in so many ways. In an instant I'd rush off, anxious to finish those daily tasks before suppertime. Then I'd have a few moments of freedom. And I'll never forget watching the spider building its net as the sun set, casting shimmering rays through each strand. Early the next morning, when I raced out to see if the spider was still there, I'd find its web decorated with dewy rainbows.

Although I was primarily raised by an iron-willed mother-and-daughter team, often at odds over child rearing, I was lucky also to have a loving grandfather. He was an intrinsically strong man, the typical American farmer. Usually dressed in overalls, he worked hard from dawn till dusk. Naturally, I was his number-one helper. Whether it was to drive the tractor or tear apart a motor or dig a ditch, my patient grandfather would be right there showing me how to do it. And he had a big double-barreled shotgun by the bed that was taller than I was, a really imposing weapon. So he taught me gunmanship and how to hunt. But I never really enjoyed shooting animals. "I don't like to see them fall, Grandpa," I told him.

"Your grandmother wants something special to fix for supper," he replied. "Let's see what we can find for her."

So we'd go out looking for pheasant in the field behind our house. On occasional cool, early mornings there would be a tall, easygoing farmer, closely followed by his eager grandson, stalking food for the table across the grassy meadow. These days were soon to fade as the fields of grain and corn that surrounded our property disappeared, along with many of the farms. Taking their place would be the new schools, homes, and blacktop roads of North Sacramento.

When I was young, I was kind of quiet, holding my feelings inside. But all the time I was absorbing my surroundings, and very early, music became a natural part my existence. No doubt, this feeling of kinship with music was inherited from my parents. But music had been a part of my environment from the beginning. After we had moved up to Sacramento, my mother bought a piano for the Jackson farmhouse, and I began to make my first stumbling attempts. Whenever Mom played it, her fingers flew confidently over the keys without an error. Her expertise was intimidating, but with shy hesitation, when I was about nine, I tried to be her pupil.

"No, Lee! Not that chord! You've missed a note," she'd say sharply. Before long it was, "No. No. Not that key!" Then in exasperation, "Your timing is off! Try it again, this time more slowly." Finally, barely able to control her patience, she'd plead, "Lee. Don't run the notes together!"

There was no way that the conscientious beginner and the accomplished pianist could find middle ground and become harmonious. This was definitely not fun! So I quit and began spending my time playing baseball.

Our lessons together had failed. But Mom still had a feeling that somewhere in her little guy there was musical talent. Remembering my father's ability on the sax, she brought home a surprise. "A saxophone for you, Lee," she smiled. "You might like this better than the piano. Play it, if you want to."

This time my mother wasn't putting on any pressure, but she was hoping her son was still open to music. Actually, I could barely keep my eager hands away from this shiny instrument. Sliding my fingers over each curve and experimenting with the notes, I blew into the mouthpiece with all the gusto my small lungs could manage. It was so easy to play. Self-expression and success! It was great!

The large radio in the corner wasn't on much of the time, so we didn't have music unless we created it. Maybe that was one reason I was drawn to it, and before long I was copying tunes that I had heard my mother play, music that seemed to be already in my head. I could memorize anything and play it all the way through after hearing it for the first time.

I kept on with the piano, too, only when Mom wasn't there because it drove her crazy whenever I hit the wrong notes.

But my grandparents didn't mind my mistakes. "Oh! Sorry, Grandma," I'd say, as I came down on a flat note. The sour tone was jarring as it rang throughout the house.

"That sounds fine, Melvin," Grandma would answer.

So I'd stay there for hours, practicing. Those times made me feel that music was something I could do, and feel good about it. Then after the sun set, leaving the room in darkness, there would be a hush, and that solitude let me be creative. I would still be playing the piano while my grandparents rocked in the cool breeze on the front porch. Without realizing it, I was learning how to play by ear, not needing to even see the keys.

My early attempts on the piano and saxophone carried over into vocal expression. On Sunday mornings I sang with the choir in the nearby North Sacramento First Baptist Church. It was fun to be there with other kids my age. All decked out in our black robes, we'd march to the rhythm of the organ music down the center aisle and then up into the choir loft, where we patiently suffered through the fire and brimstone sermon until it was time to sing. We were surrounded by a kind of music that was entirely new to me. I was learning about time signatures and about music that changes clefs all the time. This is where I was introduced to the majestic melodies originated or arranged by Bach, Mendelssohn, Handel, Haydn, and their more modern counterparts. These classic hymns were added to my slowly increasing repertoire of musical forms.

One afternoon near Christmastime, the choir director came up to me. "Lee, the Sunday night service calls for a solo. Would you sing 'O Holy Night'?" It was more like an order.

"Yes, sir," came my timid reply. And then, "It's a real hard song to sing. But I'll try."

From that moment, the upcoming solo was constantly on my mind. This difficult hymn requires a wide range and very high pitch. I practiced and practiced.

Finally the formal Christmas Eve service was beginning, as the congregation crowded into the brightly decorated sanctuary filled with twinkling lights. I marched in with the choir and almost held my breath as the prayers and sermon droned on and on. Then there was a heart-stopping silence, and I was standing before them, scared to death as I filled my small lungs and began the words, "O Holy Night, the stars are brightly shining. . . ."

In the holiday glow of the moment, my fears melted like magic. The melody kept building in a crescendo, as my clear young voice easily reached the highest notes. The grown-ups in front were smiling their approval, and soon I realized that I was singing the last words, ". . . O night divine."

A petrified little boy had made it through his first solo.

On the farm, the only playmate I had was Robert, who lived down the road. We were constantly getting into mischief. Like fledglings, we felt we could fly. We were indestructible. The innocent trees were challenges, waiting to be overcome. He and I were fascinated with stories we'd overheard about the victorious American fighting men. We'd climb the tall, leafy front-yard fig trees and then bail out like paratroopers.

"Stand up! Hook up! Geronimo!" And one of us would plunge to the ground.

Luckily I always survived, merely cracking my head open or suffering a superficial wound, which I'd carefully conceal at the day's end from the questioning eyes in the house. But, more than once, Robert struggled up from the dust to limp home with a broken bone, and we were in deep trouble. We were never to play paratrooper again!

Soon we developed a new interest, as we listened to the grown-ups discussing the latest weapon introduced into the field of warfare. Not understanding what this really meant, we heard that our country had just exploded its first H-bomb. It was less than a year later that the Soviet Union dropped the same kind of bomb. People started explaining how to design bomb shelters and talking about stockpiling food to last until the "fallout" had cleared. They even mentioned a "nuclear winter." But this grim picture was far beyond our comprehension. All we could imagine was how much fun it would be to live, like camping out, in one of those shelters.

So I was soon into Cub Scouts, learning survival skills, saluting the flag, and saying the Pledge of Allegiance. My budding patriotism was nurtured while I worked on merit badges and was taught to show respect for our country. And during those early years, I also joined Little League. This was my first opportunity to play with a team.

The Four Oaks players, all dressed in rubber cleats and grey uniforms set off by a red band on each sleeve, were determined to be winners. Pitching and fielding, hitting fly balls, and sliding into home plate, we were trying our best, and all of us were dead serious.

The hard part of being a player on the Four Oaks team was that neither Bliss nor Edna would let me travel to out-of-town games. On that one point they were in agreement.

"Hey, Lee. We need you to play. Why aren't you coming with us?"

All I could say was the humiliating answer, "My mom and grandma won't let me. But I'll be playing the next home game. Okay?"

When the Four Oaks won the regional championship and were ready to leave town to play for the title, I was crushed not to be going with my teammates. To be a part of a team effort was all-important to me. Even in junior high and high school, whenever I was asked to be on the school teams, my overprotective guardians refused to give their permission. Music was the path they wanted me to follow, and they urged me toward it with any available instruments and performance opportunities.

Soon I began volunteering for local Red Cross shows, and when I turned thirteen, my grandfather's brother Jake sent me his shiny silver saxophone. It was a proud feeling to have Uncle Jake's alto sax for my very own. Of course, I carried it with me when early the next Saturday morning our bunch of traveling entertainers left for another charity performance.

While getting ready to leave, the well-intentioned directors had piled all of us into one of those old Red Cross station wagons with the wooden paneling on the sides. We performers could barely squeeze in. Our shoulders were jammed together and there was a lot of giggling going on. With not one inch of extra space inside, the leaders stacked all the props and musical instruments in the slatted luggage rack on top.

Soon our whole troupe was happily bouncing along the rocky, twisting California road that led up the mountain to Weimar's emphysema hospital near the top.

All at once a loud, metallic crash on the pavement stopped our laughter. Instantly, the driver slammed on the brakes, pulled over, and brought the station wagon to a screeching halt. Climbing out to the roadside and gazing down the highway behind us, he said, "Lee, I've got some bad news. Somebody forgot to tie down your sax."

It had hit the hard road surface and was smashed beyond recognition. I was one heartbroken young trouper!

If there's to be a happy ending, I might add that, feeling responsible for the destruction of my saxophone, the Red Cross bought me another one. Uncle Jake never found out!

Throughout those years, my grandparents also let me perform professionally, as a member of small groups. A lot of times we played at dances for the American Legion and the Veterans of Foreign Wars. And we had music in school, too. At Las Palmas Junior High I played alto saxophone, clarinet, and drums.

Percussions meant power! Being a drummer in the Las Palmas Gauchos Marching Band brought the freedom of rhythm. "Pull out your sheet music for 'The Washington Post' and 'Semper Fidelis,'" our bandleader would direct, as we prepared for a parade.

Those two Sousa marches were stirring pieces, but it was our rendition of "The Stars and Stripes" that always brought out the patriotism of the flag-waving onlookers lined up along the avenue. As we marched past, with our heads held high, we could see emotions rising to the surface. The war in Korea had just ended, but over fifty thousand American soldiers had been killed. Although the fighting lasted only three years, it had been one of our country's bloodiest conflicts.

Playing in the band and orchestra with my friends at school was exciting. We were constantly being asked to perform for special occasions. And I guess it's natural for teenaged boys to try a few pranks, but during junior high I learned that if you do something wrong, you're probably going to get caught. Our orchestra had performed for the stoic PTA members one evening, and their meeting was still going on as we left the auditorium. Walking out through the large school doors, lugging our instruments, my favorite buddy and I were joking around. As we got to the school parking lot he came up with a seemingly wonderful idea. "Hey, let's let the air out of their tires," he whispered.

Under the tall streetlights stood rows of cars. Before long, while the parents continued their lengthy deliberations inside the Las Palmas auditorium, two young mischief-makers were hurrying from tire to tire, joyously watching each one slowly ease down to the asphalt as the air hissed away. We let the air out of almost all the tires in the whole parking lot.

"This is great!" I naïvely chuckled as my friend and I sauntered over and sat down on the school steps to wait for the results of our labors.

It was a comedy to watch. The PTA members began to emerge from the auditorium, and the ensuing scene was bedlam. The cluster of indignant grown-ups sent up angry shouts as they looked around the parking lot. They mumbled vile threats toward the unknown culprits: "Those juvenile delinquents will be caught and punished!"

Soon three or four tow trucks from the nearby service station began swinging into the lot. Out jumped their drivers, carrying pumps, and soon they were going from car to car, pumping up the flat tires. To the two kids observing their elders, hollering and screaming in outrage, it was hilarious.

But the next day, I found out that I'm no good at lying. Under pressure, I confessed and ended up spending a lot of afternoons after school in the principal's office, cringing under the ridiculing stares of my schoolmates whenever they walked past. It was a very important lesson to learn early on: don't hide your actions; just do the right thing in the first place. It sounds like the advice my grandparents had been giving me all along.

While at Las Palmas I formed my first band, the Moonbeams. Pat played the piano, and our trumpet player, Karl

Bernardo, couldn't keep his eyes off her. Mike Hartmann agreed to play clarinet, and Bob Starr joined me as the other saxophone player. Gary Hill on drums filled out the group. We were a sit-down band, all dressed up in Sunday clothes with little music stands in front, Glenn Miller-style. We guys were progressive-jazz oriented, and even went into jazz clubs, trying to sit in as musicians. Of course, being only in our early teens, sometimes we'd make real fools of ourselves.

There was one personally embarrassing moment. Mom was scheduled to perform with her quintet for a dance at Norte Del Rio High, where Pat was in school. They needed another saxophone player, and my mother was delighted to have her eighth-grader son come over from Las Palmas to sit in with them. Pleased that I was following in her footsteps as a musician, she had put her pride on the line with those folks.

In music you can learn a whole song, or you might know just part of a song. Musicians have different talents. Some can remember lyrics. Some can remember the artistic lines that make up a song, but may not necessarily be able to get all the notes. I knew little bits and pieces of many songs, but was still far from being a real professional.

Of course I was nervous, hiding my apprehension as I warmed up with her quintet. I listened to the three or four tunes they were running through, then nodded my approval at one of these, indicating that I could play it. The song was "Cherokee." I only knew the melody. I had never learned the bridge, the interlude between verses.

The group started out with this song, and my big moment had arrived. We were playing along, but when we reached the bridge, one of the quintet members glanced over at me and called out, "Take it!"

"Oh, no!" I thought as a cold shiver of stage fright tingled down my spine.

I was completely caught off guard, and soon I was totally lost. The more I tried to make my way through it, the farther out on a limb I became.

Well, my mother is a very emotional person, and she felt so sorry for me that she joined in, trying to help me through the bridge by playing musical notes that would lead me where she imagined I was going. Actually, I didn't know where I was going. But I was unknowingly leading her down an alley she couldn't get out of. Then she got tangled up, and the whole band became hopelessly lost. I'm not sure how we all ever got out of it at the end. But by that time, I was sure my mother was mortified. Feeling certain that her band wouldn't trust me with another song, I just looked at her and said, "Sorry, Mom." With my head down in dejection, I packed up my sax and left.

In spite of this experience, music was becoming the focal point of my life. Music was like a big wheel, taking me out into new places. But best of all, music was a way to escape from the house! Although I loved my grandparents, there was quite a generation gap. It was terrific to be out performing with a bunch of musicians, although I was always the youngest in the group.

As a kid growing up on the farm, I watched the adults around me, and this must have been when I found out about the dangers of alcohol. Mr. Jones, or "Jonesy," as we called him, lived behind our house and did odd jobs on the farm. He was a congenial old guy. But once a month, when his pension check came in the mail, he fell helplessly under the control of liquor and stayed soused for at least three days. Jonesy's spells of oblivion taught me what too much alcohol can do. When I was a teenager performing with bands in Sacramento bars, alcohol was everywhere and people offered me drinks all the time. But I really didn't like the smell of it, and it never even occurred to me to drink.

A similar reaction to cigarettes, around that same time, turned out to be beneficial. "Here. Take a puff!" Pat told me one afternoon while the two of us were walking home after school.

"Okay," I said, anxious to seem more grown up than my junior high years. Then I took one long, lung-filling drag. Coughing and sputtering, I managed to choke out, *"I hate this!"* So smoking became another habit I never started.

While realizing that I'd always be the youngest among my schoolmates, I was really looking forward to the ninth grade. Sacramento's junior high included the seventh, eighth, and ninth grades, so finally I'd be in that privileged group, the oldest kids in school. But just as I was getting ready for a year of being on top of the heap, my rising balloon of optimism was punctured.

My mother had married a wonderful man, Lewis D'Antonoli, who obviously loved her very much. They were moving to Anaheim, and taking me with them. I was delighted because we'd be living right across from Disneyland, a fantasy kingdom that had opened the year before. What I didn't realize was that Anaheim High School consisted of the ninth through the twelfth grades, and ninth graders were at the mercy of the upperclassmen. I would soon find out!

CHAPTER II

AT LAST THE TIME HAD COME for our move to Anaheim. As far as this thirteen-year-old was concerned, I was starting a new life. Even the journey down there was going to be like a Boy Scout adventure because my new stepfather and I were driving down together over an unexplored road.

"Hey, Lewis," I shouted out as my stepfather swung his pickup truck, pulling a small trailer, into the driveway. "I'm ready! When do we leave?"

"Just hold on a minute, Lee. Let's get packed up! It's going to be a long drive," he yelled back.

Lewis had loaded up the trailer with supplies for the hotel that he and his brother planned to build in Anaheim. Carefully, I placed my alto sax in beside some well-tied boxes. Then the two of us climbed into the truck and headed south out of Sacramento.

Rolling down the highway was a perfect time to get to know my mother's new husband. A handsome man with straight, black hair and light brown eyes, Lewis was impressively sturdy. For a little while, Lewis talked to me in his light Italian accent about his work as a missile electrician with the Air Force at Cape Canaveral, and about the stretches of sand dunes and sea oats that lie along the eastern part of Florida's coastline. The area sounded like such a contrast to the rocky highlands that we were traveling through. Then he glanced over at me and said, "Lee, you're going to like helping Salvatore and me build our hotel across from Disneyland. Our brother, Pasquale, is going to be working with us, too. Construction's a tough job, but it's rewarding, watching what you're working on as it goes up. It's a great feeling to look at a building when you finally get it finished. You've got that pride in accomplishment."

"That's pretty neat," I agreed.

It sounded good to me. I was anxious to grow and take on some weight. This was a new frontier I was headed toward, and I was plenty willing to work. I was really getting to like my new stepfather. He treated me like a man, not like a little kid, and I decided that he would be a great father.

As we continued, the road was straightening out, stretching toward Los Angeles while the radio blared out the sounds of everything from country to rock 'n' roll. Lewis knew I loved listening, so he let me turn the dial from station to station. All the hits seemed a fitting background for the journey to my new home—a California metropolitan area.

While Lewis and Bliss were getting our family settled into the Anaheim environment, I got a taste of what it was like to live in a big city. At Anaheim High, the freshmen were like first graders compared with the lordly seniors. Still two inches short of five feet tall, I hadn't gone through that growth surge that finally brings young males to at least a respectable height as they stand around the halls during those rowdy class changes, talking with bunches of smooth-looking girls. So entering high school for the first time was intimidating. The older students seemed alien to me. They were "cool" and in a culture all their own, like James Dean and Natalie Wood in *Rebel Without A Cause*. As I viewed my new schoolmates, I had no idea of how dangerous a school can be. But I got a small taste of it on my first day.

I didn't know anyone, and after one of the longest days in my young life, I realized that the school bus had left without me. How could I reach Mom to come get me? Being so new, I didn't even know the D'Antonoli phone number. So I was attempting to get it from the operator when three big seniors walked up. One of them grabbed me and muttered, "We can use your talent, kid!"

Threatening all kinds of bodily damage, he threw me in the backseat of an old Chevy. Finding two more defenseless newcomers, they pushed these terrified kids in on top of me, jumped in the front seat, and squealed off.

They drove us to a remote area. Then the three of us were jerked out of the car.

"Get to work, muchacho," snarled the biggest senior. "Wax this car. And do it right!" he added, forcing a half-dirty rag into my hands and shoving a greasy wax can in front of my face.

I glanced up at this gang of giants. There didn't seem to be much choice. One freshman stalled and stammered, "I don't want to wax your car." The other two guys snatched him up and began punching him in the stomach. "Okay, smarty. Then you can wax the engine."

Panic-stricken, the rest of us joined in, trying to help, hoping to make it out of this situation with a minimum amount of cuts and bruises. We were obviously no match for our tormentors. It felt just like being on death row.

Afterwards, fortunately, one of the seniors began to feel some sympathy for us. "Get in the car, you kids. I'll take you home," he announced. Without hesitation we scrambled in, and he made good on his promise.

To me, especially after this hazing, the seniors looked at least six-feet-nine. The only way to compensate was, like Avis, to try harder. The pressure was on to be an achiever, and this school did have a way for students to prove their ability. In physical education, we wore gym shorts that indicated our level of accomplishment. The tests were sit-ups, chin-ups and push-ups, running and hurdling, and swimming for distance and speed. Everyone wore grey shorts. But if they worked harder, they could move up into the blue category. The kids who went beyond blue graduated into silver shorts. But those with driving ambition could "go for the gold." Soon after I started in the Anaheim High program, through stubborn determination and effort, I was wearing the gold.

In spite of this, I would have given anything to be on the basketball, football, or baseball team. One day, on the locker room floor, I found a little gold football that somebody must have lost. So I picked it up, put it on a silver chain, and wore it around the halls. When some cute little girl would ask about it on the way to class, I'd give her a confident, big-man-on-campus look, straighten up a little taller, and casually say, "Sure, I used to be on the football team in Sacramento."

It was ridiculous, but I really ached to be on a team.

One of my salvations in Anaheim was Lewis D'Antonoli. Here was a continuation of my grandfather's work ethic, but on a strenuously physical level. He and two of his brothers were building a forty-two-unit motel across from Disneyland. The Anaheim vicinity was growing as a tourist attraction, and the construction business was booming.

The Jet Motel was going up on the corner of Ball and West streets. This structure, which was later renamed the Fla-mingo, was to be my testing ground, the outdoor classroom in which I learned about hard manual labor.

"You're strong enough to handle it," said Lewis. "Lee, you're in charge of maintenance on this job. See those pieces of board and broken concrete blocks? Be sure that they're all out of the way and neatly stacked over to the side."

Next it was, "These footings need to be dug so that the foundations can be poured. Lee, you jump on in that trench and start digging." Lewis was motioning to a three-foot-deep ditch that had a long way to go.

"See those avocado roots in the trench? They look pretty thick. They'll have to come out before we can pour this con-crete," he added. "Here's an ax, Lee. Cut through those things, and let's get them out of there."

Every afternoon after school, this is where I'd be, hauling de-bris, digging endlessly with a huge shovel, or chopping roots with a long-handled ax. Work like this will put some muscles on a teenaged boy pretty quick. It will also make him dog tired, and the hardest part was climbing out of bed in the mornings. But at school I was getting a chance to grow, musically. I learned how to play the tenor saxophone. It's larger than the alto sax, but by this time I'd grown big enough to handle one. So with this instrument, I joined five friends at Anaheim High to form a Dixieland band. Our group came out with all the popular tunes, a mixture of jazz, country, and rock. We just listened to the radio and played whatever we heard.

Although I was working hard in construction and with my band, life began to get a little wild. Mom was busy at home taking care of my new baby sister, Julie. But she was well aware that the teenagers in the Los Angeles area were involved in some risky activities. Drag racing at speeds up to a hundred miles an hour was the rage. It was dangerous entertainment, but even the death of James Dean, in the crash of his Porsche Spider between Los Angeles and Salinas, hadn't dulled our quest for thrills. All of us mourned for the actor who typified our feeling of being misunderstood. But adventure called, and I was learning a lot, maybe too quickly. At least it was too soon in the opinions of Bliss and Lewis. I had started staying out late with the seniors, getting caught up in their big-city ways.

The situation came to a breaking point one night when I "borrowed" their car without permission. I guess you could say that I stole it! At fourteen, naturally I didn't even have a driver's license. Also, I wasn't doing well in school. So as my ninth grade year came to an end, Bliss told me, "Lee, you're moving back to Sacramento with your grandparents."

"But Mom! I like it here!"

"The subject is closed," she said firmly.

This was not a democracy; it was a dictatorship! Soon I was packing for my return to the farm.

It was a far different trip than the trek that Lewis and I had made in his pickup truck. This time it was a lonely train ride. I felt desolate, like the first lines of "The Gambler" as he's riding the rails, seeing the stares of the other travelers, then watching them fall asleep, to the "clickity-click, clackity-clack" rocking motion of the wheels over the tracks.

First I explored most of the Pullman cars. Then I tried to while away the time playing solitaire with the deck of cards in my bag.

"Leaving Anaheim is the pits," I thought. "Here I am, being shipped back to Sacramento. Instead of coming up a notch in school, I'm going to be back on the bottom. Norte Del Rio is a three-year high school, and I'll be down in the lowest grade again." It was depressing.

While I was in Anaheim, my sister Pat had graduated and gotten married. That left me alone under the vigilant eyes at the farmhouse, and I wasn't pleased with the situation. My grandparents let me participate in sports, but still wouldn't allow me to be on the school teams. I wanted so much to be a team player, and the macho sports-idol image was probably something I longed for, too.

The image in the music world that grabbed me was the newest teen idol, Elvis Presley. Here was this good-looking young guy who wore a motorcycle jacket and slicked-back hair. Elvis was cocky, but he was so good at what he did that everybody loved him. Of course I was more reserved, but my hair was straight and dark like Elvis's. I identified with his style as a performer and drew upon his stimulating musical innovations, too.

It was during my first year at Norte Del Rio High that the Army picked up its most well known recruit. One of the guys at school was grinning when he said, "Did you hear Elvis joined the Army? Guess he won't be wearing blue suede shoes!"

"Yeah," was the comeback. "And he sure better not be telling his sergeant, 'You ain't nothing but a hound dog!'"

Even though he was only twenty-three, Elvis had already sold over forty million records, including his early song "Hound Dog" and the string of hits that included "Blue Suede Shoes," "Don't Be Cruel," "Love Me Tender," and "Heartbreak Hotel." But "I Just Want to Be Your Teddy Bear," released the next year, was the song that turned on the kids at school. Elvis was influencing my music an awful lot, but another steady source of inspiration was my high school music teacher, Fred Cooper.

Mr. Cooper was tall, thin, and only twenty-seven when I first walked into his classroom. He never let me get by without doing my best. In his band class, he gave occasional tests to see who would sit in first chair. The most capable player would get this honor, while the others sat behind. Although I had earned the first chair, I didn't have any idea of how to sight-read. Every time he introduced a new piece, I would take it home and learn it, note by note. So it was terribly embarrassing, one day, when Mr. Cooper put some music in front of me, and I couldn't play it. He just stood there, staring at me in amazement. Then he asked, "You mean you can't play this?"

"I don't think I can, Mr. Cooper," I answered. And it was soon obvious that I couldn't. I tried it and stumbled.

"Well, when you can sight-read, then you'll be back in first chair again," was his reply, as he motioned another student into my place.

So then I had to learn to do it. It took about three or four months of concentrated work at home before I was waiting after class to talk with him. "Mr. Cooper, I'm ready to take your test. I can sight-read."

"Fine, Lee. Let's give it a try," he answered. And it wasn't long until I regained the first chair.

Mr. Cooper was also the dance-band instructor, and he communicated with students on our level, joking with us all the time. This flexible six-footer allowed me to express myself, musically, as no other teacher had done before. He knew that I wasn't going on to college, although I was eligible for a scholarship to the College of the Pacific in either music or track. To make up for this, he tried to prepare me for whatever might come after graduation.

"Lee," Mr. Cooper said one afternoon after class. "I want you to sign up for my music theory class."

"Is there really a class in theory here?" I asked.

"I'm starting one," he stated simply. "You on that sax and your trumpet-playing friend are going to be the students."

It turned out to be a private class, during seventh period after most of the other kids had gone home. The two of us got what it might have taken two years in college to learn, thanks to Mr. Cooper. His music theory class turned the light on in my mind to aspects of music that I knew by instinct, but couldn't write down or describe. I began writing, arranging, and learning to play other instruments. I even tackled the big kettledrums so I could play timpani in the percussion section of our symphony orchestra. Mr. Cooper knew I had a goal, and he was anxious to help me excel.

Del Rio had a sharp marching band, too. In our blue and gold uniforms with all those gold buttons, the whole group presented intricate routines with flash and color that could be seen by an audience high in the stands. Our musical selections were strong, almost majestic. This very regimented music became a part of my writing background. But in those days, I had no way of knowing that it would influence the most significant song of my life.

Music was so easy, it was ego-building, and it was something that earned money. I was about fourteen or fifteen and was proud to be making from five dollars to twenty-five dollars a night. The musicians who hired me were almost twice my age, and I was holding my own with them. We usually entertained in dance halls or nightclubs. Back then, playing the saxophone throughout long nights, I still had endless energy. With only three or four hours' sleep, I could wake up and get through a full day at school, then go right back and do the same thing that night. And I could stay with this routine indefinitely.

The two bandleaders who kept me the busiest were Chester Smith and Del Reeves. A country and gospel star for Capitol Records, Chester Smith played the mandolin. He had a strict format, and his music was more easygoing than honky-tonk or rhythm and blues.

The more flashy group was led by Del Reeves, a famous guitar picker, singer, and comedian. A skinny, Ichabod-Crane-looking fellow, Del was a super performer and the funniest man I'd ever met. He kept joking and playing pranks all the time. The piano player used to jump up on top of the piano and play it with his feet. Seriously! People from all over the Sacramento area came to hear Del's group, wherever we were. Usually we'd be at the Rocklin Roller Rink.

(Rocklin is the name of a little town about forty miles north of Sacramento. Blink your eyes and it's gone!) It was a shabby-looking place then, but packed with feverish excitement.

Actually, it was a roller-skating rink with a turnstile out in front. Even when couples went in there to a dance, they pushed their way through this turnstile. All the musicians, too, just pushed on through into the room. In one corner was a stage, about three feet high, where the microphones were set up. Every dance in that hall drew huge crowds. Maybe a thousand people could pack in. They boogied and gyrated to our earsplitting music right there on the smooth skating floor, while Del's band played everything from country to rock 'n' roll. It was unbelievably loud in there, and we played all night long.

After an evening at Rocklin, it was hard to come down from the heart-pounding musical high. Back home, I'd lie in my bed, my ears still ringing from the hours and hours of blaring sounds. I could hardly fall asleep. But I didn't care. It was terrific to have the chance to do what I loved most: get out of the house and play rock music as loud as I could.

Another place where I sometimes worked was up near Rocklin. It was called Helvetia Park. All of us thought it had been named after the Hell's Angels motorcycle gang because of the fierce-looking gang members hanging around the area in their scarred-up black leather jackets.

Stabbings were part of the scene when I was playing with bands at Helvetia Park. Almost every time we were there someone would get knifed or beaten up. The neat game to play while we were up on the elevated stage in this big, old barn would start when one of the band members spotted a rat, carefully balanced, crawling along one of the rafters of the high ceiling.

"Hey, buddy. Can you take that one out?" he'd challenge.

"Sure. Watch me nail him before you do," another would yell.

The contest was on. Picking up empty beer cans, the opponents would begin hurling them toward the beady-eyed rodent, perched precariously above the huge room. As the crowd of dancers and music fans became aware of the action, they would take sides and make a few bets on their favorite.

Suddenly someone would shout, "Good-bye, Charlie!" and the rat, pawing the air, would fall like a rock.

Thud! Then there would be scratching of tiny toenails, if it was still breathing, as it scrambled across the wooden floor and out of sight.

This was a real tough place. The only reason I was sure I'd survive was that always, before I was allowed to go out with any group, my grandmother would take the leader of the band into our living room, and he'd have to sit down and guarantee my safety.

There was one fellow I worked with quite often. He was a very big, dark-skinned Mexican. When he closed his fists, plainly tattooed on the knuckles of those two huge hands were eight letters: *H A R D L U C K*. When I think of that rugged character, I can still see him hunched across from my small but stern grandmother, looking her straight in the eyes, promising that he'd have me back by a certain hour, that I would not get into any trouble, and that he'd protect me with his life.

"Or he won't be allowed to go with you next time," Grandma would solemnly remind him.

Hard Luck and other bandleaders needed me for the jobs. So they'd go through this little ritual, nodding their heads and assuring her, "Yes, Mrs. Jackson. Yes, I'll have Lee back at least by that time."

Sure enough, they'd have me there at the door. Grandma would be standing right inside, tapping her little foot, waiting up to make sure that they returned me safely and in perfect condition. I didn't have any problem with this because I wasn't interested in drinking or getting into fights. All I cared about was the sensational high that came from getting up on stage and playing music.

There was a drummer named Sal Salerno who played with us in Hard Luck's band, and Sal was in charge of me one New Year's Eve. We were playing at a nightclub down on the river in Sacramento. Celebrating the holiday with as much liquor as he could hold, Sal had gotten totally wasted and finally realized that he couldn't drive me home. He knew he had to; Hard Luck had told him that he had to!

The new year had been rung in hours before, as Sal stumbled toward his old Mercury with me in tow. "You're drivin' home," he slurred, as he motioned me toward the driver's side.

Not willing to admit that I had never driven a stick shift before, I slid my small frame beneath the wheel and took a look at the dashboard. I glanced nervously down at the stick shift. My feet barely reached the pedals, and I could hardly see over the steering wheel.

Taking a deep breath, I lifted the keys from Sal's unsteady hand and tried to get the car started. After a few attempts at getting the engine to turn over, we were out of the parking lot and rolling, at 2:30 A.M., just as the last bars closed down. In his inebriated state, Sal was trying to teach me how to drive. The shifting was going pretty rough as I popped the Mercury up to the I Street Bridge. Here the two lanes split off in a *T,* and I knew I had to go left to head toward North Sacramento. Glancing in my rearview mirror, I saw a policeman, following right behind.

"There's a cop back there," I muttered to myself, getting an even tighter grip on the wheel. I was concentrating with all my might to keep in the lane, and it was such a narrow road that if I went over that yellow line at all, we were going to take the mirror right off of a passing car.

Meanwhile, Sal kept up his drunken encouragement. "You gotta stay on the highway," he slurred. "You're doin' okay." He was really in bad shape.

Somehow I got the car up on the bridge, then nervously wailed, "It's sticking in this damn second gear!"

I wasn't doing so great at all. Then suddenly, I jerked it up to the stoplight. The policeman pulled his squad car right in behind our back fender. I was really worried. I wasn't even old enough for a license. If I got caught, I'd be in bad trouble, even though I was just trying to help out, at this late hour on New Year's Eve.

The patrolman gave us a long, mean look, while I held my breath, keeping my eyes focused straight ahead. But at last he eased past us and disappeared into the distant traffic. Somehow we made it to the farm in that Mercury, and Sal was real lucky to get himself home alive.

Hard Luck's group usually played at a tough bar downtown called the Tropical Cellar. It was down a steep stairway, off one of the back streets in Sacramento. Trying to look cool and casual, I would walk nonchalantly in with the group, wearing a suit and dark glasses so nobody could tell exactly how old I was. On breaks, when we finished a set, I'd go sit in a corner. Not wanting to be noticed, I'd watch as Hard Luck would go off to hit on some chick. They would disappear somewhere for a few minutes, but I knew he'd soon be back to keep a close eye on me.

"What'll you have?" the bartender asked one night, seeing me waiting all by myself against a wall near the stage.

"Oh, just some coffee will be fine," I answered, trying to sound grown-up about it. I was shifting my eyes around the seedy place just to make sure nobody was paying attention to me. I hardly glanced at the large mug and never noticed the steam rising from the coffee that the bartender had quickly poured and shoved into my hand.

"Thanks," I said, without looking up, nervously grabbing the coffee and downing it. Boiling hot liquid slid over my tongue and all the way down my throat. My mouth was scalded. In excruciating pain, I winced, reeling backwards and exhaling air from my lungs as hard as I could to help soothe my burning throat.

Back onstage, it was a suffering kid who struggled through the next set, playing that sax in blistering misery. I was just hoping to make it to the end of the evening, as my eyes caught the form of a grim-faced man striding up to the stand. Pointing at me and looking at my bass-player buddy, he shouted above the music, "Is this guy union?"

My buddy was a big, awesome figure. He just shrugged, turned toward the dance floor and kept booming away on his bass, totally ignoring the man. Not to be put off, the stranger persisted, still shaking his finger at me and pressing my friend. "We've got to know. 'Cause if he's not, he'd better sign up or you're playing non-union and this club is shut down."

Then, after a pause, "We ain't putting up with any infractions of union rules, ya hear?"

"Bug off!" my friend growled, leaning toward him with a menacing look. The man backed away and retreated up the flight of stairs.

Before long, another guy stomped down the stairs. Obviously Mexican, with slick black hair and a swarthy complexion, he swaggered up to our group and started yelling obscenities in Spanish. He was shaking his clenched fist and shouting right in my friend's face. Without a change of expression, as we continued playing the staccato notes of "Tequila," my protector turned to me and said, "Here. Hold my bass."

While I was playing my sax with one hand and holding his bass with the other, he stepped down from the stage and began to pummel the guy. I mean just beat him to a pulp. Then he casually walked back, took his bass from my outstretched hand, put the strap back over his shoulder, and started playing again.

This was a common occurrence. Anybody who hassled me got the same treatment, so nobody bothered me. I felt safe with a friend like that.

One time I had been asked to play with a rock quartet led by a guitar player named Frank. We had just finished playing a heavy-rhythm show for six straight hours. It had been an exhausting, but great, night. So I was in no mood to go right home. Putting out energy for that long makes you hungry, and it's always good to go have a breakfast in the early morning hours. This other kid, a talented steel-guitar player, and I were ready for food. Both of us were young; he was about eighteen, and I was still only fifteen. Frank, who must have been at least twenty-five, was taking us out for some well-earned eggs and bacon. This was after two in the morning, so the bars and cafés were almost empty.

Frank pulled up across the street from a lighted coffee shop and we began climbing out of the car. Just then, two guys walked up. They were menacing-looking dudes, and they wanted a piece of us. That's all there was to it. They were going to fight. Moving in on us, they confronted Frank, sizing up his lanky frame and long arms. Seeing no way to avoid the contest, Frank said, "Okay. But one of you at a time." And he stepped up to the biggest one.

These guys weren't tall, but they were plenty built, very stocky compared with Frank. We two younger kids didn't even measure up. Frank managed to beat up the big one, but in doing so he sprained his wrist. The other stud, still spoiling for some action, moved closer and said, "Now it's my turn."

"No. Look, I've hurt my wrist," Frank told him, "and I'm a guitar player. I'm through fighting now."

"Yeah. Well, you gotta fight anyway," he snarled back, making a grab for Frank.

By now I was ready to jump in, because this guy was going to beat up Frank for sure. Well, at that moment a gigantic hulk stepped out of the restaurant across the street. He must have been as tall as a house, six-feet-five or something, and 300 pounds. He had been watching the whole thing, the confrontation and the fight, through the window. Now he was shouting at Frank's assailant, "The man says he doesn't want to fight anymore. So hit the road!"

Without a word, the hood disappeared with his cohort into the darkness. Then Frank grinned at his two young musicians, and the three of us strolled across the street and into the little coffee shop for breakfast.

It seemed as if these things happened all the time, and it's amazing how many times I barely escaped getting my teeth knocked out or my head cut open. The environment had something to do with it. Alcohol or pot can put people in angry or depressed moods, and a smoky room usually adds to the feeling of unreality. Maybe the type of music builds up that antagonism. We played hard country and hard rock. It was often hostile music, and it fired up the crowds. Of course, that was our job: to bring up the heat. But a lot of times, deep down inside, I felt like an insecure young kid in a tough adult world.

CHAPTER III

FINALLY I STARTED GETTING TALLER and began to look at the world differently. It wasn't such an immense and formidable place after all. I began coming out of my shell of childhood timidity, and spurred on by this newfound bravado, I started testing the limits in the ways that many teenagers do. I've always been one of those who sort of races on the edge. The challenge is exhilarating, and although my grandparents wouldn't even let me out at night except for musical performances, I slipped out anyway.

A good friend of mine, Ted Hall, was my accomplice in after-hours exploits. He was tall; I was energized. We relied on each other for strength. Getting a kick out of testing our luck, we were seeing how close we could come to breaking the law without getting caught. We'd sneak out and be gone till all hours, exploring like a couple of rangers on the prowl. There was a ten o'clock curfew, and we'd ignore it. We'd dodge the police, quickly ducking behind trees or buildings whenever they drove by. These were rebellious times, and we were experimenting with defiance of authority during those fast-moving, careless years.

On the track at Norte Del Rio, I was the fastest guy in school. And Ted was pretty athletic, too. Anyway, we started becoming more arrogant and bold. So as we passed by a beer truck parked on the roadside one night, Ted had one of his bright ideas. "That beer truck would look better someplace else, and it has too many cans on it. What do you think, Lee?"

43

"Okay," I said. "Let's see if we can get her rolling."

Sure enough, the truck wasn't that hard to start, and before long Ted and I had it expertly placed in a secluded spot, where we stole as many of the six-packs as we could handle, and then left it.

At school the next day, Ted and I were carefree kings of the parking lot, selling beer to all the kids, who probably wondered how we had happened to come upon such good fortune.

Productive! Although they had always encouraged me to be gainfully employed, I don't think that's what my grandparents had in mind. But the next stunt capped it off.

One night, wandering as usual, long after curfew, Ted and I found a '53 Chevy in a quiet residential neighborhood. Sliding into the driver's seat, Ted found that it had a standard shift with three speeds. "She's got plenty of gas," he reported. "Let's take her for a spin."

The two of us had been pilfering a little, but we had no idea of the consequences of stealing a car. Kids in L.A. would take one for a joyride, burn it up and rip off all the parts, just for fun. We were simply going to take a little ride and then leave this Chevy somewhere after seeing how fast it would go. Ted started her up.

It was a very foggy night as we cruised past the houses near the high school, not more than a quarter-mile from my grandparents' home, and headed toward Norte Del Rio. When we reached the school and rolled around the corner in this heavy fog, the car lurched up over the curb and onto the school's lawn. Right there, parked in the circular driveway, was a squad car, its lights on and engine running.

"Oh, no! Be cool, Ted," I was half-whispering, hoping we could get by unnoticed. But he panicked, popped the clutch, spun the car around in a circle, and went tearing off the lawn. With a deafening screech, the police car pulled out after us. We could hardly see it in the dense fog as we bounced back down through the housing district, nearing the railroad trestle.

"Can we lose them?" Ted gasped desperately.

"There's no way," I answered, just as Ted pulled into a one-way street, with the police right on our tail.

"We're gonna have to ditch this baby," Ted shouted, pulling the hand brake and bringing us to a nerve-shattering halt. We were both already tugging on the door handles, and as the Chevy slammed to a stop on the train tracks, we used the momentum of the opening doors, as we hit the ground, to begin running.

The squad car squealed up behind us and jerked to a dead stop. Two huge officers jumped out and started chasing us. Ted went down the tracks, with a policeman in hot pursuit. As he reached the riverbank not more than two hundred yards away, Ted took a running leap and plunged in! Treading water for a moment, he reached for a reed and used it to suck small amounts of oxygen from above the waterline as he became totally submerged, waiting for the officer to finish his flashlight search.

Meanwhile, I fled over the railroad track. I knew I could run the 100-yard dash faster than anybody in school, but under the fear of being caught by the police, I flew like a bird.

Well, the space out in front of me was blurred. The night was still foggy white, and I really couldn't see more than three or four feet in front of my face. Somehow I found a familiar path, but it was hard to see clearly and, in my panic, I veered off to the left about six feet and slammed, at full speed, into a barbed-wire fence. The jagged wire caught me right across my face and chest, knocking me to the ground, flat on my back.

It was the only thing that saved me.

"The cop's right behind me, and he's got a flashlight," I thought, holding my breath as he dashed on down the path, right past me, and quickly disappeared into the fog. Bounding up, I ran back down the train trestle in the opposite direction and scurried across the field where I used to hunt pheasant as a child. Reaching the farmhouse, I eased open the door and tiptoed in.

By now it was one o'clock in the morning, and my grandparents were fast asleep. Creeping carefully, one step at a time, I slowly eased down the hall to my room and climbed into bed. Exhausted, I didn't even think about my bloody face and chest as I feel asleep.

The next morning, when I got up and looked in the mirror, I could hardly believe it! Staring at me was a bruised up and swollen kid, cut across the forehead, with dried dirt-stained scratches running perilously close to his eyes.

"What's Grandma going to say?" was my first thought. I was frantically trying to come up with some way to get out through the front door.

Quickly dressing myself, and casually holding one hand over half of my face, I walked into the kitchen and hurriedly said, "Grandma, I've got to be at school early."

Then I raced out to the porch, jumped on my bike, and disappeared down the road. My grandmother must have been standing there long after I was gone, wondering what was up.

Anyway, back at Norte Del Rio, Ted told me the tale of how he had avoided capture, and we laughed about the night before. We even talked about joining the Highway Patrol after graduation, and made a solemn vow that our "life of crime" was over.

Maybe I have a certain measure of rogue in my blood from unknown ancestors who lived long ago. The name *Greenwood* originated in England and has always been associated with Robin Hood. To "take to the greenwood" in olden days meant to hide out. Perhaps there was still a bit of that crafty fugitive left in this teenager until the final chase scene with the police. Robbing the rich to feed the poor must have been a thrill for old Robin, but this narrow escape had taught me that there's nothing romantic about being an outlaw. Right then, I decided that although I might follow the Robin Hood path of helping the less fortunate in other ways, I was turning straight and would never do anything illegal again.

That experience had a profound impact on me. I think it underscored the feeling that weaves itself within my spirit, an inner voice that says we should do right and obey our country's laws.

With the teenage renegade phase over, music took first place in my life again. Early that year I joined with some other musicians, and we formed a small band called the Apollos. Like always, I was the youngest. Eddie Lovato, our guitar player, was at least ten years older. With his Spanish background and dark good looks, he was a magnetic ladies' man. Eddie was a true friend and very understanding with this know-it-all kid, who had an ego that wouldn't quit. I had gotten plenty cocky by that time. But Eddie would work with me, keeping the band on an even keel. Don Reitz was our drummer until he had to leave the band. Then I called our drummer from the Moonbeams, Gary Hill, and invited him to join.

Our new member was extremely quiet, a good-natured guy. But he was plenty "vocal" on the drums. All we heard from him was the steady but imaginative beat coming from the drum kit.

Then there was Goody Javier, a Filipino and a really good man. Draw a happy face, and you've got Goody. His round, cheerful face always had a smile right in the middle. Goody was a fine musician, a woodwind player, and the two of us played twin saxes, a popular sound in those days. He could barely read music but was a perfect mimicker. He'd call the music that I had written out "papers" and he'd walk into our practice sessions saying, "You got the papers, man? You got the papers?" Then he'd start laughing, because his English was kind of rough. He shared my admiration of Earl Bostic's sandpapery sound and wailing style of playing sax. As I tried to imitate the hard-driving Bostic rhythm, Goody was right behind me, a perfect echo. But Goody had been in a bad car wreck some years before and still had a difficult time walking. Later, when the Apollos started playing dates on the road, Goody simply couldn't travel.

Bob Baumann was our bass player and a strong force on-stage. What a slapstick actor he was, with an outlandish collection of hats. When the Apollos met before a session, in would come Bob with another idea for the show.

"See all these?" he said to us one day, dropping a shaggy grass skirt, a straggly wig of straight black hair, and a pair of hairy coconuts. It was more of an announcement than a question. "This'll be super for the show. Lee, you've been talking about some Broadway play music. Well, we're going to do some of our own scenes from *South Pacific*. You can sing 'Some Enchanted Evening' and I'll be the Hawaiian dancer," he concluded.

Viewing Bob with his two coconuts in place along with the rest of his Hawaiian rig, we knew he was no compliment to the islands that were going to become America's fiftieth state in August. But as we cast a few doubtful glances in his direction, we took in the look of expectation on his hilarious, Buddy Hackett face, and we just broke out laughing. "All right, Bob. It's okay with us. But you're the comedian. Get up a routine and we'll work it in," we agreed.

It wasn't long before we found a much lovelier Hawaiian dancer. Her name was Momi, and she was a native of those islands in the Pacific. She would glide onto the stage barefoot, with orchid leis about her neck, lightly swinging her ginger-leaf skirt. Using her graceful hands and smoothly swaying hips, she shared tales of her islands accompanied by our harmonious instrumentals and blended vocals.

With the Apollos I began to develop as a singer, sometimes taking the lead. The first lead solo that I ever gave was "Mack the Knife," from *The Threepenny Opera*. It was a total copy of Bobby Darin. I was this little fifteen-year-old kid, with hair neatly slicked back, singing all the rhythms and snapping my fingers. I tried acting real cool like the gangster in the song, but before long I couldn't keep up that pretense and a smile broke out. The audience warmed right up to me. It was exciting—exhilarating! Somehow at that moment I had made a connection with them, and right then I knew that my heart was really into becoming an entertainer.

For now, it was mainly fun being a teenager. Most of the guys wore tight jeans like Elvis, with our collars turned up and our shirts open to the navel, even when it was cold. All of us were constantly defying the weather, trying to be hep. You were hep if you were one of the "in" group.

Turning sixteen, old enough to be a licensed driver, was an eagerly awaited milestone because as a member of the Apollos, I was always in need of transportation. Knowing I was working toward the goal of having my own wheels, my grandparents offered to help me buy a car. Of course, price was our main concern as the three of us searched through the used car ads. What we found was a two-tone, green, four-door '55 Chevrolet. It was a wonderful first car. I drove my Chevy all the way up to Reno, right over the California-Nevada line, looking for the right guy to paint its name — *Flying Tiger* — in beautiful Old English script across both of its back fenders.

But this newly found independence made me a little too anxious to push the pedal to the floor. Why waste time ambling down the highway?

It was during the springtime of my senior year, and all the trees and wild shrubbery seemed to blend right into the mountains in a thousand shades of blue-green as I zoomed up the highway, headed for Reno. The Apollos were auditioning for a job at the Golden Hotel, which later became Harrah's Club. We were hoping to start as soon as I graduated. Having just gotten my license at the end of October, I was a green driver with a lead foot. As my Flying Tiger sped along, my mind was already on the music we'd be playing in our attempt to impress the club manager. Suddenly I spotted a patrol car in my rearview mirror, and it was moving up on me pretty fast. In a matter of minutes I was waiting unhappily while an officer wrote out a speeding ticket.

Well, I hadn't gotten far. I was still in the jurisdiction of Sacramento, so on the following Monday I was standing nervously before a circuit judge in the city's courthouse. With me was the manager of the Apollos. He wanted me to make those out-of-town dates, and he knew that I needed my own car to get there.

"Mr. Greenwood, you are charged with exceeding the speed limit on Interstate 80. The patrolman clocked your car at eighty-five miles per hour," said the white-haired judge in a formal, stern tone. "Do you realize you have broken the law?" With his piercing eyes looking directly at me, making me want to just shrink to the floor, he waited for an answer.

"Yes, sir," was my quick reply. Then, looking up at his white hair and patient expression, I began to feel a little better. "Maybe he'll be understanding," I thought, hopefully.

"Are you ever going to speed again?" was the judge's next solemn question.

"No, sir!" I answered with all the emphasis I could muster.

Then the judge peered down at me and in his strong, serious tone said, "Mr. Greenwood, I'm going to give you another chance. But if I ever see you in my court again, you'll not drive until you're twenty-one. Case dismissed."

That was a serious threat. But with a sigh of relief, and still not daring to smile, I mumbled a grateful "thank you." Then I turned and headed for the door, followed by my relieved manager.

Everybody is caught in a mistake occasionally, but this was a lesson that left a lasting impression. It was over twenty years before I would be arrested for speeding again, and that turned out to be a case of intentional entrapment.

An international confrontation that was caused by a serious mistake occurred that spring. An American U-2 jet classified as a weather research plane strayed over Soviet-Afghan territory. The U.S.S.R. downed our plane and captured its pilot, Francis Gary Powers. When we heard about it, some of us wondered why the Soviets would shoot down a plane doing weather research, and we figured that only governmental officials knew the whole story. What I couldn't know then was that a very similar but deeply tragic action would infuriate the world years later. And it would alter my whole life.

My senior year continued along. Although I was looking forward to graduation, the Apollos were especially anxious for me to finish.

"When are you getting out of there?" Bob kept asking. "We need to start working full-time."

In fact, our audition at the Golden Hotel in Reno had been successful. The Apollos had been hired, but our opening night was the same evening as my graduation. When I realized that I wouldn't be able to make it, I walked into the principal's office to explain.

"If you aren't at the graduation, you will not get your diploma," he replied, glaring at me from behind his cluttered desk.

"But, I can't come. My band has a job. They're depending on me," I answered.

"No graduation ceremony, no diploma, Mr. Greenwood. It's going to stay right here in my safe." Then he pounded the door of a formidable metal box, which must have contained pages of evidence concerning student infractions as well as ungranted diplomas.

This seemed really unfair. I couldn't figure out why he would penalize me for pursuing my career. I realized that graduation was a significant event, and it would be fun to be there, celebrating with all my school friends. I'd miss hanging out and partying with them afterwards. But I had a commitment to the Apollos that was more important than a ceremony.

"But, sir, I don't have any other choice," I explained.

"Mr. Greenwood," he said, his words icy with anger, "you'll get your diploma over my dead body!"

There was nothing else I could say. I turned slowly around and headed for the door, my feelings tied in a knot of frustration.

He had made his own Karma. Not long afterwards, Norte Del Rio's principal died. When my grandmother heard about his death, she calmly went down to the high school and asked for my diploma. That afternoon, Grandma quietly packed it up and sent it to me, where I was on tour with the Apollos.

As I headed down the road to play my first shows as a full-time musician, I was like a burning comet, almost out of control. I was so excited to be out in the world and playing music!

I grew up fast 'cause my seeds were strong
And my roots went way down deep.
The day I left, I never looked back
'Cause I knew that I could keep
A part of home in my heart.

CHAPTER IV

AFTER MY GRADUATION, the Apollos began securing dates up and down the California coast. Many of our stops were to perform with the USO for military audiences. We were a band without a format, combining slapstick comedy and Hawaiian dancing with music ranging from pop songs of the day to rhythm-bound rock and honky-tonk. I'd warm up the hall with the seductive tones of "Harlem Nocturne" on my saxophone and give my best vocal rendition of Sam Cooke's "Chain Gang." Then, since Bobby Darin had just won a Grammy for "Mack the Knife," I'd sing that favorite of mine again. Included in the selections were heartfelt country numbers like the "Tennessee Waltz" and "Georgia," a few cool jazz instrumentals, and the newest rage, rock 'n' roll.

By now, Elvis was drawing crowds of starstruck teenagers to his film, *G.I. Blues*. His enlistment in the Army had caught the attention of his adoring fans, and in January 1960, John F. Kennedy called for all Americans to serve in some way. In his inauguration speech, our young President challenged, "Ask not what your country can do for you; ask what you can do for your country." He was especially speaking to America's youth when he told us, "The torch has passed to a new generation."

The Apollos had been traveling to various bases during my senior year, and it was at McClellan Air Force Base near Sacramento that I became intrigued with the pretty Spanish-looking girl smiling up at me from the front row. This was about the time that I had started making attempts at songwriting, and my first one was called "For You." She must have liked my song. But she had no idea that I was only seventeen. No way was I going to admit it!

"You guys better not let on," I told my Apollo buddies.

"Your secret is safe with us," they assured me.

She was so quiet and reserved behind those dark, shy eyes that the topic of our ages never came up. Maybe I was good at changing the subject. Soon we became more serious about our relationship, and before long, the two of us were involved in a dedicated commitment.

Edna was her name. It was the same as my grandmother's. Maybe that was one of the romantic reasons we were drawn to each other, but we were deeply in love. It was young, naïve love. An entertainer is like a Gypsy, continually traveling around. And where he goes, his woman goes. We were married in Reno, with Edna expecting our first child.

The Apollos were working hard, on the road almost all the time. Often we toured with the Department of Defense branch that sponsors entertainment for the U.S. military. It's called the MWR, for Morale, Welfare, and Recreation, because it deals with those needs of our service families. We also went on USO tours, performing at bases like Fort Ord, the Army base over on the coast near Monterey, as well as China Lake, the Navy missile-testing range in Ridgecrest, March Air Force Base south of Riverside, and Travis Air Force Base in Fairfield. This gave us an insight into what military life is like. I still had that longing to be a part of the team and really wished I could be in the service. But the Apollos and I were headed for a far different kind of experience.

Planning to create some stability for our families, we pulled into Idaho Falls, where we purchased a bar called Jack's Club and changed its name to Club Apollo. Our manager, who controlled the Apollos' finances, had made all the arrangements. He was married to our Hawaiian dancer, Momi, and he had evidently made plans for the two of them to reap a profit at our expense. Thinking we were sacrificing in order to make the club a successful venture, we band members worked for almost nothing while he collected the ticket and bar revenues.

We decorated the place, trying to transform it into an inviting, even romantic, nightclub. This was totally on a shoe-string because none of us had much money. So once Club Apollo was a going concern, we decided to go on the road, signing on for a USO tour. We left our manager in charge of the club until our return, and I took Edna home to California so that she could be near her family when she delivered our child.

On the tour, none of the Apollo members could bring their wives along because we were making long drives from one venue to another, traveling throughout California, then north into other Pacific Coast states. But finally our band got the chance to take a long-distance flight. It was on October 11, 1961, when the USO offered to fly us all the way to Alaska. We made the spectacular drive in our cars up from Sacramento along the rugged coastline of Oregon, then flew out from Portland.

Seeing America's fledgling state from an altitude of 15,000 feet was an unbelievable sensation. Snow-covered mountains stretched endlessly ahead, edging down to icy inlets, intermittently spotted with small villages. Then the larger city of Anchorage loomed into view. Slowly our transport plane descended and the Apollos began gathering our belongings. The plane crunched down in the light blanket of snow on the runway, and all of us started piling out.

As our group hauled down our bags and instrument cases, a friendly-looking naval officer walked briskly up to me. "Are you Lee Greenwood?" he asked.

"Yes, sir. I sure am, sir," I answered.

He reached out, gave me a cigar and a hearty handshake, then said, "Congratulations! You have a son, born in California!"

What an exciting moment for a new father! I called home right away and found out that our baby, whom we named Tedd, was healthy and that Edna was fine. From this moment on, I was a family man, a new role for me, and still so young.

Now my life would change because I had greater responsibility than ever before. Now I wasn't just a husband. I wasn't only an individual, and I wasn't just a musician. Suddenly I felt like a part of America. I was starting a family that would become part of the fabric of this country.

Having been an entertainer with the Red Cross and then the USO troupes since the age of twelve, I identified closely with America's service-related organizations. Military audiences always made me feel at home, and it was inspiring to hear the men talk about our country's latest technology. I thought it would be a super feeling to become part of such an enormous team effort. With this thought firmly in place, when I returned to Sacramento I headed for the Marine Corps Recruiting Office. Asking for an application, I filled it out and handed it to the recruiting officer. But after glancing down at the first few lines, he looked up. "You're healthy enough. In fact, you qualify in all areas except for the fact that you have a kid. So you're classified 3-A. We aren't signing up any fathers right now. Sorry."

Disappointed, I tried the Navy, but they refused my application, too. After being turned down twice, I thought, "Guess the Air Force won't take me either."

It gave me a left-out feeling, a feeling that Edna didn't seem to understand. "I'm glad they wouldn't sign you up, Lee," she said. "You'd be gone all the time."

Now I would have to find another way to become a member of America's team. President Kennedy had announced the formation of the Peace Corps, a group of young volunteers who traveled to underdeveloped nations to help grow food and build dwellings in the name of our democracy. But I couldn't join the Peace Corps. Still in my teens, I had the responsibilities of a wife and son, and I needed to keep working to support them.

Meanwhile, Americans employed in the space program were building toward a history-making event. They achieved their goal on February 20, 1962. As the Apollos were riding down the road on our way to another show, an announcement came over the radio: "John Glenn, aboard his Mercury spacecraft, *Friendship 7,* has become the first American to orbit the earth." Then we heard a playback of the U.S. Marine Corps pilot's reaction as he circled, 100 miles above us: "Oh, that view is tremendous!"

What a boost for our national pride! But later that year, for six suspense-filled days, everyone in America shared a feeling of oneness, as we waited out the Cuban missile crisis.

It happened during my twentieth birthday in October of '62. President Kennedy had just been informed that the U.S.S.R. was transporting missiles and putting them up on a small island right off the Florida coast. Cuba, under the control of its powerful leader, Fidel Castro, had become a satellite of the Soviet Union. When the President saw the photos taken by our reconnaissance planes of the missiles and bases, he immediately called his Cabinet into emergency session. Then he sent the evidence to a special session of the United Nations Security Council.

Meanwhile, the press reported the situation. Newscasts and front-page stories stated that our leaders wanted to get all the facts before they reached a decision. In a nuclear age, the U.S. was wary of the risk of a war with her rival superpower. But Cuba is dangerously close to the U.S., and allowing Soviet missiles to remain right off our coast would make us permanently vulnerable to attack.

President Kennedy realized that the decision rested on his shoulders. He ordered a blockade, halting the flow of war materials to Cuba, and he demanded that the Soviets remove their missiles that were already in place.

All Americans, and the whole world with us, waited. As in a chess game, the next move would be made by Premier Khrushchev. We listened as each report gave an update on the drama. It seemed as if the entire country was holding its breath in anticipation. The next load of weapons had left the Soviet Union, headed toward Cuba. This missile-loaded ship approached our blockade, slowed, then began to turn around. Our nation, along with the rest of the international community, breathed easy again. Premier Khrushchev agreed to the President's request, and the U.S.S.R. began dismantling its missile sites. Americans from coast to coast celebrated, and the Apollos felt like walking on air. Our country had not given in. It had met the test and had won!

While the Apollos were back performing in Idaho Falls, we met a talented musician named Joel Jeffreys.

"Joel, you're a terrific singer. How would you like to join our group?" I asked. "We're getting ready to go on the road again soon."

"Great, man, I'm ready to roll," he said.

Joel's black heritage seemed to have endowed him with natural talent, both at singing and playing his guitar, in that superb George Benson style. He was an inspiration as a rhythm-and-blues artist. It was marvelous to see Joel perform. Being a lot younger, I often watched in amazement as he stepped out into the spotlight and instantly drew the crowd to him. His charisma was astonishing as he'd grab a song with that versatile voice and capture the audience, shaking his body and swinging his head in circular fashion as he won their applause.

Paying close attention, I was trying to learn from a variety of musicians. The pop and rock singers were great, but in those days I was fascinated with the instrumentalists. Duane Eddie from Phoenix covered a whole range of moods on his guitar, from rhythm and blues to rock 'n' roll. His music ran the gamut from his hard-driving instrumental of "Cannonball" to the more loose, but harsh-sounding "Rebel Rouser."

One sax player I admired, who included a certain amount of hostility in his compositions, was John Coltrane. He played tenor and was one of the leaders in progressive jazz. I had been experimenting with his style and also trying some licks from Stan Getz, whose bossa nova rhythms blended Brazilian samba melodies with American jazz harmonies.

Traveling gave us a chance to learn from live performances by other musicians. But on our next trip back to Idaho, the Apollos got the bad news. Our manager had sold Club Apollo. We were left flat in Idaho Falls! Needless to say, that was the parting of the ways with our manager and the Hawaiian dancer. We had learned a lesson from the school of hard knocks.

Burned by the Club Apollo fiasco, Eddie, Bob, Gary, Joel, and I were looking for another home base. Feeling that we were ready for a more sophisticated entertainment setting— Las Vegas—we obtained an audition date with the Sennes brothers. They were from a Cleveland organization and pretty much ran the Stardust Hotel.

"I can't believe you called me off the golf course to look at this group," Rocky Sennes told his brother. "Okay, let's get this over with." And he flopped down into his chair in the audition room, with a disgusted scowl darkening his face.

"It doesn't look too encouraging," I whispered to Eddie. "But this is our chance."

Joel, the starring talent of our group, was a genius on stage. Instantly, he had the Sennes brothers absorbed in his every note. In fact, they were taken in by the high-powered presentation of the entire Apollo band. During our energy-packed show, I had played one instrument after another. Finally we were into our "closer," the grand finale. The two men in our audience, who by now were taking a real interest, watched in amazement as I jumped on the backs of Eddie and Bob. Suddenly we were blasting away with "When the Saints Come Marching In," which I was playing on my saxophone, upside down!

The Sennes brothers hired us on the spot, and the Apollos moved to Vegas.

These were rough times for understanding between the races. Civil rights activists were pushing to the forefront of American history with bus boycotts and nonviolent protests. Their leader, Martin Luther King, Jr., gave his stirring "I have a dream" speech before the 200,000 demonstrators who overflowed the Mall in Washington. His eloquence reached the hearts of citizens all over the country.

For years, black musicians also had held audiences spellbound with their fabulous vocal and instrumental abilities. Among them were such greats as Louis Armstrong, the undisputed master of jazz, and Count Basie, supreme bandleader of his legendary Big Band. Black artists like Jackie Wilson, Sam Cooke, Ben E. King, Gene McDaniels, and Brook Benton had already crossed over from rhythm and blues into the popular scene. Sam Cooke was probably my favorite. Starting out in gospel, he had developed a warm, romantic style as a ballad singer. Then he left the Soul Stirrers for a career in pop, where he drew an enthusiastic following of bobby-soxers and young musicians like me.

At the Stardust, the Apollos added a new singer. Merlene Garner, a brunette with long, flowing hair, was blessed with Southern charm. Her manager, the well-known Mae Axton, had brought Merlene to us, so that gave her a certain preeminence. She fit right in with the Apollos like the last piece in a puzzle. Audiences flock to excitement-packed shows, and ours were spectacular. I was doing everything on stage from saxophone and drums, to standing on a Vaseline jar with my hair on fire!

After about a year, the Apollos had an offer in Hawaii. It must have seemed like an easy choice for the others, but I had become drawn to the challenge of this town of musical professionals, and I was determined to stay. Las Vegas was billed as the "Entertainment Capital of the World." It had the cream of seasoned musicians and performers, and I realized how much more I needed to learn. Embarking on an independent career, taking a gamble in that city of chance, I was betting on my ability to make it on my own.

The next three or four years were exhilarating for me. But it was a traumatic time for America.

On November 22, 1963, I was playing with a band at the Frontier Hotel. An Ice Capades show was scheduled for that night. In front of our small wooden stage, which was slightly raised, the uncovered ice stretched out in crystal whiteness like a carpet. The whole room was very cold, and although our fingers were almost freezing, we had to ignore our discomfort and pretend that we were warm and excited. Even the stage lights were not bright enough to keep us from shivering. The people, sitting at little cocktail tables around the ice, had just finished a champagne brunch. In front of them was a dance floor about the size of two living rooms, not big. It was our job to play popular dance tunes and persuade this assortment of vacationers to move out onto the floor.

Club managers in Vegas had one thing constantly on their minds: the customers must be kept busy and happy. Otherwise, they will wander off and spend their money, usually gambling, in some nearby hotel. The competition was fierce in this city, which earned its living selling amusement opportunities. So, although it was really frigid in this ice-filled room, our band was pumping out rocking hot tunes and trying to convince these folks to come on up and dance.

It was during our break, while we were warming up in the hall, when a news broadcast interrupted the program on a nearby TV set: "President Kennedy has been shot. The President was riding, beside his wife, Jackie, in a Dallas motorcade. He was taken to Parkland Hospital, where he has been pronounced dead."

Our hearts stopped, almost in midbeat. How could it be true? Was it possible that John Kennedy, our dynamic leader with his natural charm and youthful idealism, was really dead?

"Dead" is a hard, final word. It hit with a thud in my mind, even as I was still not quite able to believe it. Yet the questions kept flowing as the news filtered out to those on the dance floor and then into the crowd sitting in the small lounge. A hush fell on the room.

Immediately the casino boss marched rapidly up to us. "Well, what're you waitin' for? Go on back in. Start that music up," he ordered, with a frown. "This show needs to keep moving."

Seeing our hesitancy, he added, "Get with it!" and then stalked out.

All the band members were reluctant. It seemed so distasteful to perform at a time like this. As despondent as we felt, the dance music was cranked up and we tried to get the audience involved. But it was a room full of depressed people, and no one was in the mood for dancing. Starting up the music at a time like that really hurt me inside; it was very difficult for all of us. We probably shouldn't have played. We should have put our jobs on the line and refused.

John Kennedy had left us a legacy: his dream of America as a "New Frontier," free from racial discrimination and foremost among nations in space exploration. He had asked Congress to appropriate the funds for our missile program and urged them to send Americans to the moon, saying that such investments "may hold the key to our future on Earth."

Just five months before his assassination, President Kennedy had spoken to a multitude of cheering West Berlin residents, who lived beyond the Berlin Wall, surrounded by Communist control. These inhabitants of the free section of their city were dependent upon airlifts for the necessities of life. They were applauding Kennedy's expressions of U.S. support, as his voice rang out, "All free men, wherever they may live, are citizens of Berlin." He congratulated them on their resolve, saying that if any people had doubts about the true value of freedom, "Let them come to Berlin."

The morning after the assassination, I picked up the newspaper with a thought that the tragedy might have been a terrible dream. But on the front page was a photograph of Lyndon Baines Johnson, on Air Force 1 in flight back to Washington. His hand was raised for the Oath of Office, and the look on his face was somber, almost haggard. His wife, Lady Bird, stood at his right side. Standing to his left was the dazed widow, Jackie, still in her pink suit, which was stained with blood.

As America slowly recovered from the shocking murder of its President, I continued working in Las Vegas as a free-lance musician, learning as much as possible about music. I put aside the trumpet, trombone, and drums, and concentrated on piano and saxophone. It was great to come upon Sam Butera, a sax player who played behind Louie Prima, setting up a fast-paced show that held his audience with its speed and verve. Butera had the same style as King Curtis, the instrumentalist I patterned my evening jazz sessions on, who was a soul player, but with a rugged attack on the notes. Curtis created a strong, macho mood and was a virtuoso on reiterated phrases. But the part I liked best was his punch at the end. He knew how to produce a heavy-hitting finale.

As a piano player, I was an admirer of Ray Charles. His music was a blend of gospel, jazz, blues, and pop, and he was also a soul-stirring vocalist. In the past, I had never really sung much, only using my voice in arranging or singing with the group. Incorporating my music into the total sound of the band had always been the primary concern. There was one main thing in the back of my mind: harmony.

Early in 1964, four young men who were greatly influencing my musical style visited America. The Beatles touched down at JFK Airport, primed for their appearance on "The Ed Sullivan Show." John Lennon, Paul McCartney, George Harrison, and Ringo Starr were all about my age, but already they had the number-one hit on the U.S. charts. That wasn't bad for a new group from Liverpool! "I Want to Hold Your Hand" was echoing all over the country. The rhythms and harmonies of their releases were creating Beatlemania, and I was learning from their graceful melodies and inventive flair.

In addition to the boys from England, artists on the Motown label were coming to the forefront in musical circles. Singers like Stevie Wonder, Marvin Gaye, and the Temptations were warming up the airwaves. Mary Wilson, Florence Ballard, and Diana Ross, who called themselves the Supremes, hit the charts that summer with their song, "Where Did Our Love Go?"

During the same year my family was growing. On October 30, Laura Rene was born at the China Lake Naval Base hospital. It was wonderful to have a daughter. But she had a father caught up in a whirlwind of jobs, struggling to make a living, yet striving to make it to the top professionally. He was a man taking a crack at becoming known in Las Vegas and hoping to earn a chance to go beyond this city of stars, out into our vast country. In these efforts he was a nonstop performer, experimenting with more exciting formats and seeking higher-profile shows.

Edna was a fine mother and I was trying to be a good father, but somewhere along the way we lost the love. I felt trapped. I had gotten married too soon, and I knew it. Probably when we met, I was reaching out for family. My dad had left so early in my young life that I had missed the stability of a family unit. But my attempt to find a lasting love somehow failed. So Edna and I wrestled with the question of separation. Then after a long, traumatic year, we were divorced.

Why do people cry when they hear the word "good-bye"
In a love song?
Tears are sure to fall when you know they gave it all
In a love song.
Sometimes two people take a chance on a beautiful romance
And you wish it could be you.
'Cause everybody's needing what the singers all are singing
In a love song.

Sometimes a momentous accomplishment shakes us from our own personal tragedies. During the following summer, Air Force Major Ed White captured the imaginations of people everywhere, as we focused on his walk outside of the craft *Gemini 4.* Floating gracefully, tethered to the spacecraft by his oxygen-hose umbilical cord, he proved that experiments or craft repair could be accomplished in outer space. I could only marvel at the expertise and courage exemplified by our astronaut. Of course, I never dreamed that in a little over a year he would be killed in the Project Apollo capsule, along with astronauts Virgil Grissom and Roger Chaffee, during a flash fire at Cape Kennedy Space Center.

But soon after Major White's historic space walk, I was back to dwelling on my situation. Alone in Las Vegas, I was deeply depressed over the breakup of my family. Hoping that getting out of town would help, I joined a group called Sandu Scott and the Scotties, which included Dino Dinelli, Felix Cavaliere, and several others. It was amid high anticipation that we received the news: "We're playing 'The Ed Sullivan Show,'" Sandu Scott told her band members.

"That's terrific! In the same league with the Beatles," we joked.

There was electricity in the air as we flew to New York City, the "Big Apple." But after we were there, Sandu had a change of plans. "Due to some personal reasons, I'm going to have to cancel our act," she said. "I'm sorry."

Afterwards, while talking it over with the band, I said to Felix, "Looks like we're going to forfeit the 'really big shew.' "

"Why don't you stay in New York for a while, Lee? There's a lot happening musically up here," Dino said. "You can stay with me."

"Sure, but not for long. I promised Henry Lenz that I'd be back to help with his show at the El Cortez. It's a commitment," I answered. As fate would have it, these two buddies of mine formed a group that was to make it big, the Young Rascals.

While I was returning to Las Vegas, America was slipping into the quagmire of Vietnam, a tiny country that most of us had never even heard of. Congress gave President Johnson the power to enlarge the U.S. role in this conflict. Suddenly our pilots were flying regular sorties off carriers over there, while planeloads of freshly trained American ground troops were being sent to Southeast Asia.

At the same time, another ominous signal went up in Asia. China exploded its first atomic bomb. A feeling of uneasiness began to settle over our country. The world situation seemed to be something we had little control over.

Emphasizing the frustration of the times, the Beatles declared it had been "A Hard Day's Night." This struck at a personal level, too. Perhaps looking for emotional security, or maybe hoping to become a conventional father and husband, I made another try at pulling my family together. Edna and I remarried.

While I was single I had met a cocktail waitress, Roberta Taylor, who was also an exciting go-go dancer. We had shared our hopes and disappointments, and I was still seeing her, even though I had reestablished my home with Edna. So it's not surprising that the pressures of conflicting personal relationships as well as the tensions of striving for a place in the entertainment field brought my marriage, once again, to an end. For the second time, Edna and I were divorced. Before long she remarried and took Tedd and Laura with her to California.

> *It can tear you apart, for a word can break a heart*
> *In a love song.*
> *They take everything you feel and they make it sound so real*
> *In a love song.*
> *There's a part of you and me in every memory*
> *That tells us who we are.*
> *'Cause everybody's needing what the singers all are singing*
> *In a love song.*

CHAPTER V

By 1966, THE PROTESTS against the war in Vietnam were getting stronger. In New York City, 20,000 demonstrators paraded down Fifth Avenue, while peace marchers rallied in Boston, Washington, and all through California and the Midwest. Ready to take the consequences, young men burned their draft cards. For the first time, American deaths in the war exceeded those of the South Vietnamese. Still feeling helpless to do anything about the international situation, I was on my way back to Vegas to fulfill my earlier promise to become the musical director for the King Henry Show.

In Vegas the atmosphere stayed light and frivolous on the surface, but there was always an underground with its own agenda. The Whiskey A Go Go was a small lounge downtown with the typical meat-market atmosphere. Beyond the long bar were a lot of cocktail tables, scattered throughout the room. The music was upbeat. The whole place had a fresh look because the club was newly painted. And although its stage was dimly lit, there was no hint of the clandestine operations going on in the club's midst.

I had been hired by a guy named Vinnie to play in the band and had brought with me a brand new tenor saxophone.

"You can just lock your sax in the dressing room," Vinnie told me. "All the guys leave their instruments in there."

I had only been with the Whisky A Go Go a short time, when I walked into the club to get ready for work one night and found the dressing room broken open. My beautiful sax was gone! A wave of anger rushed over me. How could someone take from me the tool that I made my music with? It was a personal affront, like the hurt of being violated.

"Vinnie, somebody stole my sax," I said with disgust, when I finally found him working in the bar. "This makes me really mad. I've been needing that sax for so long, and I just bought it. Now it's missing!"

"Oh. Well, don't worry. I'll get it back for you," he replied, without showing the least flicker of emotion. Picking up the phone, he made one call.

Vinnie was one of those guys in Vegas who got things done. The tenor sax was back in an hour. This lounge manager was obviously involved in some network, and his bunch of cohorts were not the best characters to be in business with. I decided to make a change.

After a short engagement at a place called the Mint, although I was playing jazz on my own around town, I realized I'd have to find a job with a regular band. Sifting through the possibilities, I thought, "The Gay Nighters are at the Hacienda Hotel. Maybe they can use a sax player."

Driving south down Las Vegas Boulevard, out to the edge of the entertainment district, I pulled up to the last hotel on the Strip. The Hacienda wasn't as elaborate as the others, and it was smaller than most. As I walked into the lobby, blinking off the sunlight from outside and trying to adjust to the glittery, festive atmosphere, I found myself in a scene that certainly didn't appear to be a typical casino. The Hacienda was the place where Vegas locals went whenever they could get time off. It was a younger crowd. Cocktail waitresses, dealers, bartenders, cab drivers, and musicians would show up here to hang out and dance.

The lively sound of the Gay Nighters drifted in from the nearby lounge. Their bandleader, Bob Patrick, was the man to see, so I stood there, listening to the music, until he came offstage at the end of their set. It wasn't long before I was making plans to join his group. As our conversation came to a close, I glanced over at a young guy who had been standing near the stage wings. Apparently he had been waiting for someone, too. Obviously a musician, he casually walked up and greeted me with, "Hi! I'm Danny Bradley. Who are you with?"

Holding out my hand, I answered, "Lee Greenwood's the name. I'm getting ready to join the Gay Nighters. Are you playing here?"

"No. Well, actually I'm waiting to talk with Paul Dino about a job on the guitar," he said, accepting a friendly handshake. "His band's on next, so maybe he'll be showing up in a few minutes."

Soon we were talking music. Being about the same age and in similar stages of our careers, we had a lot in common. The meeting was casual, but the friendship that developed was lifelong. As it turned out, one of the bonds that we found ourselves forming, besides music, was our interest in sports. We started meeting at the local high school basketball courts. They were surrounded by high chain link fences, but the gates were open, and a lot of times a bunch of fifteen-to eighteen-year-old boys would show up to join in the action. It was a rough brand of ball and a terrific way to get any aggressions out. The accent was on winning, and I was happy to have Danny on my team. He was accurate from anywhere on the court!

It was great to be outside, away from the stifling atmosphere of crowded, noisy clubs and dark lounges where hot spotlights filtered through the slowly rising cigarette smoke. And when it wasn't basketball, it was a touch football game. One afternoon, when Danny and I had a small team going against some other guys, we were losing at the countdown of the last quarter. In the huddle, Danny, who was playing quarterback, whispered to me, "Lee, go down as fast as you can. When those guys come in to cover you, drop back a couple of yards, turn around, and the ball will be in your stomach. It's called a button-hook. Just go down there, button-hook, and be ready to grab the ball."

Although I'd never seen that play before, it seemed to be worth a try. Nothing else was going to win the game for us.

So, I gave him a nod and started racing down the field at full speed.

Reaching our opponents, who were running in for the block, I did a quick about-face and was caught totally by surprise. The football slammed right into my mid-section, my arms automatically closed around it, and I was over the goal line. We had won!

Danny and I were a natural team. So although my job with the Gay Nighters came through and Danny started playing with the Paul Dino group, soon we were asking each other, "Why don't we form our own band?"

Putting together the best players we could find, Danny and I ended up with a rock group that was heavy in the horn section. The Beatles, all decked out in neat English clothes, were considered the good guys, and they were called "mod." "Mod" meant "modern" and had good connotations. The rough bands who dressed down were known as the "rockers," and they looked like street gangs.

So we called ourselves the Mod Squad Marmalade. The six of us walked in, auditioned for the hottest producer in town, and were immediately hired.

Suddenly, the Mod Squad was a real Las Vegas band, playing at the Hotel Sahara. There we were, with short hair, in our British-style blue suits with big, thick lapels and bell-bottom pants. Ascots at the collars topped off our white ruffled shirts. Danny played the guitar, and Al Para, a real likable guy, was on trumpet. Ike Clanton, our handsome bass player, always impressed us with his suave clothes. On drums, Tommy Quigley was a real showman. He managed to maintain the tempo even while twirling his sticks. Then there was Billy Monogold, a talented tenor sax player. I played alto sax, and as the arranger and lead singer, was responsible for our style. Our hearts were in hard rock, and audiences compared us with the Union Gap. So for a Vegas act, we were ahead of our time, musically.

Las Vegas has never been on the cutting edge of entertainment. When something is tried and true, then it goes to Vegas. So, in effect, the town works a little behind the times. But the Mod Squad was avant garde. We were a real contrast to the beautiful, but topless, girls in the chorus line in front of us!

"It's frustrating to work so hard on our music, and then have it upstaged by a T & A show," I told Danny one day.

"Yeah," he agreed. "All the audience seems to be interested in are those six bare-breasted dancers and sexy lead singer."

"Well, as musicians, we're obviously not very important here," I said.

"Let's face it, Lee," Danny concluded. "The casino boss is after money. We're just part of the draw. In fact, if the Mod Squad gets too good and starts taking anybody's attention away from the gambling, we're out of here."

Las Vegas was a night-life town, making its living on gamblers. People didn't travel there to sleep, and our job was to keep them awake all night long! Our two shows, each night, were the latest on the Strip. The first began at four in the morning and the second at 5:15 A.M. Entertainers in town who were through for the evening would stop by to catch a final show. Sammy Davis, Jr., Elvis Presley, Jack Jones, Anthony Newley, Flip Wilson, Don Adams, Don Rickles, Marilyn McCoo and LaMonte MacLamore of the Fifth Dimension, and a lot of others dropped by. The list of stars was endless. It was just like calling the roll!

To keep customers moving during the daytime, Danny and I put together a second band that was a total contrast to the hip image of the Mod Squad. The Pony Express, which played at the Casbar Theatre in the Hotel Sahara every afternoon at 3:00 and 4:30, featured country music. In keeping with the theme, the petite, scantily clad dancers wore boots and fringe. Some even wore Indian headdresses.

This was a light, humorous show, and one afternoon the audience got more of a surprise than they expected. Danny had hired an excellent drummer, Tony Lavello. In order to have room on the stage, the band was situated outside the fancy hydraulic-powered curtains, which were embossed with a flourish of glitzy designs. The drummer sat right next to the curtain, and we were behind him, scattered out over the rest of the stage. While Tony was setting up that day, he was in a big hurry, driving his drum spur, the long, pointed shaft of steel, into the wooden stage floor. This was to stabilize the drum kit for his performance. The curtain hem was draped on the floor, and Tony had unknowingly caught it with the spur point.

It was time to start. Tony began his timpani roll, announcing the opening of the show, and someone threw the switch to pull up the heavy curtains. When that fancy drapery started rising, the spur sliced into the thick material and caught like a hook.

"Look out!" I yelled, as the entire drum kit, including the drummer, was lifted slowly upward toward the ceiling. The look of sheer terror on his face was indescribable!

Tony's sticks stopped in midbeat as he was raised right up. Then he keeled over and toppled into the audience. While the entire drum set was rising with the curtains, it was dangling down, all jumbled together, and making unbelievable clanging and banging noises.

"The curtains!" someone called out. After moments of suspense filled with clattering sounds, a stagehand found the right switch and the curtains were lowered. The crew hurried out to untangle the drum set so that the Pony Express show could resume, this time for a well-primed crowd!

But on the larger scene, events were grim. President Johnson ordered 25,000 ground troops into South Vietnam in an operation against the Vietcong. Thousands of our combat soldiers were being killed. Naval air strikes against North Vietnam were intensified, and America was losing young pilots and planes in a distant land.

Not long before, I had watched some jets just like these, with their highly trained, gung-ho fliers, streak across the sky above the desert at Nellis Air Force Base. As a flight enthusiast, I often drove out from Vegas to see the Thunderbirds perform their daring near-misses, loops, and other breathtaking feats. It was hard to imagine those sleek aircraft falling in flames over enemy territory, and even more horrifying was the specter of our heroic young pilots being forced to eject from their plummeting jets. However, many survived the downing of their planes and became prisoners of war. The first of them had been Lt. Everett Alvarez, Jr., of San Jose, California, not far from where I grew up. In August of '64, Lieutenant Alvarez had flown his jet off the aircraft carrier USS *Constellation,* bound for a patrol-boat base northeast of Haiphong, 400 miles away. In the airspace above Hon Gay, his plane was hit, and as he ejected, Alvarez radioed his squadronmates: "I'm getting out. I'll see you guys later."

Lieutenant Alvarez had to live through eight horror-filled years of struggling to stay alive in the dreaded "Hanoi Hilton" before the North Vietnamese finally returned him, along with a group of his fellow airmen. Some of them had been held isolated in tiny cells. But they were the lucky ones. Many of our POWs never came back.

In Las Vegas, I was alone again. Roberta and I were still dating, although it had been a rocky relationship from the beginning. She was a beautiful, volatile woman, with a lot of charm. Then there was her lovable four-year-old son, Marc. They were an irresistible combination for a solitary guy.

"It sure is hard knowing that Tedd and Laura are being raised by somebody else," I told Roberta one night. "I'm their father, but it looks like I won't have much input in their lives."

"Why don't you go out there to see them?" she asked. "You and the children could spend some time together."

"Edna made me promise that I wouldn't visit the kids," I answered. "It's the arrangement she asked me to abide by. Since she was going to remarry, she felt that it was better for Tedd and Laura to have the constancy of their new family rather than go through the unstable setup of visitation. Maybe she's right, but it's tough."

Someone who understands can lift your spirits, especially when you're on your own. Love finds the lonely, and before very long, Roberta and I were married. The void had been filled and I embarked upon founding a home once more. I was strongly determined to be as good a father to Marc as wonderful Poppa D'Antonoli had been to me. Lewis had taught me to be responsible, and he had freely shown his love. I was already a teenager when gentle Lew had taken over the chore of being a stepfather, and like a willow, I had pretty much grown the way I was going to grow. Like me, Marc wouldn't have the benefit of his own father as a role model and confidant. Remembering the pain of being in the same situation as a small boy, I set out to be that father figure for Marc. He was only five when I adopted him, and my new son became an important part of my life.

Being an only child can get lonesome. "Will you bring me a sister?" was the question Marc asked us over and over.

He got his wish on August 1, 1967, with the arrival of Kelly, our tiny daughter with the laughing, dark eyes. She was the last of my children, and I took on the challenge of raising these two youngsters who lived with me.

But America was entering a period of increasing turmoil. That June, musical protest was in the air. The Monterey Pop Festival drew 50,000 "flower children" to chant slogans against the war and listen to songs of love and peace. The urgent tone of their music was a sharp contrast to the mellow sounds being heard by the tourists in Vegas. Among the peace movement's intense performers were Jimi Hendrix and Janis Joplin, who whipped the crushing mass of youthful followers into a frenzy. But while still in their twenties, both of them were taken to their deaths by drugs.

It was only three years later that I heard on the news of Hendrix's death. Two weeks after that, Joplin was dead. The double tragedy seemed so unnecessary.

The Monterey Festival also included pop culture groups like the Who, Ravi Shankar, the Byrds, the Jefferson Airplane, Otis Redding, and the Mamas and the Papas. Their cries for peace and "flower power" echoed the voices of many frustrated young people. Thousands of antiwar activists were marching in the streets in cities throughout America. Vietnam veterans were demonstrating along with them, tossing away their combat medals in symbolic gestures of revulsion at the human suffering that was still going on.

In spite of the flower children and peace marchers the war dragged on, while quite a different battle was raging in

America's streets. The people fighting for an end to racial discrimination were shocked, along with our whole nation, when Martin Luther King was assassinated in Memphis that April day in '68. Although he was only thirty-nine, his accomplishments had been impressive. Legislation for a more equitable America had already been passed by Congress, and during the same week that Reverend King died, President Johnson signed the historic Civil Rights Act.

Still sickened by the cold-blooded murder of our country's outstanding civil rights leader, I could hardly believe the news that Sen. Robert Kennedy, having moments before given a triumphant acknowledgment of his win in the California presidential primary, had been shot down in Los Angeles. I was almost numb with anger at the power that rests in the hands of unknown extremists, as I watched the TV news repeat its coverage of Sirhan Sirhan's victim, soaked with blood and dying on the floor of the Ambassador Hotel.

Wherever Joel might be, I knew these were especially painful blows to him, because our former attorney general had been an outspoken advocate for racial equality. The loss of both leaders would be strongly felt by America.

With more and more people being killed in Vietnam, our country was wrestling with a situation that was getting out of hand. Casualties were rising, and the ripples of our Vietnam vets coming home had just begun. Many of them were horribly injured and many more now felt alienated back here after going through the agony of warfare in the Asian fields and jungles. A lot of our citizens were convinced that our country's involvement in the conflict was right, but an increasing number of Americans began to speak out against our actions in Southeast Asia. America was searching for a way to pull out of its tragic dilemma.

We read the headlines and tried to keep up on the news, but those of us in Las Vegas, Reno, and Lake Tahoe were in an isolated environment. The gambling industry kept entertainers and visitors insulated as much as possible from current events. The economy was still good in Nevada, and the hotel and club owners wanted to keep it that way. Why dampen the spirit of revelry among the gamblers and show-goers? This was supposed to be a place where you go to have a good time. There were no newsworthy peace marches or demonstrations forceful enough to draw attention away from the economic mainstay of these communities. As a result, people who lived there were not fully informed about what was happening in the outside world and how badly America was being wounded. In spite of this, I became increasingly distressed by the news, and my responsibility to my country was troubling me. I wanted to speak out. But what could I do, in Las Vegas? I was looking for an answer.

Soon, the Mod Squad had added a new bass player, a nice-looking guy named Pat Dowlin. Then with the exit of Tommy Quigley, Jimmy Packard had come on board to take over the percussion section. We were still performing at the Sahara when a television show began using our band's name. We had invented the name and had proof in the form of contracts with the Hotel Sahara. "The Mod Squad" was even up on the large marquee outside. Wondering if our group could get some benefits from this mutual identity, we sent our manager to Los Angeles to negotiate with the television show produc-ers Aaron Spelling and Danny Thomas.

I'm sure we'll never know exactly how the negotiations went. However, they offered our band a few spots as a back-ground rock group in their TV nightclub scenes and a re-cording contract for four cuts with Dot Records. This seemed fair to us, and we were happy to have a shot at cutting some discs with top session players in Los Angeles. So we recorded "This Is My Woman," "Beautiful Woman," "Someone to Watch Over Me," and "Maria" from *West Side Story*. All four were fully orchestrated and released under the Dot label, but they weren't promoted at all. Dot sent us our promo copies of the songs but never distributed them. Understandably, noth-ing came of that recording contract.

However, because of our first release, the Mod Squad had the opportunity to appear on "The Dick Clark Show." After being introduced, we lit into a strong performance of "This

Is My Woman" in hopes of pushing our record. Then Dick Clark sat us down for his interview.

"Thanks, guys. That's your new recording on Dot, right?" He turned toward Al, who was still adjusting his trumpet against his knee and sliding back into the closest chair.

"Yes, Dick," Al responded smoothly. "We think our song will move right up there," and he faced the camera with a confident grin.

"This is your first release, isn't it?" Dick continued, looking to Pat for a reply.

"It sure is. But the Mod Squad has been performing in Vegas for the last few years. We've been packing 'em in at the Sahara," Pat answered, sounding cool.

Glancing over at Billy, and nodding at the sax by his feet, our smiling host went on, "I see you're a saxophone player. What kind of sax is that?"

"This is a tenor sax, Dick," was Billy's nonchalant reply. "It gives out a sound a lot like James Moody," he continued, casually tossing out a reference to the Dizzy Gillespie saxophonist who had been ahead of his time in the bebop era.

Billy was being suave, laying out his background on the sax. What he wasn't letting on was that he was still smarting from the loss of his Super 20 King tenor sax. He never had been able to replace it. One night behind stage after a show, Tommy Quigley, feeling full of it, had slid down a banister and landed with a thump right on top of it, smashing the newly acquired sax into a mangled mound of twisted brass. Billy could have beaten him senseless, right on the spot!

But that was a rather juvenile happening to relate on a TV talk show. So, Billy just knowingly mentioned Moody, one of the country's excellent sax musicians, but definitely not a household name.

"Yes. He's great," returned Dick, glibly, "And you sound terrific yourself on that tenor sax, Billy."

Trying to include all of us in his interview, Dick Clark now held the mike closer to his next guest, Jimmy Packard. "Those are hot drums you play. Is there a drummer that you especially look up to? What stick man is your inspiration?"

"Well," stalled Packard, momentarily caught a little off guard. Then after an almost unnoticeable pause, he responded, "Lionel Hampton is probably the granddaddy of jazz drums. He was an innovator and an early great. But I tend more toward Ringo and percussionists for groups like Blood, Sweat, and Tears." Jimmy was anxious to put himself forward as a knowledgeable musician with a handle on cutting-edge trends.

Giving a knowing nod, Clark began again. "Danny, tell me about this name, the Mod Squad. Isn't there a TV program of the same name? How did that happen?"

"Actually, we had the name first," Danny answered. "But we're willing for the show to use it. The producers have promised us some appearances on the program, and they've arranged a record contract for us. We're on Dot Records, as you know," he said, pushing the label of the song we had just played.

"That sounds good, Danny."

Then, about at the bottom of the barrel of his questions, Dick turned to me. "Lee, I see you're the leader of this group. It must keep you pretty busy. What's your favorite pastime when your groovy guys aren't onstage impressing those cheering audiences?"

Without even giving it a thought, I came back with what was really at the top of my mind. "Well, I'm interested in the Boy Scouts, Dick, and I'm the leader of a Webelos den. These are the ten-year-old scouts. They earn badges for citizenship, swimming, and science. My son Marc is in the troop."

Looking over at my Mod Squad buddies, I could see that they were taken aback. Their mouths had just about dropped open in disbelief. Here we were, men in our mid-twenties, working to maintain a hip image for our band, and the lead singer of their supposedly avant-garde group is saying he was a Boy Scout leader! They could hardly believe it!

Well, that's the way I really felt. I guess it just didn't cross my mind to put on a front.

It was during that summer, on July 20, 1969, that our country was given a chance to feel really good about itself. On that historic day, three U.S. astronauts landed their Apollo 11 lunar module on the moon. Back on Earth, six hundred million people watched their television screens as Neil Armstrong let go of his spaceship's ladder and stepped into the moondust on the Sea of Tranquility. As Armstrong proclaimed, this was "a giant step for mankind."

Hoping that the Mod Squad could make it to the top, I had been writing songs, usually for our shows. "Tint of Paisley" centered on a popular fabric design of the time, with love mixed in among all the colors. Some songs had messages. "Society" was about a high-class girl with little empathy for the rest of us. Understanding and communicating with others on all economic levels is an American ideal. Each individual deserves a right to personal dignity and happiness.

My happy song was "Kelly," written for the baby daughter who was bringing so much pride and laughter into our home. Then there was a philosophical song, on a theme as old as man's ability to think and project his thoughts into the future: "Time Waits For No One." It's true. And this same concern about our destiny was expressed in a far different way by the 400,000 peace activists who gathered at Woodstock in August. This multitude of young people behaved peacefully. They braved lack of food and other necessities, and waited through torrents of rain, while they listened to music and tirades against President Nixon and his "war machine." Their message was clear: "Peace Now! End the war!"

But the Mod Squad continued to entertain far away from protests, in the insulated atmosphere of Vegas. After our record on Dot didn't make a ripple in the industry, we began appearing in an early-morning slot at the Hotel Sahara. That's where we caught the eye of Kirby Stone, the intelligent, rough-looking leader of the Kirby Stone Four. They had recorded hits like "Baubles, Bangles, and Beads," making the rounds of the Nevada Circuit, which included Las Vegas, Reno, and Lake Tahoe. Kirby Stone carried a reputation for finding young talent. While traveling through Houston with his group, he realized they needed a back-up band. Hir-

ing the Bobby Doyle Three, he found that it included an excellent bass player, Kenny Rogers.

Kirby was instrumental in nurturing Kenny and pushing
him to become a solo act in the First Edition. This turned out
to be his springboard to a fabulous singing career.

After viewing the Mod Squad at the Sahara, and noting
our vocal and instrumental ability, Kirby came backstage.
"I'm getting out of the performance end of the business.
Right now I'm set up to be the entertainment director for a
new hotel at the corner of Flamingo and the Strip. It's called
the Bonanza," he told us. "It's going to have a Western
theme, and I'm putting together a review. Would you guys
like to be the back-up group for the review, plus do your own
spot?"

"Sure," was our reaction. "We'll just add it to our schedule."

At the Bonanza we finally got a taste of what the big showrooms were really like. For me, it was a fantastic feeling to get
through to a large audience and actually communicate. It was
like creating a bridge and touching on a personal level, and
it's a powerful high.

This was still early in a singing career that eventually lasted
through years of vocal strain in working with many varieties
of amplifiers and microphones. And usually it was in smoky
clubs designed without a thought to acoustics. The evenings
of entertaining under these conditions, well beyond the midnight hours, took their toll. It was a long, harsh road that
eventually led to that dust-and-gravel sound coming from today's Greenwood throat.

In Las Vegas I finally ran into Elvis Presley in person. Or
actually, he ran into me. He was starring in the Main Room at
the Hilton International Hotel. At the same time, I was working the lounge as the opening act for Bill Medley, who had
just split from the Righteous Brothers. Medley was the headliner and I was in the audience watching his show when suddenly Elvis bolted out onto center stage. Everyone was
startled, then electrified! Elvis had them in the palm of his
hand.

What a phenomenon that a star can just walk out on stage and take command! I loved seeing it, and staring up at him, among those clamoring fans, I was amazed at his magnetic power.

After the show, as I was going through the hotel kitchen on the way to the Hilton's back door—all of us entertainers just push on through the lettuce and the garbage—Elvis came striding in, surrounded by his phalanx of security guards. Then he bumped right into me, knocking me to one side of the aisle!

Elvis stopped in his tracks. "Oh, excuse me!" he said politely, that captivating grin breaking through his concentration on getting out to the parking lot.

He paused to look me straight in the eye, and I smiled back. "That's okay. Excuse *me!*"

It was a brief meeting, but at that moment I realized that I liked Elvis. I liked his music, and I liked who he was.

Shortly after that accidental meeting, I got a distressing call from my sister Pat. "Lee, Grandma's sick, and we're really worried."

"I'll be right up there, Pat," I said.

It was hard to imagine Edna as anything but healthy and busily taking care of the household on the farm of my childhood. The visit to Sacramento was both nostalgic and sad. But it was good to have that last chance to spend time with her and to share my feelings with Grandpa Jackson. Very soon afterwards, Grandma passed away.

Back in Reno and Tahoe, I had organized the Lee Greenwood Affair. I was producing our shows, planning the content, arranging the music, deciding on costuming and lighting, and developing the crescendo for the entire presentation. It was becoming clear to me that the closing number must create a powerful impact. The audience has to feel the vibrations of the grand finale.

From my earliest days in music, beginning with the Moonbeams, I had been the leader of a band. Now, in the fall of 1970, I decided to step out from the group into the spotlight as a single performer. This was a big chance to take, and it would cost almost all of my savings. But I felt it was time to do something. Time was definitely going by; I had written that in a song. So I made the decision to break up the Lee Greenwood Affair.

To announce this transition, I started writing a show that for the first time would feature Lee Greenwood as an entertainer and the band merely as background. My friend Rudy Egan was a talented piano player, conductor, and arranger. Rudy helped me assemble the charts. The two of us worked night after night, getting the music ready and working out all the details involved in a show. Finally, we handpicked some great players and assembled them for two or three rehearsals.

The International Hotel was the venue we wanted. It was the showplace on the Strip, and the entertainment director there, Bill Miller, was a good friend of mine.

"Bill, do you think you could arrange a Saturday night in the main lounge for us?" I asked. "It's larger than most of the main rooms in Vegas, so it'll hold a big audience."

"Well, I'm not sure. We have Jerry Lee Lewis scheduled to play all three shows on the only possible Saturday. He's a hot item. The word is out that he's stolen the title 'King of Rock 'n' Roll' from Elvis. But let me check with his manager about that after-midnight performance. Would that one be okay?"

"Sure, Bill. This'll be an hour-and-a-half show, with me as the solo vocalist. I realize it's something ambitious that we're trying to do because I've always been an integral part of a band. And I know that today's attention-getters are top stars like Elvis and Jerry Lee Lewis."

"I feel certain we can do it, Lee," he said. "I'll announce it: 'Bill Miller and the International Hotel present Lee Greenwood.' "

The next day, Bill let me know that the key-pounding "Great Balls of Fire" man, who always had "A Whole Lot of Shaking Going On," would be happy to let me take over the late show at the International. That was good news, and I continued planning. Since my first days as a vocalist, I had admired Bobby Darin, the clean-cut, sincere singer and instrumentalist who had just played to a full house at the Copacabana in New York. It was his type of image that I identified with and wanted to present.

Rudy and I started sending out invitations along the Strip. And because both of us had been in Vegas for so many years, it wasn't hard to get permission to put up notices in the backstage areas of the main rooms and all the lounges. These were free invitations to the casts. In other words, we comped the show, drinks and everything. The evening would cost me between five and seven thousand dollars. I was putting everything on the line.

The other motivation behind my show was that I had finally been able to express my feelings about the Vietnam conflict. I had written a song that revealed my innermost thoughts as an American. Years ago I had been turned down by the military, and now I felt powerless to help.

I had been tense and frustrated, watching from the detached vantage point of Vegas, the struggle that was raging in our country. It seemed as though the war in Southeast Asia was wiping out our national unity. Everywhere, college kids were joining with teenagers, young adults, and many of their elders to demonstrate against U.S. policies. Determined young men, disillusioned and unwilling to risk death for a cause they couldn't believe in, were disappearing into Canada to avoid the draft. At the same time, a lot of equally patriotic Americans felt that the existing policies should be followed. But it was becoming obvious that helping South Vietnam establish its democracy was a mission we couldn't complete. In spite of our original intentions, America had fallen into a pool of quicksand, and it would take some difficult decisions to pull ourselves out.

It was a depressing time for me. Like many young guys in my generation, I felt guilty not to be with my contemporaries who were suffering and dying in those Asian jungles. Villages and fields were being devastated by bombs and napalm, and thousands of innocent people were being killed, and in many ways we felt responsible. Our government announced that the war was "winding down," but it was taking a long time and a constant barrage of public protest to bring our servicemen home.

The urge to participate was strong. I felt that there was a song for me to write that would make a difference. Maybe I could have some impact. Music is powerful. There might be a chance that my voice could make a small contribution in the direction of peace. Also, I was spurred on by an urge to be creative during those days. After entertaining in Vegas for so many years, I was hungry for new horizons. I hadn't lost my music; it was still inside me. But my earlier creativity had slowly dwindled away.

The song that I had written was to be not only a gift to the nation, but also a statement concerning my own personal freedom. I decided to bring the evening to a close by letting everyone there know just how I felt about the war. I was using this show and these people in my audience for that one night, as a springboard to send out my message.

The long-awaited evening finally arrived, and by one o'clock in the morning the members of our full orchestra, in black attire, were ready for the opening number. In my dark green suit, with its V-necked shirt and leather trim, I was nervously anticipating one of my life's biggest risks. Flowing into the big showroom was a capacity crowd of guests like Juliet Prouse, Jack Jones, the Fifth Dimension, Anthony Newley, and many others, including the cast of *Hair*. Excitement hovered in the large hall as the audience anticipated the introduction of a new solo entertainer on the Vegas scene. Although a lot of them knew me as a member of the Lee Greenwood Affair, they were interested to see what I had prepared for this move toward an independent career. Now for the first time, I was being presented as a single performer. It was an electric night.

Before I realized it, my show was almost over, and the spotlight slowly dimmed. I took a deep breath and waited in center stage for the right moment to present my final song. The first notes sounded behind me, and I stepped forward. As the stage lights beamed with ever-growing brightness into my face, I heard the opening harmonies rise from the saxophone and piano behind me. Feeling with deep intensity the statement that I was about to make, I began to sing "America."

"As I stroll the countryside
And gaze upon it with swelling pride
I thank my father for his strength."

I was thinking of "father" in its broadest sense, of the gratitude we owe our forefathers, those who first established America. George Washington, leader of our first military force, Thomas Jefferson, author of our Declaration of Independence, and James Madison, who framed our Constitution, envisioned a land of liberty and strength. But America was now in a state of dissension. How could we bring the people of our idealistic nation together? My words rose up, expressing my uncertainty:

"Maybe today we'll all say
'Good-bye' to this great land.
Maybe today we'll all get together
And face our troubles, hand in hand."

A deep hush had fallen upon the crowd. Even with the piercing lights in my eyes, I could vaguely see the friends and fellow entertainers in the front rows, and it was plain that the words were touching a chord of agreement in their hearts.

"As I walk down the busy street
And the pavement slides beneath my feet
I thank my brothers for a chance to survive in this land
   that's supposed to be free.
'O beautiful, for spacious skies, for amber waves of grain.' "

Now the melody increased in volume, underscoring my words and building to a heart-shattering crescendo.

"Give me one last chance before I die
To clear the air and see the sky,

And I'll be thankful just to know
There's a home for my son to protect and to love.
America. America."

Applause and shouts of approval broke through the final phrase as the spotlight suddenly faded, and I ran from the stage. After openly showing such sadness for my country, it was hard to hide the fact that I was almost overcome by the intensity of the moment. I can remember standing in the wings with tears welling up in my eyes because of the deep, personal feelings that had just been expressed, and as I listened to the cheering audience, I wondered why I hadn't prepared an encore. But it made no difference. There was no way I could have gone back for a bow, much less an encore. My emotions had finally taken over.

Of course, "America" was a negative song, a shot at our government, insisting that the path we were following was wrong. It was saying, "This land isn't free." Underneath the words of "America" was the unasked question: "How can we call this a democracy when the people's will goes unheeded?"

I was trying to say, "Hey, world, wake up! Hey, United States, we're going through a crisis. I love my country. And I'm echoing the feelings of the people in the streets who are telling our government to stop the killing. Throngs of people are standing out there, trying to convince our leaders. There are masses out of control!"

But I had missed the target. Maybe I hadn't even said what was on my mind in the right way. Anyway, the song never was heard outside of Vegas, or even beyond that night.

The one person who really liked the song was my friend Jimmy Packard. At the time, he was my greatest ally; when we were recording, he would spur me on. For some reason, he wanted me to give "America" to him.

"Why, Jimmy? What could you do with it?" I asked, half-smiling with curiosity, although I knew very well that he was the kind of guy who sort of collected things like silver and gold, and old coins. Maybe he wanted to collect this song, as he would a painting or a boat. He obviously wanted it very badly.

"Just to keep it," he replied. "Like a work of art. I can put it in my personal archives," he teased.

"Are you serious? Just like the Mona Lisa?" I joked back. "Well, okay. You take the song. It's yours."

I never go back on my word, so I gave it to him. It was like a friendship gesture. He was a big believer in what I was trying to do, which supplied me with a lot of courage and strength. His confidence gave me faith in myself, and I wanted to thank Jimmy Packard for that. So I signed over the copyright to him, and he owns it to this very day.

During the following two years, the U.S. was finally able to pull itself from the brutal conflict. By that time, the harsh statistics were clear. Over fifty-five thousand Americans had died and thousands of our allies were dead, as well as countless numbers of the inhabitants of a pathetically war-torn land. Many young veterans who had come home to us carried incurable scars, both physical and emotional. Although North Vietnam had returned a large number of our POWs, hundreds more were still listed as prisoner of war or missing in action, and the likelihood of ever determining their fate was very slim.

The song "America," which I wrote during that troubled stage of my life, wasn't quite right. The times were not right. Maybe if a certain singer or publisher had been there at the International Hotel that night and had been especially touched by it, perhaps the song would have been taken beyond the isolated world of Las Vegas.

America was down on itself, and I had failed with what I had hoped would be a song to tie us together and give us direction. But somewhere in my heart there remained a strong statement about my country. And I wondered if someday I could write a song that could make a difference, a song that would unite us with a positive feeling of patriotism.

CHAPTER VI

THAT CONCERT PERFORMANCE at the International Hotel, with its key song, "America," had signaled my decision to reach for a broader audience. First I would go to Los Angeles to make another attempt at becoming a solo artist. Dot Records had been bought out by Paramount, and I was bound over as a single performer. This made it possible for the producers Ed Matthews and Jerry Fuller, who had worked with Johnny Mathis at Columbia, to put together a recording contract for me. It seemed like the opportunity I had been working toward for so many years.

There was no doubt that my wife would be thrilled with the idea of moving to the big city of Los Angeles, the center of lavish shops and restaurants. I was really excited as I walked through the doorway of our home that evening and blurted out, "Guess what, Roberta. We're moving to L.A.! Isn't that terrific?"

Imagine my surprise when she gave me a tense, worried look. "No, Lee. Please . . . God, I don't want to go to California, especially L.A. . . . They have earthquakes!"

Roberta had been raised in the East, and I guess she had always thought of California as falling off into the ocean. She had heard wild tales of times when the ground shook and buildings crumbled, trapping people beneath mounds of rubble and even killing them.

"That's silly, Roberta," I assured her, giving her a little hug. "Los Angeles won't have another earthquake for 100 years."

I had her convinced, totally convinced, that there wasn't going to be an earthquake while we were in Los Angeles.

Within a matter of weeks, it was time to leave. We packed our belongings and gathered up Kelly, just three and a half, and Marc, who was ten. They climbed in the backseat of the car, holding tightly to their pets, Pepper Belle, a feisty little schnauzer, and Kelly's Maltese cat. In spite of the misgivings of my family—even the children had picked up some of Roberta's fear—we headed for a new life in Southern California.

It was almost dark when we finally reached our destination and drove up to a small motel. After checking in with the sleepy desk clerk, Roberta and I settled our tired family down for the night. The following morning would be February 9, 1971, a dawn that brought the most damaging earthquake to have hit Los Angeles in almost forty years.

Asleep in our motel room just before 6:00 A.M., I felt Pepper's warm, wet muzzle pushing at my arm. Opening my eyes, trying to come out of the heavy sleep brought on by yesterday's long hours of packing and driving, I glanced down at her and suddenly realized that the dog was staring at me nervously. In her eyes was that wary look that dogs have when they sense an intruder. Kelly's cat was jittery, too, and began bounding from one wall to another. Her blue fur was standing up all over her body and those sharp claws were out, first clinging onto the drapes, and then the couch. All at once I was jolted awake by the sound of my alarm clock sliding across the dresser and plunging to the floor. The room began to shake violently.

Roberta was instantly alert, screaming and grabbing me, and then clutching the bedside table. As it moved beneath her hands, she became hysterical.

"We've got to get the kids!" I yelled, and started toward their room, holding onto the walls as I made my way to our door. Just then, the full force hit, as if a huge Caterpillar tractor had slammed into the side of the motel. The impact jarred all the furniture, sending it sliding.

"There's no way to stand up," I was muttering to myself as I tried to make it across the bedroom in a half-crawl toward where Marc and Kelly had been sleeping. The whole place was shaking like a rag doll in the teeth of a terrier.

Instantly, it was over. There was total silence, except for some terrified cries coming from the kids' room.

Marc darted into our bedroom, followed by Kelly, who was still rubbing her sleepy eyes and crying. All four of us comforted each other, then walked to the window. Looking over at the swimming pool, we saw that almost all of that once-blue water had been tossed right out. The movement of the ground had been slinging it from side to side, then up, just like liquid swirling from a glass.

The quake had put a damper on our feelings about moving to Los Angeles. Our first night in L.A. turned out to be an omen. My decision to move had been the most costly miscalculation of my life. I had put my whole entertainment career on the line, and the next two years became a total downer.

Bound by a five-year contract and determined to stay, I went into the studio to cut "My First Night Alone Without You." Before it was ever released, Gulf and Western bought the Paramount label, ending any chance of my record being made public. This left me high and dry with a contract that was meaningless. Now began the rough days of looking for a job in a city I had explored as a high school freshman, but in which I was now a complete stranger. It was impossible to find work.

The weeks progressed as I beat the pavement in an attempt to feed my family. It soon became obvious that jobs in the music field just were not available. If people would have given me any chance at all, I think I would have played for free!

We began selling our belongings. Used articles sell for almost nothing, and everyone who answered our ad got real bargains. My matched Winchester rifle and shotgun were the first to go. We took a beating on the guns. It was rough giving up our personal things for so little.

One day, I looked at my two Buffet saxophones. They were beautiful horns, and I played them in my work. Well, I would be playing them if I had any work! But my family needed to

eat, so they had to go. It broke my heart when the guy came
to pick them up.

Then our Volkswagen station wagon was repossessed. The
dealer in L.A. came and took it away. I remember walking
downstairs from our apartment to the garage below and
looking for the station wagon where it was usually parked.
"Someone's stolen our car!" was my first thought. "This city's
overrun with thefts. You hear about them all the time."

All at once it hit me: "It's been driven off by the VW people. You can run from responsibility, but you can never hide.
Not even for the shortest time. It's amazing! How could the
credit bureau find us so fast in this sea of people living in the
San Fernando Valley?"

During the summer of 1971, when the VW was taken away,
some Air Force officers had a car where you'd least expect it.
The Apollo 15 astronauts achieved Man's first ride on the
moon. Their mission was covered, live, on TV and radio from
the prelaunch lift-off of their command module, *Endeavour,*
to its splashdown two days later. To the delight of the folks
back on Earth, Col. Randolph Scott and Lt. Col. James B. Ir-
win rambled over the moon's rugged surface in their lunar
rover, from the dusty Marsh of Decay to the edge of the dry
Sea of Rains. They were like two kids with a new toy, telling
us, "Moon soil is like softly powdered snow."

It sounded like fun, but back in L.A., there was a shadow
hovering over our household. Seeking work all over town, I
would have gladly accepted anything. But it was impossible.
This desperate search was something I didn't want to burden
my Las Vegas friends with. Trying hard to keep up my own
spirits, I was the epitome of optimism. On the phone with
Danny it was, "Hey! Things are looking up!"

But I still didn't have a job. Noticing the *Help Wanted* sign
that had gone up on the place selling Dixie Chicken across
from our apartment on Woodman Avenue, I knew I couldn't
wait any longer. Walking across the street, I signed up and
went to work delivering fried chicken. Ironically, I was transporting it in my flashy Z-28 Chevrolet Camaro.

"I sure wish this Z-28 had been taken instead of the VW. The gas for the Camaro costs more than my tips and wages combined," I kept thinking.

It didn't take long to get my wish: three weeks later they repossessed the Z-28.

For three or four months, I kept on working there at Dixie Chicken, helping cook and sell the food. I was really worried about a coworker in the kitchen who seemed to be overmedicated, or something. Maybe he was on drugs. He just wasn't with it. Then one afternoon there was a piercing scream. Racing into the back of the kitchen where he had been chopping the meat, all the other employees and I stared in disbelief at the bright red blood pouring from his half-destroyed thumb.

"It's gone! My thumb! Help me, you guys!" he was shrieking, wide-eyed with pain.

"Quick! Look through that chicken!" one of us shouted. But that part of his thumb was well into the mound of meat and impossible to find. It was gruesome, even to think about.

Right then I said, "This is hogwash! This is really dumb! The job isn't even paying enough to cover the expenses of my family." Truly finished with this place, I quit.

It was so depressing to be unemployed and without music. I felt such a deep void and needed, in some way, to keep my mind alert. So in order to maintain my sanity, I began writing a detective novel. For months, sometimes working six to eight hours a night, I wrote it out by hand, penciling down a mystery story. It was like a Mannix TV episode with a complex plot. It started with the main character looking out of his window on a gloomy day while the rain was falling, making circular rainbows in the oil on the pavement below. This guy was in the Army. He and two of his buddies had stolen some gold bullion. They exchanged it for German marks, which were hidden inside some large, ornate picture frames and shipped to America. The adventure slowly unfolded until finally the three of them were reunited in a shoot-out at the end. Plenty of action!

When the book was finished, I let several people read my handwritten manuscript. It drew a lot of approval, but I never thought to have a second copy made. Anyway, I didn't have the money.

One day I showed my book to a man from Texas who said, "Oh, yeah. I work with the King family. You know, the King's Ranch? Well, I'll take your manuscript down there and get it put in proper form. Maybe it's publishable. I'll mail it back to you."

"Sure. I'd appreciate that." And I handed it to him.

Talk about naïve! I had no idea who that man actually was. From a writer's point of view, that was really stupid. But I wasn't thinking as a writer. I was thinking as a human being: much too trusting. I never saw my manuscript again.

Deep in debt, with no prospects for work, I was almost in despair. I remember very well the instant I decided to leave that L.A. environment. Continually borrowing money to support my family, one evening I was down to my last $1.60 in cash. At least it was enough to buy four hamburgers for the kids, my wife, and me at the corner Jack-in-the-Box. So, confidently strolling down to there, I brought the food back to the apartment, and Roberta, Marc, Kelly, and I stepped upstairs to have some burgers and ice tea together. Opening up the sack, I discovered that the hamburger buns contained no meat. There was nothing—just bread!

With my anger rising, a form of rage took over. I marched right back to the Jack-in-the-Box, reached out, and snatched the kid in the booth by the tie.

Leaving out the meat hadn't been intentional. It was just an oversight. He had simply forgotten to put in the meat. But I had reached a breaking point in my life and was almost out of control. Still holding him by the tie, I shoved the sack of meatless hamburgers back into his hands and in a low, threatening voice, I said, "Unless you put the meat in these, I'm coming through this window after you!"

I was serious. At this point, I was desperate!

Well, the poor kid nearly died of fright. It was probably the worst experience he ever had selling hamburgers. Of course, he slammed meat in those hamburger buns as fast as his hands would move. I jerked the burgers back through the little window and without a word, stalked down the sidewalk toward the apartment where my hungry wife and children were waiting. The scent of freshly cooked meat was rising up from the sack, and as my mind replayed that absurd scene, I started thinking: "That's it! This has gone too far. Here I am, a grown man, and I'm begging!"

Back in that rented living room, I got on the phone and called an agent in Las Vegas. "Hey, Frank. Book me anywhere, doing anything," I said to him. "I'm leaving Los Angeles."

"You're a talented guy, Lee. No problem. I'll find something and get back to you," he replied.

Within a few days, Frank called back. "I've found you a job, Lee. It's in Great Falls, Montana, playing piano bar at a club there," he said. "It's $400 a week, room and board. Do you want it?"

"When do I start?"

"I'll get the date and call you back," he said.

His return call nailed down my immediate plans: "You begin this week."

As I hung up the phone, I had mixed emotions. "Sure I play piano, but not like this," I thought. "I know a few songs, but as a single, you have to know thousands. And where the hell is Montana? Somewhere near Yellowstone National Park, I think. Well, at least I'll be back in music and making money."

With both cars gone, and having to be on the job that weekend, I managed to borrow some traveling cash, with enough for four plane tickets to Great Falls, Montana. Danny offered to take all our furniture back to Las Vegas and put Roberta and the kids on a plane to join me in Montana. Then I was out of there!

In my whole life, I had never played piano bar. Never! But I had brought along a bunch of music books and sheet music that had a lot of lyrics. Some were popular songs; others were ballads and country tunes. My mother had given me a few of these, years ago. The newer-looking ones I had bought. But I hadn't practiced. In fact, I hadn't touched a piano in years.

On the plane, I started going through these songs, wondering what my audiences would be like and which selections of music might be their favorites. The hard part would be remembering the words to all the songs in this large stack, and there was a good chance that the customers would come up with titles I didn't even have music for. Quickly, I started writing down lyrics on some pieces of blank paper. These would be easier to read while I was playing.

Arriving in Great Falls, I noticed that a girl driving an old, run-down car seemed to be looking for someone. That person was me. "Oh, yeah. You must be our new piano player," she said, motioning to the beat-up vehicle. "Get in." And she jumped back into the driver's seat.

Picking up my one suitcase and the stack of arrangements and lyrics, I climbed into the car. As we were rolling down the road toward town, she handed me the contract that had been sent by my agent. I looked it over, noticed that it covered a two-week period, and signed it, stashing one copy in my bag.

Soon my long-haired driver pull to a stop. "Well, here we are. Okay, the club's right down the street," and she pointed out the direction. "See you later." I was out of the car, and she was gone.

Grabbing my suitcase, books, and papers, I walked into the motel where she had dropped me and right up to the front desk to register. Without even glancing at me, the fat man behind the desk said, "Pay up."

Feeling rather puzzled, I answered, "But it's supposed to be on the club. . . ."

With an impatient sigh, the desk clerk looked up and frowned. Then, in a sour voice, he replied, "When the last guy was here, the club didn't pay. You pay."

There was no choice. Of course I had to pay. It was forty dollars a week for room and board, and I had, altogether, about a hundred bucks. "Here's forty," I told him, and checked in.

It was a shabby motel with about thirty-five rooms, and since I had already been through a long, dusty day, I found room #9 and decided to take a shower. It didn't take long to find that there was only cold water. "Well, for forty bucks a week, what should I expect?" I said to myself. So after a quick scrubbing in the ice-cold water, I got ready to go to the club and eat.

The 3-D International Club had once been a gambling casino. It consisted of a huge dance hall downstairs and a small key club upstairs, where I was supposed to play. Looking around to see if dinner was going to be served soon, I found a tray with the remains of some cold cuts and cheese that obviously had been there for hours. Approaching the bartender, I asked, "Is it possible to get something to eat?"

"We all get the same and you're too late today," he replied with a disinterested shrug.

I got the picture. The contract didn't specify what the food would be. So I climbed the winding staircase that led around and up to the second floor. Upon reaching the top, I found myself in a little cocktail lounge. But there was no piano.

Wondering what to do next, I finally found the manager and introduced myself. Then I asked, in an offhand voice, "Where's the piano?"

"You didn't bring one?" he answered, surprised.

He must have expected me to show up with an electronic keyboard. After a pause, he said, "Well, okay. Let me get a couple of guys. We'll go downstairs and get the one down there."

He was talking about the large upright from the main dance hall. He was simply going to go down there and bring it up.

The club was built on a hill. So the manager and his two muscle-bound helpers hoisted that enormous piano off the dance floor and, noting that the staircase was much too narrow, they took it outside and rolled it along the sidewalk. Then they proceeded to lug the piano up the side of the hill, using ropes that they had strung around it. I could hardly believe my eyes!

At the top of the hill, they carefully pushed it onto the roof of the club and across to a boarded-over opening in the middle. Lifting up a trapdoor of wood and shingles, they heaved the piano over to the gaping hole and lowered it precariously through the ceiling.

Slamming down on the key club floor, the piano took the blow with every note sounding. There rang out an earsplitting "crrraaasssh."

During this whole time, I was watching in amazement. What could I say?

Now that they had gotten the heavy instrument into the room, the workmen situated it where I'd be playing that evening. Looking around, I said, "Great! Now what about some light? It'll be dark tonight."

"Sure," answered the manager. Soon he brought in a little lamp and light bulb, which looked like a whorehouse light, and he set it on the top of the piano, over to one side.

That would be all right, but there was no mike, no loudspeaker. I said, "Well, what about the microphone?"

"Ohhh. . . . You need a mike." He pondered a moment, then said, "Okay. Just a minute." He grabbed a couple of guys and left.

He must have had some connection with the owner of the town's auction house. At least I hope so because soon they were back with a huge bullhorn they had taken off the roof of the auction block. It was just a big, wide circular speaker. Hauling it up the staircase, they carried the faded, rusty funnel across the floor and put it by the piano. There it was, just laid out on the floor. But they had also gotten one of those mikes that the auctioneer uses. It looked like the RCA Gramophone speaker, the one with that perky dog leaning into it with his head cocked to one side, listening. So they set up these contraptions, and that was it. They were through.

The manager dusted off his hands, stood there for a moment with his fists on his hips, then with a look of satisfaction, walked out.

Alone with this haphazard setup, I began to try tuning the piano, which had been totally slammed out of tune during its harsh introduction to the key club. After adjusting its strings as well as possible, I pulled out my music books and practiced for about an hour. Then I ran back to the motel and changed into my best clothes for the night. Although I was getting pretty hungry, there was no time to eat. Anyway I was excited that I'd be singing and playing for the first time in almost two years.

By seven I was pounding away at that terrible piano. It was a wreck, clinking with a hollow metal sound. For six hours a night, I'd be playing that instrument, doing my best to create a festive mood among the couples sitting at the key club tables. The patrons were cordial, frontier types, and, setting up a private goal for myself, I decided I'd try to get them on the dance floor. That way, there would be fewer people loudly talking and clanking glasses while I was playing.

"Could you play 'Galveston'?" was one of the first requests. The lady must have been a fan of Jimmy Webb.

"Of course. Just a minute. I'm sure I have it here," I said, digging for lyrics among my books and notes. From the very beginning, having learned to play by ear, I could run through any tune. But the lyrics were another matter. I'd have to find those.

Going through many of the songs I had performed with my bands, I was able to keep the audience happy quite a bit of the time. But the requests kept coming, and I'd continue searching for lyrics. By the end of the evening, my fingers were beginning to bleed because I wasn't really the best piano player. I remember my mother saying how she used to play until her fingers bled, accidentally hitting the fingerboard so many times with her knuckles as she pounded away at it.

In the dim light, I could barely see the music. I had to hold one hand up on the music sheets while singing an unfamiliar song, because the pages just wouldn't stay open. Singing all night, until I was hoarse, I was relieved when it was time for the last request.

"How about a little 'Stardust' for dancing?" the gent said.

"Great! Here it is, just for you," I said, a little wearily. I knew that one, thank God. My fingers went easily down on familiar keys and I began, "Sometime I wonder why I spend the lonely nights . . ." And I was wondering.

A little after one o'clock in the morning, the crowd of dancers began to disperse. I had gotten through the first night.

The second night was just as hard. Since I was a complete stranger in this town, I'd smile and try to be friendly with each couple who came up, asking for their special song. I would quickly look through my books, hoping to find it. Sometimes the song would be in there with all those tunes. I'd proudly pull it out, the lovers would be pleased, and I would play it.

The evenings went on like this, with the third night being a little bit easier. But by the fourth night, I was losing my voice, and the end of the week found me wearing these vocal chords raw, just getting through the six hours of singing.

Finally the first week was over, and my wife and kids were flying up from L.A.

But nobody had warned us about the weather. Montana can plunge down below zero in the winter, and just as my whole family arrived, the freezing weather hit!

None of us had any warm clothes. So I took what little money I had and bought jackets for Marc and Kelly. That left thirty dollars in my pocket to buy food. I knew I just had to find the owner, who had been conspicuously absent on payday. Obviously, he was avoiding me. But I was walking back to the club when suddenly I spotted him ducking around a corner, headed for his car. Sensing that this was the only way I'd have a chance to get paid, I jumped into the cab that was parked in front. It felt rather melodramatic to be telling the driver, "Follow that car."

As the club owner pulled up in front of his house and slid out of his car, I jumped from my cab and ran up to him. "I've finished my first week, and you've got to pay me," I demanded. "My family's here, and I have to get my paycheck."

Without even hesitating, he shrugged and said, "Okay," then reached in his pocket and pulled out my first week's pay. He handed me $400 in bills. Now, at least I had the cash. And this was a two-week contract. That's all it was.

I went right back to the hotel and phoned my agent. "Book me somewhere else," I said. "Quick!"

"What's the problem, Lee?" he asked.

"This isn't working out," I told him. "I don't think I'm going to get my money for next week. I'm lucky to have this week's pay."

Not getting paid was something Frank immediately understood. "I'll see what I can find for you, Lee. Don't worry," he said.

Throughout the following nights of playing piano bar, it was getting increasingly rough to sing for six straight hours. But what was really a load on my mind was whether I would get paid for that second week. Before long, I was plenty worried and was looking for the owner again. When he finally appeared, down in the main lounge, I went right up and confronted him.

"I know you're not going to pay me this week," I said calmly. "But if you'll give me as much as you can, that's all I want. Just give me what you can, and I'll get out of here."

Maybe he appreciated my forthright approach, or it could be that he felt it would be a relief to have one financial responsibility off his case and gone. Anyway, he reached into his pockets, pulled out a wad of money, and counted it.

"Here," he said, and handed it all to me. It came to $360, and the last $20 was in rolled coins from his cash register at the 3-D Club.

This was enough for plane tickets to San Diego. I finished my final night of playing and the four of us were off to the airport. As our jet left the runway and headed skyward, I searched the faces of my wife and kids for some indication of how they felt about me, after the hassle their breadwinner had just put them through.

Without a job again, I was still trying to establish a meaningful career and, at the same time, provide security for my family.

But it was rough. Still owing a lot of money because of the Los Angeles fiasco, I had almost lost faith in myself. But somehow I just kept hanging in there, clinging to the hope that I could pull out of this downward spiral.

There was a feeling of instability throughout the world, too. The news was spattered with photos of people torn apart by war. There was a wide breach between the democratic and Communist nations, and a lot of countries were separated by icy silence. Since shortly after World War II, Nationalist China, on the island of Formosa, had been accepted as the voice of the Chinese people. But just before 1972, hoping to establish communication with the world's most populous country, on China's mainland, the United Nations formally granted membership to the People's Republic of China. Now our leaders could at least have a forum where they could exchange ideas and talk over their disagreements. For the world, it was good news.

But that spring, President Nixon put out an order to increase the bombing of Hanoi and Haiphong. The North Vietnamese troops were pushing southward toward Anloc, only sixty miles north of Saigon. By mid-August, American B-52 bombers were pounding North Vietnam with the most concentrated bombing raids of the war, and soon they were targeting the Mekong Delta inside of South Vietnam.

Back home, the spirit that it takes to win a war was just not there because, in the eyes of many Americans, this war couldn't be justified. Even though our country was helping defend South Vietnam, we knew very little about it. We hadn't been given enough information about the situation in Southeast Asia to be convinced that what we were doing there might at least make some sense. The people of America needed assurance that the sacrifices being made by the men and women of our armed forces were essential. Were they losing their lives for a cause that was right?

As I had said in my song "America," we owe a debt of thanks to those who have worked and fought to make our nation free. Now it was up to us to make wise decisions in the name of that freedom.

CHAPTER VII

In the midst of grim news reports, featuring continual war coverage, the Greenwoods moved to San Diego. Waiting for me there was a job as a piano player in the Syndicate Restaurant lounge. It was a Roaring Twenties-looking place inside, decorated in red velvet. The club was one wide-open room, encircling the lounge, so the sound of my piano could be heard throughout the entire dining area. The manager would talk at the top of his voice. Then he would look over toward the piano, give me a real mean look, and start badgering: "Quiet down! Quiet down!"

I got so frustrated with the continual harassing that I quit and gathered together a group of musicians to form the Burgundy Express. You might say our music was Spanish rock 'n' roll! Even though I was working six nights a week in San Diego, our family had a chance to spend a lot of quality time together. Down by the ocean, we took walks at night along the rugged shoreline. We could smell the salty Pacific air and watch the waves crash against the jagged rocks, spraying up against our faces. It felt so good. The sea breeze was refreshing, renewing.

Those were some of the best days of my life with Kelly. Waking up, alert and full of unspent vitality, even after an endless night of playing with the Burgundy Express, I'd start clanking around in the kitchen, making a cup of coffee.

"Daddy!" my five-year-old would shout, as she ran right

into my arms, reaching up for a "good morning" hug. "Marc's already gone to school. There's nobody to play with."

She already had me wrapped around her finger, and after serving her a large helping of Dad's pancakes I asked, "Well, Kelly. Would you like to go to the playground?"

What a question to ask a little girl! She was jumping up and down in excitement as I went on. "You can play on the swings and I'll shoot some basketball on the court. Okay?"

"Okay!"

Taking hold of her tiny hand, I walked with Kelly to the local park. Sometimes I carried her piggyback, for what turned out to be a frequent pastime. Back then there wasn't much prosperity at our house, but what a rare opportunity to strengthen the bonds between parent and child. Wealth comes in many forms. I'll never forget telling her one day as the two of us were slowly wandering back home, "Kelly, maybe someday I'll have lots of money and no time. Right now, I've got lots of time and no money. But one day, when your life gets too busy to slow down, I hope you'll remember our afternoons together."

In San Diego, I began to climb the ladder slowly. Obviously, there was a long way to go, but I was on my way back up. During the time Roberta and I were there, we worked as hard as we could, but there were still some payments due. Our creditors eventually caught up with us. There were knocks on the door. We had to avoid the strangers, dodge them, or pretend we weren't who we were. There was just no way I could make enough money, all at once, to pay off the debt that I had piled up by going to Los Angeles to begin a recording career. It would take time, and because I've always been one who pays all my bills, the fact that I couldn't do it now was eating away at me.

The U.S. was down, too. President Nixon had been steadily increasing our bombing of North Vietnam. But during the two weeks between Christmas and New Year's Day, 1973, we reached the point of losing twenty-seven aircraft and ninety-nine men. This was just too much—even for Americans who hadn't been demonstrating and speaking out against our involvement in Southeast Asia. In past years, all the attempts to reach a peace agreement had failed. But on January 27, in Paris, our leaders signed a cease-fire treaty. Not many of them were smiling, but at least the pressure would begin to lift.

Valentine's Day was terrific! The first planeload of prisoners of war coming home from Hanoi landed at Travis Air Force Base, California. One of them, Navy Capt. Jeremiah A. Denton, Jr. had made a suggestion during their flight, and the returning servicemen filed out of their plane whistling, "California, Here I Come." It had seemed like an eternity away from their families.

Over the nation's radios, Tony Orlando and Dawn were singing, "Tie a yellow ribbon 'round the old oak tree," the theme for a lot of happy parents, wives, and children, whose men were among the returning. Bright yellow bows on all kinds of trees throughout the country welcomed them home. After all the pain, it was great to have something to smile about.

America's initial disengagement from the war didn't take long. By March 29 our troops were home, and Hanoi declared that all our POWs had been repatriated. But the fighting kept going on in South Vietnam, Laos, and Cambodia. We were wondering how the conflicts were ever going to be resolved. And the relatives of the men still classified as POW or MIA were pressing for more information. Deep in their hearts, they felt certain that Hanoi must be secretly holding some of the missing Americans. It was a feeling like, "What if my son is over there, suffering? We've just got to get him home." A ground swell of support for their cause began to grow. People everywhere wanted to help, signing petitions, writing letters, and speaking out to remind Hanoi that the issue wasn't closed.

Although I was deeply concerned about our injured veterans and unreturned servicemen, I was glad to see America beginning to recover. I was slowly making my comeback, too, and I was anxious to square away my debts. Still not wanting to declare bankruptcy, and determined to repay every penny,

I decided to return to Las Vegas, which had always been good to me. A call to Billy Monogold got me one of the hardest jobs I've ever played.

"It's at the Palomino Club, a glittery burlesque house on the north side of town. I'm playing sax, Lee, but we need a singer and organ player. We play seven hours a night, seven nights a week. It's not big bucks: only $140 a week. . . ."

"Well, it's a way to get back to Vegas," I said. "When can I start?"

"As soon as you get here," he answered.

Those were wonderful words to hear. So I headed back to the city that had always provided a job and a life for a Gypsy like me.

Soon I was walking through the door of the Palomino Club, which lived up to Billy's description. It looked like Glitter Gulch: elaborate, with sparkly decorations everywhere. Billy and I were joined by two other guys, a drummer and Red, who played two trumpets at the same time and told vulgar jokes. Sometimes I could wedge in some pop melodies from Chicago and numbers that most musicians entertaining in a place like this wouldn't be able to play. But usually the nights found me doing the typical bump-and-grind stuff and crooning "House of the Rising Sun."

When I had decided that Las Vegas would be the best town in which to find a job in music, I was underestimating the opportunities. At the point when the Palomino Club job was starting to dissolve, and I was looking for employment again, Jimmy Packard called. "Lee, our bass player is leaving the Bare Touch of Vegas at the Stardust. It's a rock 'n' roll show. How about taking his place? You could play keyboard bass."

What I didn't mention was that a very different job had just come my way. A good friend, Sammy Sams, was casino manager at the Tropicana. Years earlier, Sammy had tried to get my first record played in Chicago, but all his efforts had failed. Disappointed that he hadn't been able to help my career, and knowing I needed another job, he promised that I'd be hired as a baccarat dealer in his casino. First he had to teach me to deal!

Sammy gave me the initial moves and rules, then suggested that I practice at home on an ironing board, a surface with cushioning, which helps the dealer pick up each card. After practicing far into the late hours, trying to become a smooth dealer, I went back to the Tropicana the next day for my audition. But when I walked up to Sammy, he gave me an apologetic shrug with a palms-up gesture of helplessness and said, "Lee, I've got no control over this, but there aren't any openings in baccarat. You're gonna to have to deal twenty-one."

A startled expression must have crossed my face. "I've never dealt twenty-one!"

"Go ahead. Try it!"

Not only had I never practiced dealing twenty-one, I didn't even know how to get the cards out of the shoe, that little box the cards are dealt from. I was scared to death.

"Audition," they call it. They step you up to a table, move the dealer aside, and let you deal to real customers. Of course, the patrons don't really know what's going on until you start dealing, and you can't deal worth a damn. Then they say to themselves, "Aha! A break-in!"

This is the situation I found myself in—dealing twenty-one, with the clued-in gamblers trying to get me, to cheat me in some way. All the time, the other dealer was watching, hoping to prevent them from taking money from this raw dealer at the Tropicana's expense.

If I had been the boss, young Mr. Greenwood would not have been hired. But Sammy had said, "You will be a dealer." And he made good his promise.

That afternoon, Kelly and I spent a lot of time learning twenty-one together, perched on stools, face to face across an unlikely-looking card table. After a break, it was, "Daddy! Let's play that game on Mom's ironing board. Just one more time, please?"

"Sure, honey." Reaching over for the still-warm deck of cards, I gave Kelly a smile. "You're a real good customer, baby. You keep coming back to my table!"

For a little girl, it was a special treat to be learning a game and getting the undivided attention of her father. To me, although I loved laughing and counting up the cards with my daughter, this was more serious. It was to be our livelihood. I found that dealing is primarily a matter of dexterity and the mathematical ability to figure the payoffs. Soon I could manipulate the cards with the quickness of a veteran dealer and gained confidence in handling the money. I was ready for the position as dealer.

So when Jimmy Packard called me with the Bare Touch of Vegas offer, I was placed in a quandary. Should I take the job in music, which was my strong suit and real love, or would the gaming tables prove to be a better path toward bailing me out of debt? In keeping with the atmosphere, I decided to flip a coin. If the quarter landed "heads up," it would be the casino job, something entirely new. "Tails" would keep me working as an entertainer.

Hastily I tossed the quarter. Up it went, then dropped down with a light "clink," and rolled underneath the bar. Heads or tails? How could I know? Then it struck me: why not take both jobs? I found a phone and made a call.

"Hey, Jimmy. I'll take the job at the Stardust."

As fate would have it, Paul Anka was at the Stardust one night. Impressed with the Bare Touch dancers, he decided our girls would liven up his show at Caesar's Palace.

The next evening, our producer came up to me. "Lee, would you like to make some extra money?"

"How?" I asked.

"We want you to double, to take on another job. Can you do it?"

"Sure, I can do it," I told him. And the Caesar's Palace gig was added to my schedule.

Working three jobs at once takes a lot of finesse. I learned how much you can do if you really put your mind to it, and I gained a greater appreciation of the grueling efforts that are often required of surgeons, astronauts, and others who are in highly demanding positions. It was amusing to overhear people in Las Vegas complaining about how hard they worked. At the card tables, they would gripe. In the showrooms where I was performing, they would grumble about their work, too. Silently, I would just laugh at them. As for me, I was determined to keep all my jobs as long as possible. Nothing, not even fatigue, was going to drive me out.

But the schedule was backbreaking. At the Tropicana, the dealing job was either from 11:00 in the morning to 7:00 P.M. or from noon to 8:00 at night. The later shift was better because it gave me a little time in the morning with Kelly and Marc, whenever they weren't in school, and a chance to see Roberta. It was also the only time available to do the ordinary chores such as go to the bank and pay bills or put gas in the car. But it was rough at the other end of that shift because the show at Caesar's Palace started at eight o'clock. Without twenty minutes' leeway, it was impossible to make the show. So whenever they booked me on the twelve to eight shift, all day long I'd be pestering the foreman and the pit boss, "Can I have the early out?"

Although I never mentioned it, they knew I had another job at Caesar's Palace. Moonlighting is one thing, but two extra jobs was ridiculous! They had the power to say, "Take it or leave it. Go by our schedule or you're out of here. You're fired."

But each time, they gave me those extra twenty minutes. I would rush out, jump into my cargo van, and race off to the Palace for Paul Anka's opening show. My featured vocal was Joe Cocker's song "Feeling All Right," with the eye-catching girls dancing in their colorful but almost nonexistent costumes.

As soon as the show was over, the show girls and I had just a couple of minutes to be onstage at the Stardust. The only way to get all of us there was my Dodge van. These six glamorous girls would scurry out and pile helter-skelter into the van, which had been left running while we were doing the Caesar's Palace show.

"I know there aren't any seats, girls, but I've thrown some blankets on the floor. And you'll find a few jackets back there to put around your shoulders."

"Lee, you're a doll. We appreciate it, 'cause it's kind of cold in here." And they'd pull off their high, plumed hats and giggle as they crowded in and stretched out on the van floor in those elaborate, feathered costumes.

These were six of the most gorgeous women you've ever seen, dressed in scanty bras, G-strings, and net nylons. Their hair was either short or drawn back into a bun, to fit beneath the orange and purple feathery headgear.

Off I'd drive with my load of girls lounging luxuriously in the back. Usually they were wound up, filling the air with animated gestures and chattering excitedly about whatever they expected might happen that evening.

It was comical. After a frantic five-minute drive to the Stardust Hotel, I'd dump them out by the stage door, leave my van with the valet, and run in to get my equipment ready for the first show with Bare Touch. All the musicians in the show had to wear bell-bottom pants, and hip-looking net shirts, with tight belts around our waists, to make us look muscular. I was the one with a very short haircut. As a casino dealer, I couldn't wear a beard or long hair like most of the musicians.

At the same time, the girls would bounce into their dressing room, rushing to put on their fresh makeup. There was no time to change costumes, and that fit in with the producer's plans. It saved him a lot of dough. But those in the audience who had seen the Caesar's Palace opening show, and then had come over to the closing show at the Stardust, were looking at the same girls and the same singer, doing a similar show. They were probably saying, "Hmmm. . . . This looks familiar."

All together, we'd close the show with the Fifth Dimension's "The Age of Aquarius." As the final notes of "let the sunshine in" were still fading, we were ready to run off the stage and out the stage door of the Stardust, leap into my van, and rush back to Caesar's Palace for its second show. Then we had to repeat the process, bolting out the back door, flinging ourselves into the van, and dashing back to the Stardust for another show. That performance of the Bare Touch of Vegas wasn't over until four o'clock in the morning.

Back home, I would wearily drop into bed, wondering if I would get to see the kids in the morning. I knew it would be: wake up and do it all over again, seven days a week. Considering our schedules, it wasn't surprising that Roberta and I had separated.

But this killer routine was going to enable me to pay off the $10,000 L.A. debt, I felt certain. Added up, the salaries for my three jobs totaled $300 a day. Danny and I had a running joke about it.

"How's it going today, Lee?"

"Oh, just another lousy $300 day!"

Then the hint of a smile would show on Danny's face.

Knowing that this couldn't last forever, I was making the money while I could. Anyway, one thing was certain. I had to get four hours' sleep. That was my minimum. If I got less than four, I was in trouble. So my agreement with Roberta was, "I'll take the money for the family each week and leave it out on the table for you, in the living room of my apartment. Come in, take the money, go out, close the door, and lock it. But do not wake me up. Because if you wake me, I can't get my four hours' sleep. And I've got to have it."

Now, I always slept with a gun under my pillow—a Ruger .22, nothing serious. Living near the Vegas convention center, which had a lot of transients and wasn't the safest place, I kept it as a precaution. And maybe it was a carry-over from the days when my grandfather always had a gun in the house for protection. Anyway, I came home from work at the end of one of my exhausting weeks, after putting aside my debt payment, with $600 in cash. I was going to lay the money for Roberta on the living room table, but being so wiped out, I walked into the bedroom, took my clothes off, and totally forgot. I just lay down, put my clock on "snooze," which I always do, checked the weapon under my pillow, and started off to sleep.

As I was in that grey area between consciousness and sleep, the door slowly opened and the living room light switched on. Then I heard some rustling around on the living room table, sounds of keys clanking, and objects moving. Half-awake, I thought, "Why would she do that? Why would she make noise? She knows she's not supposed to wake me up!"

So I sleepily opened my eyes and glanced over to the mirror, which reflected the living room area. Just then, the image of a man's head bobbed past! Realizing there was danger, I was struggling to come awake.

The trespasser peered into my bedroom. It was so dark that he didn't see me. Then he walked into the bathroom and looked in there. I just stayed very still, as the radio was slowly fading out, diminishing in volume as I held my breath.

Carefully, I reached for my Ruger and pulled it out from underneath the pillow. I couldn't see whether he had a weapon or not, but I knew he was invading my territory. My gun was a single-action revolver, which I had practiced shooting with fast-draw accuracy.

A loud, piercing click rang through that silent room, as I cocked my gun. The intruder hit the floor and desperately scrambled around the corner. He raced out the front door, slamming it behind him. Chasing after him, I put two shots through the wooden door, dashed over to it, and whipped it open.

"Damn! I missed him!" I muttered.

The prowler was leaping down the stairs, bordered by a railing, and heading for the first floor. I shot twice between the stairs and railing, but missed again. That was hard to believe because I'm a pretty good shot! But I was shaken up and anxious.

"I'm going to nail this thief," I mumbled, as I ran out onto the balcony.

Then I said to myself, "I'm totally nude, and I've got a smoking revolver. I'm going to be running down the street, shooting at this guy. . . . People are going to think I'm crazy!"

That ended the chase. After checking to see where the bullets had gone, I fell into bed and was out like a light, for what was left of the night: three hours.

Bullets had been flying and people were desperately running on the other side of the world, too. It was 1975, the year of a humiliating helicopter escape from Saigon's American

Embassy of the last remaining Westerners and their South Vietnamese cohorts, their arms filled with struggling, frightened Asian children, as they made their final desperately chaotic exit from a land being taken over by North Vietnamese troops. Our forces had pulled out, but we were still insisting on a full accounting of our POWs and MIAs.

However, that July an encouraging example of international cooperation took place in the sky. American and Russian astronauts worked together for two days, on scientific experiments, after docking their Apollo and Soyuz spacecrafts. It seems that people can get along better 140 miles above the earth than on it.

Our thoughts were in the heavens with Elton John's hit "Lucy in the Sky with Diamonds." The Doobie Brothers brought us right back down to Earth, in '75, with their song "Black Water." But the dynamic recording by the Bee Gees, "Jive Talkin'," was the one packed with high-pressured energy.

Regardless of what I've been involved with, everyone has always remarked about my energy level. Whether I'm racing down a basketball court, performing onstage, or pumping out a song in a recording studio, they will say, "Where does all that power come from? Man, you're wired!"

They're talking to someone who wouldn't even consider drinking or using drugs. From the earliest days, my energy level constantly stayed at a peak. Impatient at any pause, I was the first guy through the stoplight at an intersection, jumping ahead at the hint of green. I don't know why. It was just an inner desire to get going. But after working almost around the clock for four years, I felt the strength sapped from me.

By the time 1976 rolled around, for the first time in my life I really felt tired. My energy was just not there, and my voice was gone. The move to Los Angeles had left its mark on my life. It had taken four years to pay off that debt, and my marriage had been blown apart in the whirlwind of my relentless pursuit of success. The years that Roberta and I had spent in a struggle to be good parents and providers had left us both exhausted.

It had been a marriage of confusion. When Roberta and I married, I was still trying to find my own way, to establish a direction for my life. And somehow I had gotten caught up in feeling responsible for someone else's life. I hadn't waited long enough to feel confident about our relationship and know that it was right. That may have been my greatest mistake. So our marriage didn't have a very good chance of surviving.

It seems unfair, too, because that family sacrificed so much as I was striving to become an entertainer. Roberta, with Marc and Kelly, followed me so many places and tried to stay with me. They gave as much as they could and never said no to any decision I made.

But I had angry feelings inside of me that said, "I've made another mistake! I've married wrong again!"

Before I could put that anger behind me, I had to raise my children. That was the most agonizing challenge of being on the road.

Being unable to keep my marriage together laid on a lot of guilt. And Roberta probably felt guilty, too, that she couldn't be as good a mother as she wanted to because I was away so much. I think the children sensed the tension and the struggle. They never had the love and security of a unified home.

Roberta and I were like strangers. The bond between us had been broken, and I was facing a painful divorce once more.

With mixed feelings, I went through the motions of another workday on our country's bicentennial. The Fourth of July, 1976, was a stirring milestone for Americans and the millions abroad who watched the televised festivities as fifteen tall ships and two hundred others from nations throughout the world moved slowly into New York's Hudson Bay. In Washington, D.C., laser guns sent the message, "1776-1976, Happy Birthday, U.S.A." But that Fourth of July in Vegas I was deeply depressed. All around me were people pushing and shoving, angry they'd lost a lot of money . . . drinking heavily. I just tried to stay out of their way, hoping for rest after the last hand was dealt and the final show was over.

It has always been hard for me to live my life alone. There is a need to have someone near me. While working my unbelievable full-time schedule, I had found a special friend. Melanie Cronk was an accomplished dancer with an understanding heart and a shoulder to lean on. Knowing that I was going through a divorce, she was sympathetic. At first we were just friends. Then that friendship slowly grew into a romance. But it's difficult to establish a relationship after failing twice, and I was wary about getting involved again. It was taking a while to accept the fact that my quest for a music career had again left me on my own.

> *You can't fall in love when you're crying.*
> *Please don't try to look into my eyes.*
> *If I said, "I love you," I'd be lying.*
> *'Cause the memory of yesterday is still in my mind.*

CHAPTER VIII

FROM MY POINT OF VIEW it was time to make a change. In spite of all those years of disappointment I was still wrapped up in my music and even more determined to reach a broader audience. Although the Bare Touch had become the longest running hit show in Vegas, I could feel it folding. So I was happy when an offer came from Breck Wall and Patrick Maes to put together a band for "Naughty but Nice," a show at the Nugget in Sparks, Nevada, near Reno. It was a welcome transition, and this was where something happened that completely changed my life.

One night around 10:00 I was totally absorbed in playing the piano, singing, and trying to connect, from up on our platform, with the folks at tables throughout the room. I didn't even notice Mel Tillis's bandleader walk in to unwind and catch a performance before his second show. The next segment of our routine featured my vocal of "Short People," so I left my piano where I had been conducting the orchestra, slipped backstage, and came out through the curtain. Then I jumped to center stage and burst out singing, stumping across the floor on my knees. In comparison to everyone up there, I definitely looked like a short person! Finishing the song, I put down the mike, picked up my saxophone, and lit into Boots Randolph's "Yakity Sax."

At his table near the stage, Larry Lee McFaden called over to his cocktail waitress. "My God, Doreen! Who is this guy?"

"Oh, that's Lee Greenwood."

"Who's Lee Greenwood?"

"Oh, you know. He's been a fixture around the Nevada circuit for the last fifteen or twenty years. He sings and plays all the instruments, puts together shows, and writes songs. A little of everything."

"Well, doesn't anybody here look at what this guy's doing?" Larry went on. "Don't they hear this guy's potential as a . . . I hear him as a country singer. Would you please introduce me to Lee?"

Needing to be in the main room for the Statesiders' one o'clock show, Larry left. But an hour later he was back. By that time I was singing a special arrangement of Mel Torme's "Christmas Song." Decorations and other signs of the holiday season reminded us that it was late in December. So when Larry walked back in with several of his musician friends and took over a booth near the back, I was sitting on the edge of the stage, singing, "Chestnuts roasting on an open fire . . ."

This was the closing number. As the music ended, Doreen came up to me and said, "There's a guy in the back who says he has to meet you. He's the bass player with the Statesiders."

As she led me through the lounge to the booth, a broad-shouldered, smiling fellow stood up. Holding out his hand in greeting, he enthusiastically said, "Hi! I'm Larry Lee McFaden. I'm with Mel Tillis."

"How are you?" I replied. Then, since it had been a long night, I added, "Well. Got to go. Good to meet you, Larry Lee."

"I know you've heard this a hundred times," he went on, stepping slightly forward to slow my departure, "but you really sing great. I'd like to talk to you about your future."

Trying to be polite, but ready to get some rest, I just said, "Sure, man. Fine," and started walking toward the stage to get my sax.

"I'll call you tomorrow," he was saying as I headed for the door.

It was at least 3:00 A.M. when my head hit the pillow and I was gone.

During those nights of playing lounges I sang myself to death, usually doing four shows. Getting up the next morning was really hard, and I never got up before noon, or I'd put the next night's show in jeopardy.

At nine o'clock sharp the phone rang: "Hi! This is Larry Lee. Could you meet me down in the coffee shop?"

I could have killed him!

Later, when we did get a chance to talk, he asked if I would consider coming to Nashville to perform and write songs.

"Larry Lee, what I want is a career as a singer. The only way I'd come is if you could arrange a recording contract for me."

There were a lot of unanswered questions when we shook hands and said, "So long. Enjoyed talking to you."

Larry Lee left town with Mel and the Statesiders, and I moved to the MGM to play piano bar. When his band returned to play the Frontier six weeks later, he drove up to the Nugget in Sparks. I had left.

"Doreen! Where is he?"

"Oh, you mean Lee? He went over to the MGM. You can probably find him there."

"Thanks a lot, Doreen." And Larry Lee was on his way to the MGM.

"You've got the greatest voice, and you sure know your way around music," Larry Lee started telling me again, the minute he found me. "You sure can rip the cover off 'Yakity Sax'! And the twin sax number—where in hell did you learn that?"

"Well, I was experimenting when I was about twelve years old . . ."

"Those songs you've written," he interrupted, "like the one you just sang, 'Where in Heaven on Earth?' . . . I just know they're good, man. You've got potential as a writer."

"Well, thanks. . . ."

"It seems like I've been Mel's bass player forever, away from home all the time. I'm thinking about getting off the road. And if I've ever seen a guy with so much talent that I'd stake my future on him, it's you. I'd even put up my job and house, too, 'cause I just know we can make it. Would you come to Nashville and record some of your songs? I really think we can get a grant from a publishing company there."

"Let me think about it," was my initial reaction.

Since I had been raised on a farm with country music flowing out from my grandparents' radio, the idea of returning to my roots was appealing. From that moment, Larry Lee and I started talking about our dream of bringing my career to Nashville. Whenever I was performing, if Larry was in town, he'd be there with Mel and some of the Statesiders, Dottie West, T. G. Shephard, or anyone he could persuade to come hear me sing. He'd be out there in the audience with a crowd of his buddies, laughing and joking and sounding off about me, in between numbers. Other times he'd walk in alone, sit down at a table in the lounge, and listen until the last customers had emptied their glasses, paid the waitress, and left. By 2:30 in the morning, the only ones remaining would be a few tired souls, a keno runner or two, and Larry Lee, out there urging me to keep on singing. Even as it was nearing three o'clock on my watch, Larry's excitement hadn't dwindled.

"You're a natural country singer, man. You've got that different voice, that raspiness. Nashville's a town that appreciates a unique sound, and I just know that your talent is ready for something 'left field.' I mean, you're not the typical country act. But we have the individualists there, the Ronnie Milsaps, the Crystal Gayles. And there are some Eddie Rabbitts, who aren't ultracountry. You're a stylist. That's what makes Willie Nelson a great country performer. He's a stylist. Kris Kristofferson is a stylist. Johnny Cash . . . These are not perfect singers, and they'll be the first to tell you. But nobody else sounds like them."

It was obvious to me that one thing Larry Lee McFaden had was enthusiasm!

Well, I'd had my ego stroked pretty good. On one hand, I was really skeptical about this guy. But on the other hand, I was very taken with him. He was a nonstop pitchman, and he had this laugh that would just drive you crazy.

It was a time when my confidence needed to be reinforced. But as great as it was to have Larry's unrestrained encouragement, job security had to be my first concern. After our contract ran out at the Nugget, Melanie found a job as a waitress for the Showboat in Lake Tahoe. Since she was paying most of our bills, I was again in need of work, not only for the money but for the self-esteem that comes from being productive. Driving through town, I spotted a *Help Wanted* sign outside a club called Barney's Casino. I walked in and asked the owner, "Is the job still available?"

"Sure. Come back tomorrow morning, dressed just like you are."

"Okay, I'll be here," I answered.

Since I was wearing a white shirt and tie, with my best slacks, as I walked out the door I was telling myself, "This is great! I can use my dealing experience. I'm going to deal!"

When I came back the next day, the manager led me, along with another kid who had applied for the job, to a small room in the back of Barney's. Then he brought in a huge sack of quarters and a couple of magnifying glasses.

"Just separate the silver quarters from the sandwich coins. You'll get forty dollars and three meals at the club," he said, as he walked out.

The two of us started sorting through those quarters, carefully examining each one. After eight hours, and looking at $10,000 worth of quarters, I had found only six made of solid silver.

When we showed the results of our labor to the boss that afternoon, a look of surprise crossed his face, then a scowl. "This is ridiculous," he told us. "There's no profit here. Sorry, guys, but your job's finished!"

It was just one day's work at Barney's Casino, but at least we got paid.

Thankful for the forty-dollar check, it was hard for me to believe that the world was now spending $300 billion each year for arms. The companies putting together military equipment must have been making a mint! Two-thirds of their output was being bought up by the United States and the Soviet Union. But a sobering fact was that in the Middle East, purchases of war-making machinery had increased by 800 percent. The newspapers said we were in an arms race that was out of control.

Meanwhile, still job hunting, I decided to form another Lee Greenwood Affair. This would include Sally Waldo, Jeff Cornell, and Melanie. All of us were working anyplace we could, scraping up enough money to get it off the ground. Finding a piano playing job in a small club, but needing an amplifier, I went to the C & M Music World in Sparks.

"My name's Lee Greenwood. I have a job here in town and my own piano, but I need to rent an amp," I told the owner.

"No problem. This one's a twin reverb, a fine piece of equipment," he said. "And I'm Cal McBride. Good to meet you."

The amplifier was exactly right for my piano. It was about two feet high by two feet wide, with twin speakers. "Great!" I said, and signed the rental agreement.

So the next day, I picked up my piano, drove down to C & M Music, and loaded this expensive amp into my orange, four-wheel-drive Chevy truck. The club wasn't very far away. Pulling around behind it, I backed my pickup over to the rear dock, where most of the lettuce, tomatoes, and other vegeta- bles were brought in for the restaurant there. First, I carefully took the amp out of the truck and used it to prop open the back door. I pulled up my heavy piano, then dragged it into the club and out onto the stage. After pushing the piano over to the right spot, I turned and walked back to get the amp. It was gone! Somebody had stolen the brand new amp that I had just rented! I stared at the empty deck behind the door, almost in shock. Not only did I not have any money, now I was in debt to someone who was probably going to put me in jail!

I was beside myself! It had been a tremendous effort to get the job and work out all the problems. Now fate had stepped in and taken it away. I gave Cal McBride a call: "Cal. You're not going to believe this. I'm loading into the club and some- body walked away with the amp you just gave me."

"Come down and get another one," he said.

I couldn't believe what I had just heard. What blind trust! I went back and picked up a new one, signed a note, and cautiously placed this second amp in my truck. Over the years that followed, even though work was sporadic, I would send Cal ten dollars. Or I'd just let him know, "I can't make a payment this week."

Cal would say, "Okay. Fine. Just keep in touch."

Together, the amplifiers were about $400 (I kept the second one for performances), but in time I paid off both of them. I deeply appreciated Cal's trust. Belief in each another is part of the glue that holds our country together. Anyone who is honest and accepts responsibility becomes a productive part of the American puzzle. Each person puts in a little something, and it all works.

Cal's trust was uplifting, but I was still looking for a way to finance our reorganized Lee Greenwood Affair. It would cost $5,500 for equipment and costumes to underwrite a successful show, and we'd have to come up with the cash. Still $2,500 short, Melanie and I sold our jointly owned Lincoln. After giving Melanie her half of the money, I decided, "I'll just take my car money to the tables and get more for it."

I had gambled some in Vegas, trying to figure out how you beat the game. As a former dealer, I knew what the theories were, and I'd seen guys win big. Well, the tables taught me their lesson. Even with a dealer's expertise, I was behind the eight ball from the beginning. After losing one hand, I was uptight. Before it was over, I had lost almost all of the cash, in what turned out to be a heavy downer. The whole experience brought me to the depths of despair. It must be the feeling someone gets after losing a drug high—extremely depressing.

The four of us finally got our show off the ground. But success was short-lived. After the Lee Greenwood Affair had run its course, I received an offer for a job in Fort Wayne, Indiana playing piano bar once again. Looking forward to the fresh environment, I flew east to a section of the country I had never seen before. On St. Patrick's Day, I opened for Bud

Miller at the Three Rivers Apartments on Spy Run Avenue, playing in a little lounge called The Retreat. This was just the retreat I'd been needing. Bud, along with Jim Price of Honeywell and his wife Sandy, and Mike Watson, a local businessman, took me under their wings, sharing their companionship and bringing in their favorite music, like the hits of the Commodores. When another job opened up in Columbus, Bud drove me out there in his own car. The manager of the new club was Herman Spruit, a Hollander and European-trained chef. The Bodega, his exquisite little dining establishment where I played piano, featured white linen tablecloths and napkins. There were candles on each table, and he served delectable American and Continental cuisine with an elegant flair. These days were an enriching time for me, providing an opportunity to look within and reassess my life.

After this refreshing break from the pressures of the night-life circuit, I traveled back to Reno. During my time away, Larry had kept in constant touch by phone. Both he and his cousin, a country singer named Ray Pillow, had begun scouring Nashville, seeking opportunities for a record contract. They had convinced some of Mel Tillis's boys to sit in on a demo session at the Old Music Mill. So I flew to Nashville, bringing my music charts, including songs like "W-Bar-X Rocking Horse-Y," and "Home Away from Home," written while I was trying to imagine what life as a Nashville picker would be like.

It was the day of our session, and as we were going into the studio, Ray said, "Before we record, you need to sign this publishing agreement."

"Well, why?" I asked.

"Because Larry and I are paying for this. You'll get half the royalties as the writer, and we'll get half as owners of the Sycamore Valley Publishing Company."

Well, that didn't sound very good. But I thought it also had the positive aspect that they were really that confident. I was in my mid-thirties, and I figured this was my last shot. If I didn't make this one, there would be no more.

After a moment of thought, I said, "Okay. I really want this chance. Where do I sign?"

Truthfully, I'd have signed away my first three albums if they had asked me to!

As soon as the demo was finished, we took the master tape to Dell Bryant at BMI Music. At that time, he was the music listener, the man who decides whether or not a music group would receive a grant for the publishing company because of the writing talent within their organization.

Dell, Larry, Ray, and I crowded into one of those little listening rooms, which looked like a tiny, sound-absorbing padded cell that you might keep a lunatic in. It had a reel-to-reel tape recorder, and Dell put the two reels on, evidently neglecting to snap one of them tightly into place. He flicked on the machine, turned his back, and the reel jumped off the spindle. It rolled all over the room, unwinding all the time, running tape loosely around everybody.

"Oh, no!" I said to myself as my heart dropped. These were all the songs that I had just cut, hoping to make my dream of being a recording artist come true. Now they were rolling around on the floor!

But it was a riot. "Switch off that reel," Dell yelled. "What a mess!"

All of us were laughing as we picked up the tape, which was heaped in a jumbled mass of circles. Dell wound it back on the reel and got the whole thing stuck back on the machine so that he could finally listen to it.

Walking out of the sound studio, Larry and Ray were still chuckling. "Super, Lee. You did it! That was a doggone mishmash in there! I've never seen so much tape on a studio floor," Ray said, shaking his head.

"One thing's for sure," Larry added. "Dell Bryant is not going to forget you tomorrow, Brother. You and your listening-session scramble made an indelible impression!"

He was right. After hearing our demo, Dell said, "It's very good. And we'd love to have you with us at BMI."

The hardest task was still ahead. It would take a lot of persuasion to get on a record label. But this meant a $500 grant for me and a grant for the Sycamore Valley Publishing Company. The money paid for my round-trip plane ticket to Nashville. Like so many other times in my life, my bank account was scraping bottom. But with the hope of a challenging future in Nashville, I flew back to Las Vegas to work and, quite honestly, to be near Melanie. I never have been able to get used to being alone.

Back to the Tropicana! But this time not as a dealer. The entertainment director, Lenny Martin, had gotten me a position in Vegas playing background music for the casino in the Atrium Lounge. It was a luxurious setting under an attractive gazebo, just below the casino. Meanwhile, Larry was calling every day. "We're talking to everyone in town, Brother," he told me, "taking your demo wherever we can get through the door and past the receptionist." Then in a serious tone, which was rare for Larry, he added, "Growing up, neither of us had a brother of our own. So, I guess that's why I call you 'Brother.' "

When Mel Tillis was playing in Las Vegas, in between shows my self-appointed future manager would grab anyone he could, urging them with, "Come on over to the lounge a minute. You've *got* to hear him! This Greenwood guy is *the* greatest singer in town."

It was an entirely new experience to have a one-man cheering section. Larry would hype me to his friends, then stay all night till the last tones of "Don't Fall in Love with a Dreamer" faded away.

The three of us shared waffles and strawberries at the Frontier breakfast lounge: Melanie, who was now my wife, sat at a small table with Larry and me, as we talked of a career that wasn't even there yet. We were planning, back then. Buses, band, the whole ten-two-four. Just dreaming is what we were doing, but we knew it would come true.

During the days that followed, Larry kept in constant touch while he was on the road with Mel or when he and Ray were beating the pavements of Sixteenth Avenue with our demo. It's a rough place to gain first acceptance. They played it for any producer who would listen. Bob Montgomery didn't have a need for a new singer in my category. Neither did Larry Butler, who was producing for Kenny Rogers. And Jimmy Bowen said, "He sounds too much like Kenny."

It was discouraging, but we weren't giving up.

In the search for a recording company, Ray and a friend of Elvis's, Lamar Fike, took my tape to Jerry Crutchfield, the Nashville senior vice-president of MCA Music. It seemed as though months passed.

Finally Ray's phone rang. "That's a unique voice," Crutchfield was saying. "And there's some raw talent there. Let me talk with Jim Foglesong."

Taking my demo to the Nashville president of MCA Records, Crutchfield started pushing for a recording contract. He gave the reasons why a Greenwood single might be another newcomer success, like the rising hit of MCA's Terri Gibbs, who had just released "Somebody's Knockin'." He mentioned, too, that the quality of my voice would blend well with the newly written songs of his brother, Jan Crutchfield.

The next day Ray got a call from Jerry Crutchfield. "I've got him on MCA! You had to give MCA Records half of your publishing company, but Mr. Foglesong just signed him!"

"Give him half our publishing? That's typical business, for Nashville. But it's great! I'll pass the word to Larry."

"Larry! We've got it!" Ray was jubilant.

"Man, that's terrific! I'll call Lee and let him know."

The message flew along the telephone wires, and soon my phone was ringing. "Lee! We just got a record deal with MCA!"

As it turned out, MCA had just set up a new in-house production division, Panorama, and mine was to be its first record. With Jerry Crutchfield as producer, the recording session to lay down the tracks of four songs was held at Larry Butler's Sound Emporium. Sitting in with us was Nashville's well-known and gifted, blind piano player Harold ("Pig") Robbins. He was particularly chosen for the very rural sound he gets on the keyboard. Openness is his style, real steady and cool, just like Ronnie Milsap. It's amazing to watch him play.

As unknown beginners, we hadn't drawn a crowd. Only Larry, Ray, and Crutch were there to listen. But I was cautious, suddenly very much an introvert. The band struck up the intro and I began the words, "In a way I'm glad it's over, even though it's going to hurt me once you're gone." There was a hint of tenuousness in my voice. It was very raspy. I was nervous, and this mood blended with the sincerity of the song "Inside Out." But the song itself was the key. Jan Crutchfield had written a simple melody with heartrending lyrics.

As the musicians were packing up their instruments and walking out of the studio, Ray Pillow gave me a direct look with his unconditional opinion: "That is a smash hit!"

It would take some time to find out.

In the meantime, I was headed back to my job in Vegas when suddenly the music world was hit by a terrible shock. A twenty-five-year-old fan, who had even been given an autograph by John Lennon, waited outside the Manhattan apartment of the Beatles musician and shot him to death. Lennon, who was only forty, had been a strong advocate for world peace. He had written the song "Imagine" as a tribute to the possibility of human understanding, so his death by violence was coldly ironic. But there's nothing we can do to prevent tragedies like this because they're totally unpredictable.

Far from New York City, in hopes of establishing my career as a country singer, Larry and Ray were doing their best to publicize our single. Overconfident as usual, Larry was already making plans to put down his bass for an attaché case! "You'll be taking a chance when you leave Vegas to let me manage your career," Larry told me on the phone. "I'm not accepting one penny from your earnings in this town 'til you're making at least as much as you are right now. That's only fair. Still, leaving Mel's band like this, I figure I'd need some support until we're rolling," he went on. "Well, when I was playing with Mel down in De Land, Florida, I met a Leesburg guy named Keith Padgett. He grew up in Mel's hometown, Pahokee. When he and his friend Walt McLin listened to my tape of 'Inside Out,' they were so impressed with your singing that they're forming a group to help me get a start as your manager."

"That sounds great, Larry."

"And I've rented a little office in Faron Young's building on Sixteenth Avenue. I don't have a secretary, yet. I just sit there all day, praying for the phone to ring. But we're going to make it, Brother!"

That's when it started. Requests for information, interviews, and appearances began to pour in. Larry hired a secretary and moved to a two-office suite. "Lee, this schedule is filling up," he told me during a call to Vegas. "It's getting busy. You're going to have to move to Nashville."

So we turned the page from Lee Greenwood the piano-bar singer to Lee Greenwood the entertainer, and it was like a shock of cold water in my face when I got out from behind my piano for the first time and walked out onstage at the Tampa Fairgrounds before 22,000 people. Inside my mind was rolling an unbelievable realization: "They're not here for the gambling or to see the nude girls. They've come to hear me sing! This is incredible!"

Watching our first single struggle its way up the charts was a roller coaster experience. We had spent all our money to promote the record. Larry and Ray, and even a few professionals they'd hired, had been calling radio stations, asking them, "Have you heard the new song? How do you like it? Would you play it?"

As long as a single is going up in the direction of #1, you're okay. That's called a bullet; it's headed up. But if it ever begins to drop down, it's pretty well gone. After the song's release, "It Turns Me Inside Out" climbed to #77.

Then one day Larry called me. "Lee. We've lost our bullet."

It was as if someone had died. "Oh, no. You're kidding me."

"No, but I've hired a record promoter, Peter Svenson, to help us get it back. That doesn't happen often. But we're going to give it everything we've got."

"Inside Out" regained its bullet and headed up to #50. We were ecstatic.

Then it stalled. Our emotions were teetering as we watched the slowing momentum. Then it rose to #30, and fizzled. Our hopes were dashed.

But during the Annual Disk Jockey Convention, I sang my still-staggering first release onstage on the "MCA Show" at Opryland. It turned around and zoomed to the Top 20.

Three times, "Inside Out" had climbed up the charts. This was unbelievable. By the time the roller coaster ride was over, early in 1982, "Inside Out" had reached #17 on the Billboard charts and #11 in the Cash Box ratings. This is a huge success for an artist's first single. Some singers' first records don't even get played. But more importantly, it had been on the charts for twenty-two weeks, an achievement that was unheard of in country music and that caused more talk in Nashville than any other record in recent memory. Nobody could believe it!

The voice in the song was unusual, and people all over were asking, "Who is this singing fool out there? What do you think he'll come up with next?"

"Ring on Her Finger, Time on Her Hands" soon answered that question. It was time to begin putting together a band so that we could go on the road and meet all the country radio listeners who had turned around our opening single and sent it up the charts with a bullet, not once, but three times.

When we moved to Tennessee in 1981, Melanie became the original choreographer for Nashville Network's show, "Dancin' USA" and started teaching dance at Vanderbilt University. My wife was understanding about the heavy schedule I was about to take on, and she was ready to step into a new role, giving guidance to thirteen-year-old Kelly, who was coming to live with us.

It was about this time that Larry introduced us to his neighbors, Jimmy and Betty Gayle, in nearby Ashland City. They grew to be our close personal friends. Sometimes when Jimmy would hear about a boy or girl who'd been injured or was suffering from a painful illness, he'd call me up and the two of us would go over to the hospital to bring some courage or strength for the ordeal ahead. Jimmy was soon my confidant, as I started becoming a part of the Nashville community.

At a showcase down at the Stockyards, a gathering place for Nashville's musicians and country music fans, Harry Robinson came up to talk about my budding career. A hefty six-feet-four, Harry was already well known as a versatile guitar player, seasoned in the music business. After remarking on the down-and-up roller coaster victory of my first release, Harry asked, "Have you hired your musicians yet?" He followed that with, "I'd be interested in joining your group."

"Great! Will you be my bandleader?" I replied. I was delighted. This impressive music professional, who had been a member of Dolly Parton's ensemble, certainly couldn't imagine what he was volunteering for.

It was a skeleton band, to say the least. This first band was just Harry and me, in my half-ton Chevy pickup, booking for $700 a night. Once, the two of us loaded up our equipment, Harry's guitar and my keyboard and sax, and drove almost three hundred miles to the Hitchin' Post in Bristol, where the folks gave a warm welcome to their two-man entertainment team. Putting together our musical styles, we spent the evening playing "Inside Out" and a combination of "Don'tcha Hear Me Callin'," a few songs I had written, and anything else we knew.

After that long day of driving and performing, Harry and I stayed overnight in Bristol. Waking up to a cloudy morning, we climbed into the "Orange Crush" truck and headed down Highway 40, back toward Nashville. It had been raining during the night, and the air was filled with a light mist. As we approached an intersection, right before our eyes was a brilliant rainbow that stretched across the highway like an arch. Staring at its radiance in fascination, I said, "Look! You can see the exact spot where it goes into the ground!"

Then my eyes traveled up and around this multicolored band. "Harry! It goes straight into the ground on the other side of the road, too!"

As we approached it, the colors became more vivid. It was luminous, ethereal. Then we drove right under it!

That horseshoe rainbow seemed like a good omen for the future.

Anxious to play for the people out there who were calling up our office for appearances, Harry and I added on a drummer, named Tom Jones, and a bass player. Our band, called "Blackjack," was booking for $1,500 a performance. Then one morning Larry got a call: "We'll pay $3,500."

"Three thousand, five hundred," Larry repeated, slowly. "Right. I'll get right back to you." Then he hung up the phone and went crazy!

While our first single was helping to fill up "Blackjack's" schedule, Kenny Rogers released "A Love Song," which I had written and put on my album. Then Mel Tillis and Nancy Sinatra decided to cut another of my songs, "Where in Heaven on Earth?" Sycamore Publishing Company was getting a boost.

"It Turns Me Inside Out" peaked early in 1982, followed by the release of "Ring on Her Finger, Time on Her Hands," "She's Lyin'," written by Jan Crutchfield, and "Ain't No Trick." All four of these singles from the *Inside Out* album were hits in the Top 10, and the album eventually went gold.

A career that had been so many years developing was finally in an upward spiral. There were two special people I wanted to thank: Melanie and Larry Lee.

Counting all the times I've been down
In between the night and the day,
Now I realize how I've changed—
All you did was show me the way.

You're changing my life into living.
You're helping me out of this world I've known.
I hope that you don't mind my saying
Thank you, for changing my life.

CHAPTER IX

Now we were ready to start rolling. The Jim Halsey Agency of Tulsa had been booking us, and back in our Nashville office Larry was besieged with calls from venues all over the country. We got a Travel Craft motor home with a trailer to carry our instruments, and the band hit the road. But it didn't take long to outgrow our first vehicle. Adding a fantastic pianist from Vegas, Gene Lorenzo, and a new drummer, Mark Edwards, we bought Merle Haggard's old bus. Before the year was out we were a group of thirteen people, including the Trick Band, named after our song, "Ain't No Trick," a sound crew, security, and drivers. Like a bunch of musical rovers, we were traveling in two buses, Thunder and Lightning.

By late 1982, the Trick Band was opening shows for the Oak Ridge Boys, Alabama, Tammy Wynette, Janie Frickie, Charlie Pride, Don Williams, and Loretta Lynn, everywhere from Syracuse all the way down to the Panhandle of Florida.

This was the "Forever Tour." At least that's what all of us doing the traveling called it. In 1983, we spent 287 days on the road, playing in barns and clubs, at auctions and rodeos, all over the country.

Life on the road is exhausting. Every afternoon upon reaching the destination, you check into some generic motel to get cleaned up for the show. Right after the performance, you check out. Then it's back on the bus to jostle and bounce all night as you roll along to the next venue. You miss the comfort of a real bed as you duck through stiff curtains to a bunk and ease your legs carefully down into the small space.

"Lee, there's no way this is going to work," Harry said, exasperated. He was striving to squeeze his gigantic frame into a comfortable position so he could read a book, beneath the tiny spotlight.

"Can you stretch a little sideways in there?" Gene suggested.

"Maybe I just wasn't built for this kind of traveling," our bandleader concluded, laughing at his own frustration.

Mark and Gene would play some poker as Jeff Jones at the wheel kept our lead bus barrelling down the dark highway, following the yellow line in a determined quest to run out of road. "Do you think that yellow line ends somewhere?" he joked.

I've played in every town from here to Fort Wayne, Indiana,
Singing all the songs I know that folks all like to hear.
Each and every honky-tonk is somehow like the last one,
Just another place to call a home away from home.

"We'll be home someday," is what we told our wives and children. It was as if our personal lives had been suspended, put on "hold" for the duration. The families we'd left in Nashville were just waiting. I guess someone's wife would wait forever, but it seems almost impossible to be away for that long and keep a shred of cohesiveness. Having gone through this experience, I have a lot of respect for the armed-service families down through the years, who have maintained their devotion through seemingly endless tours of duty. Those are the real "Forever Tours." And the heartbreaking fact about military tours is that for some, the term "forever" proves to be true. This was what our nation faced with the death of 216 Marines, stationed in Beirut. A terrorist, driving a Mercedes truck loaded with 2,500 pounds of explosives, raced past the sentries and crashed into the Marine headquarters. Only six months earlier, our embassy in Beirut had been bombed, killing forty people. The U.S. was battling these unseen enemies, the terrorists who appeared with deadly unpredictability to underscore their causes. All we could do was increase our surveillance capabilities and hope to uncover each plot before the assassins struck. In spite of America's strength, our citizens were still at risk.

But we were all blessed with a beautiful country. And traveling through America by bus gave our group a chance to see a lot of it. The Trick Band made a swing through the South, then rode from the East across the wide expanse of states to the West Coast. We found out how extremely diverse America is, and even discovered that there are some cities in Texas that are separated by such endless stretches of land that you can't get from one to the other to play consecutive shows. It's almost impossible for a bus-riding group to play in Texarkana and be in El Paso for a show the next night.

Tyler was one of the places in Texas that we did play:

> *Well, I took a job that sent me down to Greenwood,*
> *Mississippi.*
> *Two nights with the Gatlin Band, and on to Baton Rouge.*
> *One more stop in Little Rock, then on to Tyler, Texas.*
> *Every club I play becomes a home away from home.*
>
> *Lord, I miss the sea breeze and the coast of Carolina.*
> *Why she waits, I'll never understand.*
> *The road has gotten longer since I left for West Virginia.*
> *I wonder if it's really worth the time I put in.*

One thing that made traveling seem worthwhile was the chance to see some of my family in California. Since Grandma had passed away, my grandfather had grown quite feeble. We were scheduled to play in Roseville, a little town right outside of Sacramento, so I called up my sister to see if they could come. When Pat phoned back, she said, "The girls and I can hardly wait. But Grandpa thinks he's too weak to make it."

"Pat, tell Grandpa we're picking him up in the bus and taking him to the show. I'm sure the guys in the band and I can get him to ride with us."

"Okay, Lee. We'll have him ready," she said.

It worked like a charm, and that night we got Grandpa to the Lonesome Armadillo. It was a large, dark hall with tables and chairs around a big wooden dance floor. Choosing the closest spot, Pat and her husband, Jose Coronado, were sitting on the smooth floor in front of the stage with a crowd of music fans, including three of their daughters, Tammie, Pattie, and Lorrie. The oldest, Debbie, had joined the Army. It seemed like such a short time ago that I had watched her graduate from Sacramento High.

Opening the show, I said, "Folks, I'd like you to meet my grandfather Thomas Jackson. He practically raised me. This show is dedicated to him."

Coming down from the stage, I put my arm around him. Beaming proudly at the applause, Grandpa smiled up from my grateful embrace while I sang for him and then dedicated "I.O.U." to Pat, who was all excited with her family down there in front.

It was the only show my grandfather ever saw. He missed Edna so much that he just slowly withered away after she was gone.

Our San Francisco venue was the scene of another reunion. My father, Eugene, was living there with his second family. So this is where I first met his children, Julie, Bobby, and my special truck-driving brother, Ken.

Back in Nashville things were happening. In February, *Somebody's Gonna Love You,* our second album, had been released, along with its first single, "I.O.U." The title song, which was released next, became #1 in the country. That month, we won the Best New Artist Award of Radio & Reader's Poll. Invitations were offered for appearances on "The Merv Griffin Show," Johnny Carson's "Tonight Show," and "Entertainment Tonight." Life was becoming a constant shuttle as I flew to some large city, then back to the bus.

Then something happened that threw my mind into an entirely different frame of reference. It was September 1, 1983, and I'll never forget the sharp announcement that came over the radio: "The U.S.S.R. has shot down Korean Air Lines Flight 007, off the Soviet island of Sakhalin. The Korean 747 jet, on a flight from New York to Seoul, had 269 passengers, including 63 Americans aboard, when it disappeared from radar screens. Soviet officials expressed their belief that the airliner was on a spy mission."

"That's outrageous! How could the Russians commit such a deplorable act?" was my first reaction. "Jeff, could you turn up the volume?"

The voice of Secretary of State George Shultz was angrily detailing the facts that our government had been able to put together. He was saying, "A Soviet pilot reported visual contact with the aircraft at 1812 hours. The Soviet plane was, we know, in contact with its ground control. At 1821 hours the Korean aircraft was reported by the Soviet pilot at 10,000 meters. At 1826 the Soviet pilot reported that he fired a missile and the target was destroyed. At 1830 hours the Korean aircraft was reported by radar at 5,000 meters. At 1838 hours the Korean plane disappeared from the radar screen." Secretary Shultz went on to say that the passenger plane was unarmed.

As soon as the bus rolled into our next destination, I found a phone and called up Larry. "Why would the Soviets intentionally murder a huge planeload of civilians? I can't believe it!"

"I know, Brother. It's terrible," Larry replied.

"There were sixty Americans on that plane," I continued. "How could they do that?" I couldn't figure it out, but I was burning with rage.

During the following few days, the headlines repeated various official versions of what might have happened. The facts as to exactly whose fault it was were confusing. Soviet officials insisted that the large jet from New York was flying without navigation lights and that the crew refused to acknowledge signals from pursuing Soviet fighters.

In a public broadcast, indicating that this matter would be taken up by the United Nations Security Council, President Reagan observed, "Our government does not shoot down foreign aircraft over U.S. territory even though commercial aircraft from the Soviet Union and Cuba have overflown sensitive U.S. military facilities."

To complicate matters, when congressional leaders were briefed, they were told that a high-speed U.S. spy plane, an RC-135 had been in the area and had even crossed the path of KAL 007. The Soviets would have been trying to identify both of these "intruder" planes, which appeared on their radar screens.

But there were also the pictures of weeping relatives of the airliner's passengers. All the people I talked to were shocked by this atrocity, just as if somebody had shot the President. And for some reason, it wouldn't leave my thoughts. The action, which seemed to have been directed against our country, kindled something deep inside of me. I thought that somebody had to do something, but it looked as though we were just going to let it go. It was an atrocity that we were letting an aggressor get away with. They were reaching out and taking a part of our power away from us, and it felt like a slap in the face, saying, "I dare you to do something."

That terrible act was a catalyst, the event that triggered something inside me. It was this strike against innocent citizens that actually made me put pen to paper, a few days later, and write "God Bless the U.S.A."

The song just about wrote itself. It was as if, within my mind, a strong personal statement had been formulated. It's quite possible that my subconscious had been working on it for a long time. Perhaps the song's roots go back as far as my childhood memories of World War II stories about how the U.S. rescued our allies. And maybe my scouting experiences reinforced these patriotic feelings. They certainly were reflected in those first attempts to express my concern for our country in the song "America." But suddenly, inflamed by this seemingly unprovoked attack upon some of our people, I felt that emotion find its release, and the song came out almost in final form.

A similar phenomenon must have occurred with Paul Simon's writing of "Bridge Over Troubled Water." President John F. Kennedy had been assassinated. Then that summer, one of Simon's Queen's College classmates, Andy Goodman, a civil rights advocate furthering the cause in Mississippi, was murdered. As the years went on, rocked by equal rights struggles, these events may have remained in his subconscious mind until the assassinations of Robert Kennedy and Martin Luther King unleashed the sadness expressed in the words, "When darkness comes and pain is all around, like a bridge over troubled water, I will lay me down."

The melody of "God Bless the U.S.A." appeared on the spot, right along with its lyrics. My musical background, originating with Beethoven and Bach from the church hymnal and my days of playing with the Red Cross band and school bands, is American march oriented. It draws from Sousa marches as well as the more formal compositions. Therefore a lot of changes in the music are strict, as if you were to stand and salute with a solemn, proper attitude.

But the chords were also influenced by the traditional country feeling of the acoustic guitar and the contemporary sounds from my background on the West Coast. They even drew upon the early Beatle harmonies, which helped me build that climactic structure, so the melody blossomed like a flower.

The words seemed to flow naturally from the music, and came out with total honesty. They were an expression of my feelings of pride. To me, America seemed just like a rookery, a place where we have a chance to grow, unmolested and free.

Really, the lines of the song are nothing more than a reliving of America's past: "If tomorrow all the things are gone I've worked for all my life . . ." In the back of my mind, I think, were my grandparents and the farm they had lost to the pressures of urbanization. But I could just as well have said, "We've worked for all our lives," because America has gone through the Revolutionary War, the settlement of the wilderness, the bloody Civil War and two World Wars, with the economic crash in between. And it seems as though we have been constantly dealing with world politics, suffering in a lot of wars since then. I guess every country goes through

the same kinds of hardships, only we're lucky to be in a place
that puts freedom as our highest priority.

Extremely serious about the strong commitment expressed
in my song, I showed it to Jerry Crutchfield.

"This is beautiful, Lee. But in the second verse, how about
using the names of cities that include the far corners of the
country? And why don't you choose a few of the largest or
maybe some industrial centers that are especially important
to our economy?"

Crutch helped me in naming Detroit, the center of Motown and the auto industry, and Houston, the center of the
oil industry. Then we put in New York and Los Angeles, two
of our highly populated cities, representing the East and the
West. You're talking about a number of choices, but those sort
of flowed together best, poetically. The song was completed.
Now we'd have to record it and persuade MCA to include it
on an album.

At the same time, passing through my mind was: "The
country music professionals won't think this is a country
song. . . . Coming out with it when I'm just trying to get
started might be a career suicide move." Then a stronger
thought moved in: "The song's how I feel, and it's something
I really want people to hear."

Committed to the song and the risk, I began working on
the difficult part, getting it on an album. The president of
MCA Records, Irving Azoff, who lived in Los Angeles, was
the man who could give "God Bless the U.S.A." a chance to
reach the listening public. As a new musician in the recording
business, I felt hesitant to confront MCA's president, especially to push a song I had written that didn't even sound like
country music—but I finally decided, "I'll just gut up and go
see him."

On Halloween night I was in L.A. to play "Solid Gold." After the show they gave me a bottle of champagne. So I got
into a limo, drove over to Azoff's house, and was up there
knocking on his door just as his small children, dressed as
bumblebees, were leaving to go trick-or-treating. They
walked past me with their cute little black and yellow cos-

tumes on, and I saw Irving standing right inside the doorway. Lifting up the champagne bottle, and showing him the tape of "God Bless the U.S.A.," I called out, "Trick or treat!"

He replied, "I'll take the tape. Come on in."

As I walked into the living room, he said, "What have you got?"

"This is a new song that I've recorded," I told him. "Just listen to it, and I'll get out of your hair."

He put my tape in his machine and let it play. Then I explained: "This is a song I've written, and I think it's extremely important for America to hear it."

He said, "It's good. Very good, in fact. Let me get back to my office, and I'll talk with you."

Calling him the next day, I said, "I'd really like for it to be released as a single immediately because we don't have another album coming up until next spring."

"I'm afraid we'll have to wait for the album, Lee," he said.

It was a disappointing answer. I knew that this song would move people because I had already performed it onstage, and the response had been overwhelming. And I was pleased with it as an artistic creation too. "Well, I guess I'll just have to bide my time, 'til MCA puts out the next album," I thought to myself.

During the same month that I made my trick-or-treat visit to Irving Azoff, our group was hit with a surprise we'll never forget. The Country Music Association awards were to be announced in Nashville. Larry, Ray, and I were in the packed auditorium with our wives, Judy, Joanne, and Melanie. Nominated for Male Vocalist of the Year were Willie Nelson, Ricky Scaggs, Merle Haggard, John Anderson, and myself. As a fresh recruit to the country music business, I had no expectations of winning over this impressive list of well-recognized pros.

Actually I was thrilled to have been invited to sing a medley of tunes, right after the award was given, with Anne Murray, Ronnie Milsap, and Larry Gatlin. Anxious to make a good showing, I was worried about our upcoming performance.

Could I uphold my part with these three singers, whose vocal abilities were so widely respected?

The four of us were waiting in the wings, and Larry Gatlin was smiling and laying on some encouragement: "Lee, I hope you win. Good luck, kid."

Then all at once someone was saying, "Male Vocalist of the Year . . . Lee Greenwood," and a roar of applause filled the room. I could hardly believe it! Larry and Ray were clapping and cheering as I walked up, in a total daze, to receive the award. Then I heard myself saying some kind of "thank you" to CMA. In looking back, I wish that I had thanked Melanie and Larry, too, for their constant support and strength. It was wonderful to receive this coveted title, but all I could think of was, "The medley is coming up next!"

It was a total surprise to be accepted so readily as a country performer. I had sung country and played it when I was a boy, but suddenly to be on top of the heap was hard to believe.

Now it was time for our next album, *You've Got a Good Love Comin'*. Of the songs we'd recorded in the studio, ten were included, and according to Irving Azoff's earlier promise, "God Bless the U.S.A." was one of them.

Aboard the plane headed for the West Coast, Crutch and I were taking our album to get the acceptance of the people of MCA Records in L.A. "Summertime will be here soon. I'm confident that our title song will be released first off the album," my producer said. " 'You've Got a Good Love Comin' ' is a cheerful summer song."

At this point, "God Bless the U.S.A." wasn't even considered as the first single. Maybe second or third off the album, but definitely not first.

The next day we were sitting with about five men from MCA's Los Angeles Division, deep into a discussion about the album. All at once, Irving Azoff turned to me and asked, "What song do *you* think we ought to release?"

Well, I wasn't going to name my own song, the one I had written—even if I believed it would be the best single. I wanted to leave it up to him. And so I turned it back over to

Azoff, and said, "I don't know. And that's why we're here. You tell me."

When he came back with "God Bless the U.S.A.," I could have picked my face up off the floor! But I think he had a vision of what this song could mean to the country at that particular time in history. I think Azoff got the song's message. He, like a lot of other Americans, after the song started getting radio play, caught the feeling. They understood that the music had emotion. It had movement. It expressed a form of healing for our people, and especially for the veterans from Vietnam. But beyond that, it had spirit. Because "I'm proud to be an American" says something very positive for the United States.

So I think all these factors played a part in Azoff's choosing this artistic piece to release from the album *You've Got a Good Love Comin'*. It was the first single . . . and I was shocked, elated! I mean, I was just beside myself. I wanted to jump up and shout, because it was *my* song! For the first time, I had written myself a hit. I'd been singing other people's hits, but now my song own song was going to be the first release.

While the Trick Band was continuing its "Forever Tour," the U.S. was sending close to two thousand troops to the small Caribbean island of Grenada to get rid of Cuban infiltrators. After only two weeks, the Defense Department announced that the "war" had ended. Peace advocates spoke out against our military intervention and started protesting our first shipment of cruise missiles to Britain. This was right at a time when we were involved in the Geneva Arms Negotiations with the Soviets. Our government announced that because the Soviets had placed missiles along their own frontiers, we were going to install in Europe almost twice that many within the next five years. Already West Germany was preparing to accept our medium-range missiles on its soil. This is "escalation," and it's a grim process the superpowers go through, hoping that when a mutual level of arms is reached, they can bargain away armaments on an equilateral basis. Our leaders have to make these awesome decisions, with input from citizens all over our country.

Those same citizens were generously welcoming our music. The office was hearing from country music lovers in distant places, and a young music fan, Debbie Durham, approached me with the question, "Do you have a fan club?"

"Well, no. I'm not sure what that entails."

"Would you like me to start one?" she asked.

"Okay. Sure. Go for it!"

Debbie and several of her friends began developing an organization of vivacious supporters, and it was one of their early members who especially touched my heart.

Judy Harris was sitting in our audience one evening. She was in a wheelchair. Her soft brown hair and the bright look on her face outshone the obvious fact that life had given her a heavy burden. She was terribly crippled, with hands that were bent up and almost helpless.

"Hi! What's your name?" I said, coming down into the aisle to greet some of the people who had come to the show.

The words "I'm Judy" were accompanied by the most radiant smile I've ever seen. Although she must have been about twenty-six, it was evident that tonight was a rare treat.

"Well, Judy, the Trick Band and I sure want to thank you for coming to hear us play. How about meeting us backstage after the show?"

"Oh, that would be fun!" she replied, with her eyes sparkling.

Afterwards, when Judy wheeled past the stage and over to where the band members were organizing our instruments to be loaded on our bus, her face glowed with joy. Harry greeted the young lady, while her father quietly said, "Judy was afflicted with polio and muscular dystrophy when she was a little girl, and she has a badly damaged nervous system."

But Judy was concentrating on the positive.

"Oh, I love 'Think about the Good Times,' and 'Wind Beneath My Wings,' and especially 'A Love Song.' All the songs were just beautiful!" she was saying in her lightly affirmative way. It was obvious that though her body had been weakened, her spirit had remained untouched. Judy cherished the

Eugene Greenwood, father of Lee Greenwood, played the saxophone and the bugle for the U.S. Navy.

Edna and Tommie Jackson, Lee Greenwood's grandparents, on their Sacramento farm.

Lee with his sister, Pat.

Lee and Pat at their grandparents' farm.

AT RIGHT:

Lee with his mother, Bliss.

Lee Greenwood's mother, Bliss, with her husband, Lewis D'Antonoli.

Lee at age thirteen.

Lee as a teenager.

Lee Greenwood's first band, the Moonbeams (April 7, 1957).
Left to right, front row: Karl Bernardo, 14; Lee Greenwood,
14; Bob Starr, 14; Mike Hartmann, 17. Back row: Gary
Hill, 17; Pat Greenwood, 17.

Lee Greenwood's senior picture.

The Apollos, 1961. Left to right: Don Reitz, Eddie Lovato at
top, Lee Greenwood, Goody Javier, Momi at center.

Lee Greenwood as an entertainer in Las Vegas.

The Lee Greenwood Affair, Lake Tahoe, 1979: Lee Greenwood, Sally Waldo at top, Melanie Cronk at right, Jeff Cornell.

The Trick Band: Mickey Olson, Marc Greenwood, Nick Urhig, Gene Lorenzo, Lee Greenwood, Harry Robinson, Paul Urhig.

The crew of the USS Kitty Hawk in formation: "Proud to be an American."

Lee Greenwood performing at a college football game in 1987.

Lee Greenwood's USO tour in the Mediterranean, March 10-26, 1987. (Photo by Lisa Berg)

Lee Greenwood playing saxophone, 1988.

Lee Greenwood with Vice-President Bush, November 1988.
This photo was signed, "To Lee — Thumbs up for you!
Thumbs up for America — Many thanks, George Bush."
(Official White House Photograph 02. G23019-07)

President George Bush and Lee Greenwood on Air Force One, December 7, 1989. (Official White House Photograph 07. P8651-10DV)

Soldiers in the audience during Lee Greenwood's 1989 Panama USO tour.

On the plane in Panama.

Singing to troops in Panama.

Lee Greenwood, August 1989. (Photo by Jo Ann Wolfe)

Lee Greenwood, August 1989. (Photo by Jo Ann Wolfe)

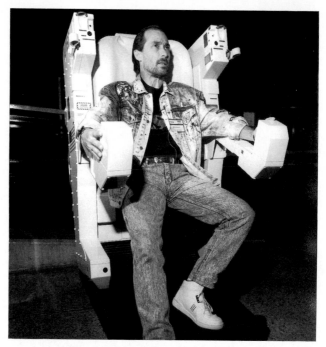

Lee Greenwood at the Marshall Space Flight Center, Huntsville, AL, October 1989. (Photo by Dennis Keim)

Gentry Lee, Lee Greenwood, Georg von Tiesenhausen, Rick Chappell, 1989. (Photo by Dennis Keim)

Lee, preparing for a performance with his son, Marc Greenwood, on drums.

(Photo by Jo Ann Wolfe)

(Photo by Mark Taylor)

simple pleasures she was able to enjoy, like warming to the rhythms of a country music concert as she sat trembling with excitement in her stiff wheelchair.

This was the beginning of a genuine friendship. Whenever the Trick Band was playing near her home in the Carolinas, we'd see Judy, perched up near the stage in her wheelchair, luminous with delight just to be there, drawing strength from the exhilaration that music can bring. One night, while playing at Possum Hollow in North Carolina, I walked over to our security guard, Tom Prue, who was a superstrong gymnast. "Tom, how about dancing with Judy? I'll bet she'd be so glad to get out of that uncomfortable-looking chair."

As the band struck up the first chords of the "Tennessee Waltz," Tom strode over to Judy. Whisking her up, out of her wheelchair, and effortlessly holding her high in the air, he whirled her around and around by the stage to the sounds of "I was waltzing with my darling to the 'Tennessee Waltz.' "

"Oh, that was wonderful!" she breathlessly whispered, radiant and laughing in spite of her helplessness. Tom gently replaced her in the mechanical prison as the final notes brought their dance to an end with, "the night they were playing the beautiful 'Tennessee Waltz.' "

Months passed, and then a full year. Judy was at every possible show, and her favorite song was our new patriotic finale, "God Bless the U.S.A." Then one evening, we had a performance in North Carolina. Judy was there, of course, with her father. Tucked under one of her arms was a gift.

"This is for you," she smiled up, awkwardly trying to reach out to offer the large picture. It was a meticulously painted oil portrait of an American bald eagle.

"Thanks, Judy. This is beautiful! And you painted this yourself? It's magnificent!"

Her eyes were shining with pride.

The painting was perfectly executed; each stroke was flawless. For someone who couldn't even write her name without extreme discomfort, I'm sure that the picture was a labor of love. How her gnarled hands and stiff arms could have accomplished this striking achievement is a wonder, but it was obvious that Judy had put a lot of heart into her masterpiece.

"This eagle portrait will always be special to me, Judy," I told her as we said good-bye.

Resting in my hands was the picture of a vanishing national treasure. The eagle represents our country's independence and strength, but it was disappearing at such an alarming rate that our own national symbol had become an endangered species.

Aspects of our way of life were becoming endangered, too. Our newly released video of "God Bless the U.S.A." featured a heartland American farm family gathered around their dinner table, sharing the bounty of their fall harvest. For me, it brought a grim reminder that a lot of American farmers were losing their land because of economic hardships. I couldn't help remembering that my grandparents' small Sacramento farm was now paved over with buildings and roads.

About seven o'clock one morning, I woke up with a song running through my head. Maybe the upcoming tour with Barbara Mandrell was sifting through my thoughts, because by 9:00 A.M., when I had finished writing it down, "We Were Meant for Each Other" seemed like a perfect duet for us. Calling Vicky Carricoe, a free-lance singer in Nashville, I said, "Hey, Vicky, can you come to the studio and make a demo today?"

"Okay, Lee. Meet you over there."

It was that quick. The demo was ready that afternoon, so I carried it to Florida, where Barbara and I were appearing together. As darkness began to fall and the first fans started gathering for the show, I was wondering if she'd like my new song. I didn't know how she'd react to it because she was a much bigger star than I was. I thought, "She'll probably look at this like I'm horning in, trying to get something for my career." But I thought because of the magic of it all, it might really happen. So I swung down from my tour bus and walked over to the Mandrell bus, which Barbara used as a dressing room.

"Come on in." Barbara was standing in the back of the bus, busily combing her hair for the performance. It was kind of like, "I really don't have time now," but she was gracious and said, "Go ahead and put in the tape, Lee. Let's hear it."

The tape started turning and the opening words, "I've been searching all my life for someone like you," filled the room. She listened attentively until it was over, and I just popped the question right away: "Would you like to do it as a duet, Barbara? I'd really like to sing it with you."

And she said, "That would be wonderful. I'd love it!"

Barbara and I were on the same label, so when we got our two producers, Tom Collins and Jerry Crutchfield, together, we talked about doing an album. They agreed, and whimsically decided to call their team Tom and Jerry Productions. As it turned out, another duet, the fabulous "To Me," was the one released as a single.

"Good morning, Sunshine," is what you feel like saying to Barbara as she bounces into the recording studio. She's a vibrant, talented lady, who is a delight to work with. It was a real pleasure to present her with the People's Choice Award on her own television special in Kansas City.

Like the "River of No Return," our Forever Tour was still rolling down the highway. Regardless of other commitments, the Trick Band and I were maintaining our almost full-time schedule on the road. Probably about the time that AT&T became our only connection with what was happening in our lives, the personnel at Halsey booking agency made a telephone bet with Larry Lee, Ray, and our accountant, Michael Vaden, in our Nashville office. "There's no way those guys are going to stay out there that long. We have their schedule. And it's a killer. Bet they won't make it to the end!"

"It's a bet!" Larry answered. "Lee and the boys are going to finish."

"They can't keep this up. Why don't you give 'em a break?"

"No way," Larry answered. "You just cannot wear Lee out. He loves to work. He's not happy any other way: he loves to be out there. I've told him, 'Hey, let me know when you're getting tired.' You won't believe this, man, but Lee's sad when the bus is headed back."

"Well, I'll bet they won't make the last twenty days," said the Halsey agent as he hung up.

The agent was almost right. It was in those last few weeks that I called Nashville: "Larry, the engine of our bus burned up."

"Well, it's no wonder, Lee. Look how many miles you've put on it. What do you guys want to do?"

"Don't worry. Jeff found some vans we can borrow, so we'll just drive ourselves around to the last venues. We're finishing up this Forever Tour!"

> *Well, the bus broke down just south of town*
> *And left the whole band stranded.*
> *Not much chance of going on, so we tried to hitch a ride.*
> *Half the band got lucky on a diesel bound for Denver,*
> *Just another place to call a home away from home.*

CHAPTER X

NINETEEN EIGHTY-FOUR ENDED on a high note, with a Christmas present for all of us. In January, the Trick Band was going to be featured as a headliner at the MGM Grand Hotel. This was a perfect opportunity to take our wives and children to Las Vegas for a holiday.

Slipping into our Sixteenth Avenue office to join Larry and me for lunch, Melanie was bubbling.

"It'll be great to see our Vegas friends again. I know Danny and Joanne will be there. Lee, do you think your mother and Lewis will be able to make it to the show? Bliss would be so thrilled to see you up on that stage in MGM's main room!"

"It sure will be a thrill for me to see your name up on the marquee," chimed in Larry. "This time it's going to read, 'Lee Greenwood and Crystal Gayle.' Those will be the big letters, the ones they have to bring in a truck to put up!"

Glancing over at Melanie, he grinned. "Remember when I used to go hear him play? The sign was 'Liza Minnelli,' then '.99 Buffet, All You Can Eat,' then '$25,000 Keno.' And right down at the very bottom, in tiny print: 'Lee Greenwood, Piano Bar-Atrium Lounge.' "

"And that was even after he had been promoted!" Larry added, with that crazy laugh of his.

"Well, yeah. It's going to be nice," I agreed. "All year, the guys in the band have been away from home for those long stretches of time. Well, this time our families will be coming, too. Melanie, are you ready to go on the road?" Then we all laughed and headed out the door for lunch.

Moving up to the main room at the MGM was a great feeling. The audience's welcome was led by my still-petite mother, a spritely fireball beside her attentive husband. Bliss had never been shy. Bolstered by the thrill of victory, she couldn't resist telling the woman sitting beside her, "I didn't really believe it would happen when Lee told us he was going to Nashville. He'd had so many things almost happen, for so many years. I'd get real sad, because I'd see heartbreak. Every time, something went wrong. I got to the point where I didn't want to hear anything at all, because I knew it was going to fall through. I remember when he said, 'Mom, this is it. I'm coming out with this record.' Then the earthquake hit L.A. You would think he'd be discouraged and want to give up. He'd been playing at Vegas and Reno hotels for twenty years, just going round and round in a vicious circle. . . ."

Bliss still had a listening ear as she reached her triumphant conclusion: "Persistence! He was battling all the time, trying to get to the top of the water. Trying to get air. All the time, you could just feel it. No wonder he broke out of that. Persistence!"

At that point, Lewis leaned over to her and whispered fondly, "You've got that quality yourself, Bliss."

She stopped and looked up at him. Then with a private gleam in her eyes, she nodded her head. "You're probably right, Lew." Then, "Shhh. Lee's about to open the show."

After the performance was over, as the stage lights began to dim, quite a few in the audience crowded over to greet the members of the Trick Band. In addition to Harry Robinson and Gene Lorenzo, the group now included Mickey Olson, our keyboard player, and the Urhig brothers, Paul on bass and Nick on acoustic guitar. Joining them, looking like a rock star in his tight black pants and silver shirt, and bringing out my genuine paternal pride, was our hot new drummer, Marc Greenwood.

Smiles of recognition were warming up the backstage as a cluster of old friends gathered. "Hi, Danny. It's great to see you," I said. "It sure has been a long time."

"Lee, it's just terrific to have you back here. And in the main room. Great going, buddy!"

"Well, how's life treating you, Danny? You and Joanne ought to think about coming to Nashville. How about coming to work with us in the capital of country music?"

"You don't know how tempting that sounds, but we've got kids in school here. How about keeping that offer open, okay?"

"Sure, Danny. We've been friends a long time. Stay in touch!"

Shortly after we left Vegas, another friend from the past touched base with me as the band was closing our Sacramento performance. From among the well-wishers a tall, slender man stepped forward. With his hand extended, he calmly said, "Congratulations, Lee. It certainly isn't a surprise to see you here. You've always been serious about your music."

"Mr. Cooper! Thanks for coming. You helped me more than anyone else at school. You made music challenging, and you forced me to learn to sight-read."

"Yes. I remember when you were sitting in first chair and couldn't read a note! I had to demote you 'til you could!"

"Well, that was a milestone. Thanks for being a great teacher!"

It's not only our teachers, but also our scientists and researchers who lead us toward a better future. Some of them even risk their lives. In February, I could hardly imagine the sensations that must have been rushing through the minds of Navy Capt. Bruce McCandless and Army Lt. Col. Robert Steward as they floated outside their space shuttle. Totally unattached, they maneuvered freely in an experiment to prove that astronauts can function as mechanics and repair their spacecrafts. Away from their base in an ocean of emptiness, both men were satellites themselves, circling around the earth like microscopic moons. These astronauts were showing the kind of individual courage that moves our nation forward.

It was that same month that the Nashville Academy of Recording Arts & Sciences, or NARAS, announced their Grammy Award to "I.O.U." Larry and I were elated. "This is like an Emmy or an Oscar!" he beamed. "What a stroke of luck that we found this song!"

Actually, it had been "I.O.U." that I had started to sing at the Music City News awards live TV show the previous June, when I noticed that the guys near the controls were beginning to scurry around. The words kept coming, but I wasn't hearing my voice on the house audio, just the instrumental. Frantically sizing up the situation, I was guessing: "My mike isn't working. I'm pretty sure we're live, on TV. Damn! Should I keep on singing?"

The cameras kept rolling and I was standing on a podium with people sitting all around me. There was nowhere to go—no escape! The music kept playing, and all I could do was make a helpless little gesture and give an expression, like, "I'm embarrassed. Is there another mike?"

Trying to keep cool, and continuing to sing, I was thinking, "Good. Smart band director. He realizes that we might be able to solve the problem if he doesn't stop the music."

But he kept glancing at me with a worried look. He obviously couldn't hear me. Before long, one of the sound men slipped up and handed me another mike.

"Thank God!" I thought, as those in the front rows near the stage gave visible sighs of relief.

" ___ ___ ___ , " came my words. No sound.

"Oh, no. Not again!" was the unspoken, shocked reaction of the crowd. They had expected my voice to flow triumphantly through the mike. Instead there was only my agonized expression. In their faces I could see their empathy. They could feel the humiliation I was going through.

"This can't be happening!" rolled through my mind as I kept on singing, feeling like a fool for appearing to mouth the words.

There was more scrambling among the sound-equipment guys, and then another crouching hand-off of a third mike. The audience in the hall, and certainly the television viewers, too, waited in expectation. Would it work?

Suddenly my voice rang out: "And I.O.U. the sunshine in the morning. . . ." Perfect timing! Exactly with the first words of the chorus. Everyone breathed easy, and they appreciated the fact that I had hung in there. That night, as the crowd filed out, the conversation wasn't about who had won their Male Vocalist award, but about that poor kid with the broken mike. Maybe some the sympathy carried over, because in 1984 I won the NARAS Grammy in February, and the Male Vocalist of the Year from Cash Box Programmers' Choice in March, the Academy of Country Music in May, the Music City News in June, *Cash Box* magazine in July, and the Country Music Association again in October. Now, that's a lot of sympathy!

"I.O.U." was one of the last country songs to cross over into the contemporary category for quite a while. It was about this time that the country music industry slammed the door on music that appealed to a broader audience and began concentrating on the "stone" country sound, a revival of the earlier version, which emphasized the banjo, fiddle, and steel guitar. Dominating the scene were New Traditionalists like Randy Travis, Ricky Scaggs, and George Strait. Previously, Kenny Rogers, Eddie Rabbitt, and some other singers who were classified as country also appealed to the contemporary market. Kenny's "Islands in a Stream," with Dolly Parton, was a cross-over tune. Ronnie Milsap had crossed over with "There's No Gettin' Over Me" and "Lost in the Fifties." The last song I remember crossing over was Dan Seals' "Bop with You, Baby." Probably the only reason that it became a hit was because of an Adult Contemporary programmer in Texas, Betty Bop!

Pointing out my common ground with artists whose style exceeded the bounds of country, Larry was saying, "When you hit Nashville, you were definitely different. First of all, you played sax and piano, not guitar. You had grown up with some blues and rock 'n' roll. But you'd spent a lot of nights coming out with that smooth swing sound that is close kin to country. And you sure have been playing the 'Tennessee Waltz' all your life. Since you've been recording here you've covered the waterfront, Brother, from 'Ain't No Trick' to

'Fool's Gold.' By the way, what category is 'God Bless the U.S.A.'? Is that only for the country music deejays to play?"

"I don't know, Larry. We'll have to wait and see." After a moment, I added, "Larry, do you know what a columnist wrote in the *St. Pete Times* about it? She said, 'When my kids sing those words at the top of their lungs, I think Lee Greenwood has brought a new meaning to country music.' The song's definitely 'country' in that sense. And it's surprising, Larry. We met some country fans last year on our swing into Canada who were so much on our wavelength that if we didn't close the show with 'God Bless the U.S.A.,' they wondered why. And they requested it. A lot of Canadians seem to identify with America. We're one and the same people, really—North Americans."

"Well, Brother, they can tell it's a true statement from you . . . not just a wave-the-flag, throw-the-baby-in-the-air hurrah, but your bottom-line feelings for your country. Did you know, someone just told me that at a lot of our naturalization centers, when new citizens are sworn in, they swear allegiance to the flag and get a copy of the Constitution? Then the first thing they hear is 'God Bless the U.S.A.' This happens whether it's just a few taking the oath or a group of hundreds."

"That makes me feel great."

Another good feeling was to be a part of the Arthritis Foundation telethon at the Gaslight Theater at Opryland. Mickey Gilley of *Urban Cowboy* was the host, and Ralph Emery and I were co-anchors. The telethon raised over a million dollars to help conquer that disease, but sometimes it just isn't possible to battle illness and win. A letter arrived at my office from the parents of Judy Harris. My fragile friend, who had kept up her spirits through so much pain, had died. Music lifted her heart, while art was the talent that kept her striving toward a goal. Her portrait of the American eagle will always be one of my treasured possessions.

Artistic endeavors were in the news as President Reagan flew into China to endorse cultural and scientific accords and to encourage business transactions between our two nations.

While he was there, he was struck by the existence of free-market souvenir stands on Communist soil. He couldn't resist remarking that capitalism seemed to be flourishing in China! In some ways, the nations of the world seemed to be growing together.

The Olympics provide one of our opportunities for shared experience. That July they were held in Los Angeles, and although boycotted by the Soviet Union and several other Communist nations, they drew athletes from 140 countries. It was there that an American, Carl Lewis, set a record for the 200-meter finals, with gold medals also in the 100-meter dash and the long jump. Being a runner who somehow had gotten off the track, I identified with Lewis's amazing accomplishment and felt a surge of pride in his triumph.

All of us who watched the televised performance of Mary Lou Retton were captivated by the agile gymnast as she flipped gracefully through her intricate routines, racking up a perfect 10 in the vault and winning the Women's All-Around Individual Competition.

But during July, the Trick Band and I could only catch snatches of the TV replays of various events. On the road, opening for Don Williams, we were appearing throughout the South. In Memphis, all of us were hustling around backstage, getting ready for our show at Mud Island, when one of the security guards brought in an assortment of messages, flowers, and gifts from some of the fans attending the concert. These were put on our bus. So it was late that night after the show, as we were wearily packing it in and heading for our next destination, when I found among the treasures a thin, red bracelet accompanied by a note. Stretching out on a bunk, I began to read the printed material that was with it: "About 2,500 Americans—military, civilian, and dependents—remain unaccounted for in Southeast Asia, from January 1961. This bracelet honors the individual whose name is inscribed. It includes his or her Rank, Name, Home State, Branch of Service, Incident Date, and Country of Loss. When you assume the one-to-one bond with a stranger who is unable to even ask for your concern, and enter the pain of his family, something happens to you. You are taught new lessons about old concepts: Unity, Caring and Brotherhood. You can help achieve the desired accounting by becoming actively involved in your area POW/MIA program."

Then I read the inscription: "Captain John Consolvo, Jr., Virginia, U.S. Marines, May 7, 1972—South Vietnam." Without hesitation, I put it on, making a resolution to keep it on, so that it was not something that I wore occasionally. It was a serious commitment I was making. To me, this bracelet represented not only the Marine whose name was engraved there, but the 2,500 Americans who were still missing.

The band traveled all summer, so we couldn't watch the television coverage of the Olympics' closing ceremonies. One night I received a surprise call from Larry: "The Olympics are over! And you won't believe this, but the TV stations finished with a super montage of the American athletes. It was really touching. These were the special moments, like when they were accepting their medals, or congratulating their teammates for winning, or just standing there hugging each other, laughing or crying. It was fabulous! And guess what background music they played."

"Oh my God! Are you kidding? Was it 'God Bless the U.S.A.'?"

As heartwarming as it was to have my song included in a televised patriotic event, I was really surprised when, not long afterwards, President Reagan called me, asking if he could include it in his film presentation at the national convention. The song had come to his attention due to a coincidence: Nancy Reagan and Merv Griffin have the same birthday, July 6. Just before that date, I had sung "God Bless the U.S.A." on one of Merv's TV shows, and Merv decided that the videotape of my performance would make a suitable gift for the First Lady. She evidently had shared it with her husband, who thought it carried a message he wanted his supporters to hear.

Ronald Reagan told me, "It is to be shown in the Convention Hall to the delegates only. We will not use it at a rally for the general public."

It's difficult to say no to the President. Anyway, I thought that it would be all right. But when the press covered the Republican Convention, they included film clips from President Reagan's video, so in a sense, it was shown publicly. I really hadn't planned for it to be used to endorse a candidate. But I guess we all should feel lucky that we can be involved in the political process without being afraid of reprisals.

About the same time, the industrial democracies were holding a conference in London to discuss world economic policies. They signed a declaration endorsing "elections freely held, free expression of opinion and the capacity to respond and adapt to change in all its aspects." Their meeting marked the fortieth anniversary of D day, the invasion of Normandy on June 6, 1944, and included the United States, Great Britain, France, Canada, West Germany, Italy, and Japan. The irony that the last two nations are now our friends points out the irrational nature of wars. As if to emphasize that fact, outside the conference hall a large crowd of peaceful demonstrators protested nuclear proliferation and the escalating arms race.

By now in America, many radio and TV stations had begun using "God Bless the U.S.A." as their sign-off music, and as we looked toward early fall, it was time for the CMA Awards night.

"Mom. It's going to be just about on your birthday. You and Lewis should come out to Nashville for this," I told her.

"You know we want to be there, Lee, but the drive to Tennessee is too long."

"You're right, Mom, and I know you've never flown. But how about trying it, just this once?"

"Fly? Lee, I don't want to be in the air. I can't do it! But Lew and I would love to have a video of everything that happens."

"Okay, Mom. I'm sure we can get the video from the producers. I'll send it to you."

When that last award of 1984 was called out, "CMA Male Vocalist of the Year, for the second year in a row, Lee Greenwood," Melanie was clapping and screaming, along with the audience. And Larry yelled, "All right! Getting these back to back, Brother . . . this shows it isn't any accident!"

Stepping up to the podium, I said, "Thank you," all the time wishing my mother could be here to receive her birthday present. I had inherited this gift from her, and I knew it.

The Reagan-Bush ticket won in November. "I hate to tell you this, Lee," Larry told me over the phone. "You just got an invitation to sing at the inauguration."

"That sounds like good news, Larry. What's the problem?"

"Well, we're already committed for January 21st. Sorry."

"There's no way we can change that date?"

"I'll get on the phone, but probably not. Damn!"

So Mac Davis sang "God Bless the U.S.A." instead. But a consolation prize soon arrived: an invitation for dinner and to entertain at the White House in February.

It was a black-tie affair in honor of the governors of the states and territories. While the rest of the Trick Band was setting up in the adjoining room, Melanie and I gingerly made our way into the formal dining hall. Looking gorgeous in her long gown and shoulder-length, auburn hair, Melanie charmed the White House staff members who were there to greet us. We were the first to arrive and felt a little awkward, so we began strolling over to the silver-laden tables, glancing at the flowers and white linen tablecloths. Melanie gave me a questioning look and asked, "What do you think we should do now?"

"Let's find our seats, okay?"

Noting the place cards, we could see that Melanie was to be seated beside Tennessee's Gov. Lamar Alexander, whose wife would sit next to the President. Nancy Reagan's card was to the right of mine.

After what seemed like a long wait, we nervously wondered if it would be proper to sit down. Finally the various guests wandered into the hall and started gathering at the tables, finding the right places, and standing behind their chairs.

You don't sit down until the President sits down. I had no idea. We almost made that mistake! Everyone was waiting for the President and Mrs. Reagan to arrive before being seated.

Then amid quite a stir, they walked in. The first person to sit down was the President. This was my cue; I was supposed to hold the chair for the First Lady. But I didn't know that, either. Everyone in the room was waiting for her to sit down, and she was waiting, too. Finally, I noticed the Marine guard behind her, gesturing, trying to get my attention: "Pssst! Pssst!"

The message came through, and greatly embarrassed, I quickly pulled the hand-carved chair out for her. At last, the governors and their wives could be seated. Then, all during the meal while I was trying to politely focus my attention on Nancy Reagan to my right, waiters kept holding dishes of food over my left shoulder. So I was going, "Excuse me," to her and "Thank you," to the waiters. "Excuse me, . . . thank you. Pardon me, . . . thank you."

But the performance went off without a hitch. After "It Turns Me Inside Out," we made a transition into "Ring on Her Finger, Time on Her Hands," and then "It Should Have Been Love By Now" and several others. Our half-hour concluded with "God Bless the U.S.A.," and as the music ended, President Reagan rose to speak. "We're pleased that Lee Greenwood and his troupe are here," he said. "They've come all the way from Texas to play for us."

"Tennessee, Mr. President," I interjected. Then looking around at the sea of faces, which suddenly wore expressions of polite shock at my audacity, I realized that you don't correct the President.

"Whatever you say, sir," I quickly added.

The tense silence turned into laughter.

It had just slipped out. I was merely being honest. We hadn't come nearly as far as from Texas!

This evening of faux pas concluded as the entire band and crew were invited to join the gubernatorial group in the foyer to greet the President and Vice-President Bush. The White House photographer placed Melanie and me in front of a feathery green palm for a photo. "Melanie, where's Marc? He should be in this with us."

"Lee, I saw him come in with the band . . . . Oh!"

At the same time, both Melanie and I spotted my aggressive son. There he was, on the far side of the hall with the President, vigorously pumping Mr. Reagan's hand as though he were saying, "Hey, prez. How're you doing? Howdy-doody!" Although I had the urge to hide somewhere, Melanie and I looked at each other, both of us suppressing a laugh. Leave it to our outgoing Marc to jump right in there and lead the scene!

Meanwhile, another young man was leading his wife, Hillary, to the receiving line. Arkansas's Bill Clinton had been his state's governor since he was thirty-two, six years earlier. That night he was saying, "I feel like I'm the oldest man in America my age. I've been in it so long. I'm greyer than half the people here. But I love it!"

"Good to meet you, Lee. That's a great song you wrote," Vice-President Bush told me, as I walked up to him to shake his hand.

That was my first contact with George Bush. In less than three weeks, he would be on his way to Moscow on a diplomatic mission. The Soviets' Premier Chernenko had died, and now the reins had fallen to a much younger man, fifty-four-year-old Mikhail Gorbachev. Representing our nation at the funeral near the Kremlin, Vice-President Bush seized this opportunity to establish a rapport with the newest commander of the U.S.S.R. Gorbachev talked about his intentions to make some major changes in Russia's economy, a restructuring that he called "perestroika." He said he was reducing their stockpiles of arms, and he stressed his new policy of openness, or "glasnost." Encouraged by his meeting with Gorbachev, our Vice-President told the press that this was "a time we can move forward with progress."

This was about the time that some of us in country music were treading on thin ice. The morning after I had performed in Tampa, Florida, *The Tribune* said in bold headlines: "Lee Greenwood—The singer has emerged as one of the leaders of country's brave new wave." The subheading read: "At age 42, the California-born superstar is giving his field of music a shot of energy and pop potential."

It was something Larry and I had realized was coming. Already in the planning stage was "Streamline," our most AC-looking album ever. Along with others, we were moving out of the old-fashioned, traditional country sound, and that scared some of the regulars in Nashville. They didn't want anybody breaking the mold. They wanted it to stay exactly the same. In the minds of the folks who ran the industry, country music should remain unchanged in order to keep Nashville as its hub and to maintain Opryland as a thriving mecca of country shows. So those of us who had our hearts into broadening country's appeal were growing concerned.

But keeping it light, the Trick Band and I started on a springtime tour with Exile and Dan Seals. For the first show, we were heading down to Gainesville, the home of the University of Florida. However, there was one commitment I had to fulfill before leaving Nashville.

"Lee, this year's Easter Seals chairman needs a little help, and I'm that guy," Buddy Killen, the owner of the Stockyards restaurant, had told me. "John Lindahl of State Industries in Ashland City and I were talking. We thought we could put together a fundraiser, like maybe an auction, to make some money. It's a worthy cause. We sure could use your assistance."

"That sounds great, Buddy. What can I do?"

"Well, someone came up with the idea that since the ladies are always screaming when you come on stage, reaching up and grabbing at you, and they bring you flowers and little gifts . . . Well, anyway, we decided those ladies would pay a bundle for your clothes."

"What?"

"Only the main articles. What do you say?"

"You're asking me to strip, in public?"

"As I said, it's for a good cause, Lee. We'll have items from other stars at the auction. But you'll be the only stripper."

"Thanks a lot," I replied sarcastically. Then a nervous laugh escaped as I said, "I'm game for almost anything for a good cause, Buddy. When the time comes, I'll try to follow your lead."

The Easter Seals auction evening arrived, and I was dressing carefully for the occasion. Purposely, I donned my new hand-painted denim jacket, considering it my donation to Easter Seals. Under that was one of my very best Western shirts. It would probably go. As a precaution to overzealous bidders, I pulled on some blue jogging shorts, with white stripes down the sides, underneath my smooth-fitting jeans—just in case things got that far. . . . I was beginning to understand how the volunteer amateur strippers in Vegas must feel. Only I wasn't going to win any prize for this act. But I kept telling myself, "Lee, remember it's for a good cause."

Down at the Stockyards, it was a standing-room-only crowd, a packed house. What followed was six hours of well-orchestrated entertainment and fundraising, during which a lot of expensive clothes and keepsakes went to the highest bidders. As the night was nearing an end, Buddy Killen, acting as emcee, brought me forward on the stage: "Ladies and gentlemen, here's a guy who's willing to give his all for Easter Seals. Let's hear it for a first-time stripper, Lee Greenwood!"

Breaking through the applause, he reached out to push me closer to the audience and began, "This gorgeous jacket that Lee's wearing was made especially for his stage performances. And it has the star's name embroidered inside the collar. What will you pay for this beautiful, one-of-a-kind jacket?"

When the spirited bidding reached $1,000, Buddy yelled, "Sold for one thousand dollars." Then he started pulling off my shirt. "How much for this good-looking shirt, folks? It's a beauty. Prettier than what's inside it!" His joke at my expense brought in $400 for the shirt. But he wasn't finished with me yet.

As I was trying to wriggle out of my shirt, he continued.

"Now, who would like to buy Lee's fine, hand-tooled boots? They're exquisitely made."

Someone paid $850 for the boots, and that left me standing, in front of almost everybody in Nashville, shirtless and barefoot.

"Okay, Folks. Now it's going to get interesting," Buddy went on. "Do you think we can persuade Mr. Greenwood to hand over those fancy jeans for such a worthy cause?"

"Yeaaah," roared the transfixed throng. He had their complete attention.

"Only if the purchase price is high enough," I blurted out, getting into the spirit of this process. "These are designer jeans, you know." And I grinned.

Now the bidding started in earnest, with me feeling not only a little insecure, but cold. It's drafty, even in the Stockyards, without clothes. Melanie, of all people, started the bidding on my pants. But a woman in the front row won. It was John Lindahl's wife who came rushing up and personally unzipped my jeans. A gasp went up from the crowd, as well as a few shouts of encouragement from the men. To the amazement of the hundreds of bidders watching, she took the jeans right off me!

"You're no shy lady, ma'm!" I said. Then glad to at least have on my blue and white shorts, I edged out of the spotlight.

"Thanks, Lee. You made the supreme sacrifice for Easter Seals," Buddy was saying, as I leaped off the stage, fervently hoping that Melanie had brought some replacement clothing.

After almost three months, the band's springtime tour came to an end, and I was faced with another request for charity. The organizers of Nashville's Special Olympics, an annual sporting event to benefit the mentally handicapped, gave our office a call. "We realize that Lee and Melanie are always captains for the teams to help our youngsters. They're good sports. But do you think Lee would accept a challenge? One of the Oak Ridge Boys, Richard Sterban, and Gary Morris are sure they can beat him through a maze we're setting up on the field."

"Accept a challenge?" Larry shot back. "You must be kidding! You know Lee. He's going to be right out there in the middle of it."

"Okay. Then you're sure he'll come. Now, it's going to be rather different . . .," the caller said, not willing to let my talkative manager in on their real intentions.

"Are you forgetting that Lee ran track in high school? He even had a scholarship offer. This guy can beat Morris and Sterban. No problem, man. He'll be there!" And as he put down the receiver, Larry added, "Great! Lee can win that sucker!"

Well, it happened during Fanfare Week. Melanie and I, dressed in our warm-ups, were having a sensational time competing in relay races and other events at the Special Olympics. Then it was time for the Country Singer's Maze Race. Bringing me over to a gigantic plywood maze, the referee said, "This is where you start. We'll put a stopwatch on you, one at a time."

"I'll go first if you want," interjected Gary.

Looking over the setup and nodding that this seemed reasonable, I watched as the starter's gun sent Gary on his way through the innocent-looking complex. The assorted fans who had gathered around started yelling, "Run, Gary! Run! You can win!"

Even Richard was hollering, in his tunnel-deep voice, urging him on. In no time at all, Gary was out. He was quicker than I had expected. I said to myself, "Boy, that was pretty fast!"

Then the Oak's bass singer said, "It's my turn, guys."

Again the excited spectators were shouting, even those watching the video monitors of Richard winding his way through this puzzle of wooden slabs. It was easy. In no time at all he, too, was out, clasping his hands above his head in a mock gesture of victory.

Absolutely certain that I could beat the times of those two

show-offs, I was chomping at the bit. I could hardly wait to streak into that maze.

"On your mark. Get set. Go!" The gun sounded and I was off. Pouring on the steam, I dashed through the entrance and raced toward what looked like the next turn. But as I reached it, suddenly it was a blank wooden wall.

"Damn!" I wheeled around looking for the path. "There it is," I thought as I ran straight toward an opening. But no. It was a dead end.

Hundreds of people outside were screaming at the tops of their lungs. Fiercely competitive and dead set on winning this, I was getting frustrated. And angry. Heading for another apparent turn in the labyrinth, I was confronted by a newly erected wall. Tightening every muscle in my body, I was determined to run right through it: "There is no way I'm going to be a loser, if I have to knock down this whole plywood jungle!"

It was beginning to dawn on me that this was some kind of hoax. Jumping up to peer over the top, I kept seeing people out there, and they were pointing like, "This way out." I was frantically pushing on the stiff walls and jumping again, and they were pointing in the other direction, indicating, "No, this way!" Then I knew that something was up. I desperately threw my body against a wall, one more time, with full force. The whole panel fell down, and I ran out.

Boy, was I hot! Really mad! Everyone was dying laughing and I almost lost my cool. But fortunately I tried to say something clever. I came up with, "Now I know how a mouse feels!"

The onlookers were applauding in glee, pointing to the video monitor, which was rolling a replay. I looked up and saw what was so funny. There was no way to keep from laughing with them. Then the emcee walked up. "Surprise! You're on 'TV Bloopers and Practical Jokes.' If you'll let us use this film on our program, you'll get $2,500."

"Okay. I'll take it." But I was still trying to shrug it off, struggling to hide my disappointment in having lost . . . and to Richard and Gary!

The Music City News announced their Male Vocalist of the Year and Single Record for 1985. It was exciting to win that award for the first time. I was so pleased that "God Bless the U.S.A." had finally won. The feeling goes back to the days when it was first written. There are givers and there are takers. I'm a giver, and always have been. I wanted so much to give something to my country.

Also, I have never overcome the void of not being able to serve in the military. I'm a team player who never got to be on that team. So in a way, my song is a contribution to America and to its important military team. It goes beyond that, because I believe our nation is the leader for world peace. It's a tough role to play, but Americans have always been willing to take on difficult challenges.

The Greenpeace group found out firsthand how difficult those challenges could be. These campaigners for the protection of our environment had their 160-foot vessel, the *Rainbow Warrior,* tied to a dock in New Zealand. They were planning to take it on a protest voyage against France's nuclear testing. But without warning the *Rainbow Warrior* was wracked by deafening blasts. The crack and roar of explosions rang into the air as flames and smoke rose from its hull. One Greenpeace member was killed, and the ship was entirely destroyed. Several months later, France's prime minister admitted that French intelligence officers had sneaked explosives aboard the cruiser.

In contrast to that sabotage of nuclear protesters, the Nobel Peace Prize of 1985 was awarded to the International Physicians for the Prevention of Nuclear War. In its presentation, the Norwegian Nobel Committee stated, "This organization was formed as a joint initiative by Soviet and American physicians and it now draws support from physicians in over forty countries all over the world."

Walter Cronkite endorsed the award, saying, "It is not pleasant to look death in the face. But unless we do, we are doomed. No group is as qualified to present the terrible facts as these physicians who, with admirable courage and tenacity, have taken into their hands the formidable task of educating

the public, the governments, and their military to the ines-
capable results of the nuclear arms folly."

But nuclear war is usually far from our minds, especially
during emotional occasions. A summertime garden wedding
gave the Greenwood family a rare opportunity to come together. It seemed hardly possible that my baby daughter
Kelly was actually this lovely vision in white, ready to float
down the aisle. But it seemed natural to be singing "You Are
So Beautiful" to her at the beginning of the ceremony. Then
her arm rested in mine as we walked slowly toward the minister and her husband-to-be, standing between two altar candles. Could I really be "giving her away"?

Gazing around at this gathering of those closest to me, I
thought about the many years of living that were represented
here. Tedd and Marc, handsome in charcoal tuxedoes, stood
among the ushers. Laura was seated near the front row, in a
sisterly gesture to Kelly. And of course Roberta had come for
her daughter's marriage. As I saw her sitting next to Melanie,
I realized that time was beginning to fade the sharp hurt of
separation and divorce, and now the family was becoming a
unit again. My four children knew each other and accepted
the idea that love can blossom and love can die, but responsibility remains. And caring remains.

October brought a triumph, the long awaited recognition
for "God Bless the U.S.A."! The competition had been stiff,
and because of its broad appeal there were some who
doubted that this patriotic song could win in the country music category. But CMA named it 1985's Song of the Year. Although two years had passed since it had been written, I was
grateful that its merit was finally being acknowledged.

This happy feeling was totally wiped out by the tragedy
that struck just before Christmas. Two hundred and fifty-
eight people were aboard a DC-8 as it took off from Gander,
Newfoundland. All but eight were soldiers from the 101st
Airborne Division in Fort Campbell, Kentucky, who had been
stationed in the Sinai Peninsula with the international peace-
keeping force. These young paratroopers must have been jubilant. They were coming home for the holidays. But as their

jet reached 1,000 feet, it quivered, lurched, then plummeted to the snow-laden forests of birch and spruce trees below. Carving a trench through the thick woodland, it skidded violently along the terrain for a mile, then exploded. There were no survivors.

Those of us in the U.S. were grief-stricken. The warm anticipation of a joyous Christmas holiday had been shattered by the finality of death. The home of the 101st is close to us in Tennessee. In fact, part of the base is in our state. So like neighbors, we shared the burden of mourning with friends and relatives there and throughout the country.

By now, "God Bless the U.S.A." was being included in many military programs that require spirit. Airborne units form a brotherhood based upon their mutual courage. These skilled parachute troops are trained to back up maneuvers on a battle's forward line. Such military tasks depend upon esprit de corps, and a strong element of that high morale is patriotic pride. The Eighty-second Airborne Division at Fort Bragg, North Carolina, had been using "God Bless the U.S.A." as their jump song. They would link up arms and sing it together. Then bolstered by a feeling of unity, one by one, they would leap out into space.

The Army Golden Knights Parachute Team adopted it, too. As a guest, I sang for their synchronized air show in Kansas City. At the song's first sound, streams of troopers hit the empty sky, filing in perfect cadence out of their plane's doorway. While I was singing, they performed aerial formations and unbelievably perfect maneuvers. Slowly they floated earthward. As the last note trailed off, every Golden Knight paratrooper had landed and their plane touched the runway, simultaneously. Incredible! It would be wonderful if we could all work together so harmoniously.

The album *Christmas to Christmas* appeared during a holiday season that was painful for many. But it included a comforting ancient melody, one that reminded me of a scared little boy trying his best as he sang his first solo at a Christmas Eve church service, so long ago in Sacramento. The hymn was "O Holy Night."

CHAPTER XI

ANOTHER TRAGEDY FOR AMERICA marked the beginning of 1986. On a frigid day in January, a morning so cold that even temperatures at Florida's Cape Canaveral had dropped far below freezing, the space shuttle *Challenger* was waiting for its journey into space. For three days, workers had been scraping thin sheets of ice from its sides and the ground support system below. Clusters of dignitaries, tourists, Kennedy Space Center workers, and families of the astronauts were still there, riveted in suspense, in spite of the ordeal of continuous delays. The window, or opportune moment for the mission, was closing. After their long months of preparation, space officials were anxious not to miss this chance for a glorious send-off.

By midmorning, the time seemed right. The Command Center ordered, "Ignition." Clouds of flames billowed against the pad underneath the *Challenger.* Then came the words, "Lift-off!" The huge rocket with its precious cargo pulled up slowly in a struggle for momentum, then hurtled skyward.

Inside the shuttle's cockpit, pilot Mike Smith shouted, "Here we go!" Comdr. Frank Scobee confirmed, "Go, with throttle up."

Then something happened that took a moment to comprehend, even for seasoned television reporters. The *Challenger*'s straight, steady path suddenly split into two smokey white plumes, as smaller streams splintered off like cloudy jet trails, and all of them curved toward the earth below.

The dreadful realization crept over one viewer and then another. Newscasters were shouting questions. A heavy, dull feeling sank into the hearts of everyone watching, and then the tears began to stream. A team of our nation's brightest space explorers had been instantly annihilated. Killed with the *Challenger*'s flight commander and pilot were crew members Judy Resnik, Ron McNair, El Onizuka, Greg Jarvis, and a representative of America's teachers, Christa McAuliffe. Looking up helplessly from below, the families and friends in the stands near the launch pad were devastated.

Along with millions of others who watched the live television coverage, I was struck by a feeling of deep loss. There was grief for the families and also the bitter realization that America had experienced a failure. Our leaders believe that space exploration is a vital method of gaining information to shape tomorrow's world. So it was a crushing blow to lose the *Challenger* crew, who were pioneers in our quest for knowledge from space.

It was only a few months later that I was high in the clouds, holding my breath and getting ready for a spine-tingling mid-ocean rendezvous. The officers and crew of the USS *Kitty Hawk,* our aircraft carrier now stationed off the West Coast, were celebrating her twenty-fifth anniversary. Their public information officer had given our office a call to see if we'd be able to participate in the ceremonies.

"By coincidence, Lee will be in California during that time. He's playing a few dates with Kenny Rogers out there," Jerry Bentley had told him. Jerry, who worked in our office for Larry, added, "Just work out the logistics. We'd be happy to come."

So early one May morning, a Navy twin-engine turboprop picked us up at Mather Air Force Base in Sacramento. This Carrier Onboard Delivery, or COD, is set up to transport cargo or troops. As it turned out, Jerry and I were the only passengers, besides the flight crew.

"Here. Take your life jackets. We need to go through a few emergency procedures in case we ditch," the First Officer said, in an offhand manner. "We have a raft, too. Just buckle your seat belts, and it'll be about ninety minutes. The *Kitty Hawk*'s out there," and he pointed toward open sea.

An hour and a half later we reached the ship somewhere in the Pacific. "We're going to circle the carrier two or three times. Then we'll go in for a landing," he told us.

Through a little window, I could see the *Kitty Hawk* floating like a miniature toy in the ocean below, and I was thinking to myself, "That looks small! And we're going to land on *that?*"

The time came for the COD to make its final approach. "Brace yourself. We'll be coming in fast," the First Officer told us. "The approach speed is 120 knots. When the wheels hit the deck, you'll hear a real loud scraping sound. That'll be the shock absorbers giving in a little. When they sink down, the body of our aircraft will slide on the deck for a short distance. No problem. The hook will be down, and it'll catch the cable." Then he added, "Be ready. When the hook catches, we're going to stop real quick."

About that time I was saying under my breath, "I don't know if I want to be here or not," and I shot a quick look at Jerry. He wasn't saying much, either. Then he came up with a nervous smile, and said, "Well, I never thought about going this way!"

Our plane was diving at high speed right toward the carrier. The wheels touched, the plane's belly scraped, and with a body-crushing yank, we were standing still—not moving at all. I looked over at Jerry and heaved a sigh of relief. We gazed across the broad flight deck, lined with Navy jets, and realized that we were on an immense floating city.

"Welcome to the USS *Kitty Hawk*. The flight deck you just landed on covers over four acres and can accommodate eighty-seven aircraft," Capt. David Hoffman told us. "The *Kitty Hawk* has a crew of 5,300. Would you believe we serve over seventeen thousand meals a day? The galley crew will be happy to serve two extra meals today. Glad to have you aboard!"

Our time on the *Kitty Hawk* was short. After a quick tour of the ship and a fast game of basketball with some enlisted men who were super shots, I sang "God Bless the U.S.A." for a group in the hangar, in honor of the carrier's Silver Anniversary. Then our host said, "Lee, we want you to know that when we reach port and pull into the harbor, our crew will be in uniform, standing at attention along the deck in a formation spelling out the words, 'PROUD TO BE AN AMERICAN!' We feel it very strongly."

After lunch it was time to leave, but Jerry and I were not looking forward to the experience. This time it was going to be *really* interesting.

"We're going to be catapulted on takeoff," our hosts informed us. "Just strap yourselves in."

If you can imagine being belted in your seat and going from 0 to 120 miles an hour in three to four seconds, you know what catapulting is. It's just like being snapped forward by a slingshot. I've never felt that much pressure slam against my body. We were sitting still. Then we were zooming up into the sky.

Suddenly our plane came to a dead stop in midflight. At least it felt that way. All the pressure was gone. It was the strangest sensation. Filling my lungs with air, I quickly glanced over at Jerry and breathed a sigh of relief. It was the most awesome kick I've ever taken!

Developments in aeronautics have come a long way in only a few years. But it's just as important to make progress in getting along with our fellow man. The ties of understanding have to be strengthened. It was a good feeling to have "God Bless the U.S.A." sung by the young choral group in their worldwide "Hands Across America" program.

I hate barriers. It would be wonderful to reach people all over the world, communicating through song. In 1986, a large collection of widely recognized musicians came very close to doing that with "We Are the World." But there are so many people out there who don't listen to each other, let alone to music.

On the Fourth of July, America threw a gigantic centennial celebration for the Statue of Liberty. Our colossal "Liberty Enlightening the World" had been presented to the U.S. by the people of France in gratitude for our friendship and to acknowledge our trailblazing efforts in the cause of freedom. So today, an unforgettable extravaganza was going on in New York Harbor. Ships from all over the world were streaming toward Liberty Island, setting their sights on Liberty's torch, rising over three hundred feet in the air. In a little enclosed booth, I was giving a television interview for the CBS "Good Morning, America" program. We were situated high at the top of a building on Governor's Island. From this vantage point, we had a bird's-eye view of the flotilla of crafts entering the harbor. The official count was twenty large U.S. warships and twenty-one from foreign nations. The tall sailing ships were impressive, and from our spot looking down on the enormous aircraft carrier, the USS *John F. Kennedy,* we could see hundreds of miscellaneous boats filtering in, turning the water into a solid mass of decks, turrets, and masts. Fireworks were flaring, while sleek French fighter jets performed aerial stunts.

"The Carrier *Kennedy* below us is hard to believe, isn't it, Lee?" the emcee asked.

"Awesome! It's about the largest thing I've ever seen," I replied.

"This is a patriotic time. I see you have on an MIA bracelet. Would you tell us about that?"

"Well, it has the name of Capt. John Consolvo on it. He's still missing. Over two thousand of our people haven't been accounted for. I've worn this bracelet for two years, and I'm going to keep on wearing it until Vietnam gives us a full accounting of these men."

"This is certainly an ongoing issue, and we hope it can be resolved. Now, would you sing the song you wrote for our country?"

Sitting at the piano, which the crew had managed to squeeze into that treetop booth, I started the opening verse of "God Bless the U.S.A." While I was singing, a gigantic ship slowly moved into the background behind me. Bigger than anything I could imagine, it was the *Queen Elizabeth II*, arriving from England. Across her bow and all the way down her side was draped an unbelievably large American flag. It was beautiful! The *QEII* had made the voyage all the way across the Atlantic and had arrived right behind me, during this TV performance, just as I was singing. Timing is everything!

Having been invited to perform aboard one of the ships, the Trick Band and I spent the evening right next to the USS *Kennedy* with the throngs of celebrants watching white-hot rockets streaming toward the sky and bursts of red and blue filling the night. Afterwards we were on our way west to Longmont, near Boulder, Colorado, for a benefit to help raise funds for the Statue of Liberty's restoration. Then we were headed back to a benefit in Indiana for the Vermillion County War Memorial honoring all American veterans. Introducing my song, I told them, "In this country we, as a people, have had our heads hung down about hostilities that we probably shouldn't have been in. There are some people who call what happened in Vietnam a conflict. Because it caused so much suffering and death, we use a stronger word. We call it a war. The men and women who served there made as great a sacrifice as any of our soldiers in the World Wars. Today we're honoring the memory of all our patriots who died for freedom."

This was a time for looking to the past and remembering. One warm recollection that surfaced during August was the thought of my Uncle Jake. I'll never forget the gift of his silver saxophone, even though it ended up smashed on that winding road in the Sacramento hills. Now we were releasing a new album, *Love Will Find Its Way to You,* and one of the songs included was "Silver Saxophone." The image of Uncle Jake and his sax came flooding back.

It was on a chilly day in mid-September that one of those unusual happenings of a lifetime occurred. In Biloxi, Mississippi, as I was having a meal with my band before our evening concert, a young lady walked up to our table.

"Hi! I'm Dana Gates. May I have your autograph?" she asked. Then, pressing a bright silver dollar into my hand, she added, "This is for you."

Rather startled, I stopped eating. "What's this for?" I asked, totally puzzled.

"It's a long story," Dana answered. "But this silver dollar rightfully should be passed down to you. It's from my aunt. She gave it to me only last year, just before she died. In the afternoons I would bring records to her bedside and play them for her. We both loved hearing your songs, but then when you sang 'Ring on Her Finger, Time on Her Hands' and came to the part that says, 'It's just a ring on your finger when there's time on your hands,' she almost burst out crying. She was an elderly lady, and I'd never seen my aunt show that much emotion."

"Gosh. I'm so sorry to have made her sad," I interjected.

"But she said it was all right, that somehow it made her feel better, and that she wanted to talk to me about a secret in her life, when she was only about my age. That's when she took out this silver dollar and gave it to me."

I gazed down at the silver dollar resting in my palm. "Did she tell you the secret?"

"Yes." With that, she said good-bye and turned to go.

That night, after our Biloxi show, a letter appeared on our bus. Traveling down the road to our next venue in Hiawassee, Georgia, I cradled the silver dollar in my hand as I learned how it had found its way to me.

Upon returning to Nashville, I made two calls: to Mary Ann Kennedy and Pam Rose, the songwriters who had helped Don Goodman write "Ring on Her Finger, Time on Her Hands."

"There's a love story that really should be told. Will you help me write the song?" I asked them. And they agreed.

> *The sun was shining on Biloxi Bay.*
> *Wedding bells rang out that day;*
> *The sweet refrain echoed through the night.*
> *Songs of love and chapel bells:*

Love was sweet, so the story tells.
Jake and Jessie, 1929.

Well, Jessie's heart began to sing.
She was proud of her golden ring.
Everything seemed to be all right.
Then a stranger came Biloxi way.
Jessie fell in love that day,
This time, in the shadows of the night.

Their love was like a burning torch.
Late one night on Jessie's porch
He placed a silver dollar in her hand.
He looked deep into Jessie's eyes
And without a word she realized
The magic of a circle as it turns:
When love is given, love returns.

The stranger left, alone, one night.
Jessie finally saw the light
As she chose between the silver and the gold.
And the love that was born in '29
Somehow was sweeter down through time,
And in their final days
God took Jake away.

Holding that secret, all those years, must have been a heavy burden. The silver dollar with its message of love remained hidden, like a treasure. But when the forgiving words of "Ring on Her Finger" melted the guilt, for the first time she could bring herself to talk about her past. That was when she gave the cherished coin to Dana.

The moon was shining on Biloxi Bay;
A young girl came to hear me play.
She said, "A silver dollar for your autograph."
I listened as I signed my name.
She said her aunt had passed away
And she told her a secret no one else had known.
As I looked surprised, she said

Her Aunt Jessie had confessed
Of one time having loved unfaithfully.
The secret love was in her youth,
And Jake had never known the truth.
"And no one would 'til Jessie heard you sing,
'Love is more than just a ring.'"
And she said, "As you were singing,
It was just like Jake was saying,
'Jessie, I forgive you, come on home.'"
She said, "Take this silver dollar.
In trade, it's not enough
For the gift of understanding,
The greatest gift of love."

I could still see the earnest look on the face of Jessie's niece, as she had placed the silver dollar in my hand.

O the circle of a silver dollar
Passing down from one heart to another,
O the circle of a silver dollar—
When love is given, love returns.

Looking down at the shining circle, I thought, "Thank you, Jessie. Your message is still with us."

Another concert, that fall, brought hidden emotions to the surface. At the Capitol Theater in Wheeling, West Virginia, our show was being broadcast, live, to seventeen states and Canada. Due to the fact that we were on the air, our audience was especially turned on by the music, and the atmosphere seemed to be charged with electricity. The hour slid by, and the expectation of my final number intensified as the time came to close the show. I raised the mike a little closer and looked into the crowd, trying to come up with the right words.

"We're Americans. But we can't walk down the street every day waving the flag. And we can't always sit around talking about politics. But we've got to stand up for what's right . . . for what's important. And that's our people. The backbone of this country is our people and their strength. And woven in, is their pride—pride in their work, and pride in themselves."

A murmur of agreement filtered through the room as I continued: "In this world there'll always be some countries that can't get along. Maybe even if the whole world was a democracy we'd still be against each other. But if we can preserve America's point of view, our free way of life, maybe other countries can learn by our example. And then someday we may all come together and there won't be a reason to fight anymore."

And I began to sing "God Bless the U.S.A."

As I was finishing the first verse, my eyes focused on a giant of a man, a Marine in blue jeans, boots, and a well-worn camouflage jacket, coming down the center aisle. All at once he stopped and stood at attention. One fist was clenched upward, as if in an emotional military salute. He seemed to be remembering his days in Vietnam, or maybe his fallen buddies. It struck me that he must be acknowledging that he was one of the few who had somehow survived. But the song obviously had a profound effect upon him.

Then he slowly began pulling off his field coat, which looked as if it had been through a lot of rough experiences in the war zone. While I continued singing, he moved steadily on down the aisle to the stage, stopped, then handed the heavy coat up to me.

Unsure of exactly what to do, I stretched out my arms to put it on. It was so bulky and long that it practically engulfed me. But neither of us noticed. We were both standing there, looking into each other's eyes and bawling—just unashamedly crying. He reached up and grabbed my hand in the clasp of brotherhood. The audience became almost hysterical. Everyone in the room was standing, just about overcome by the force of emotion.

Backstage after the show, the towering Marine walked up to me, and without a word, threw his huge arms around me in the embrace of a comrade. Gathering his composure, he said, "I'm Terry Wildman. I was in I-Corp, in the DMZ. It's such a proud feeling to hear you sing that song. It's like after all the things we've been through, here's a man who supports us. My whole heart was with every word you were singing."

"Terry, it's good to know you," I replied. "Here's your field coat. I'd like to return it. And, by the way, your keys are in the pocket."

"Oh, thanks! And would you sign it? Whenever we can, my Vietnam buddies and I get together at the VFW Club in Martin's Ferry. It seems like we understand each other. Anyway I'd like to hang this coat up there."

"Sure," I told him. "I know that you guys have been through a lot for your country. There's no way we can really thank you."

To me, this had been an unforgettable way to make a friend.

A set of coincidences converged at the end of October. It was Navy Day, and it was also Theodore Roosevelt's birthday. Because of "God Bless the U.S.A.," the 6,000-member crew of the newly built nuclear aircraft carrier USS *Theodore Roosevelt* had voted me as the mascot of their ship. The *Roosevelt* had been commissioned two years earlier, and now for its formal recognition ceremony, the officers invited me to participate.

Arriving at midmorning, I was taken on a tour of the mammoth vessel. Much larger than the *Kitty Hawk*, it was like a complete flat-topped metropolis, floating there moored to the dock in Norfolk, Virginia. Then my escort explained, "As mascot, you are now a plank owner of the carrier."

"A plank owner?"

"Yes. A plank owner is a member of the crew. In the early days, when the ships were wooden, the sailors used to come up at night to sleep on deck, because there was no air conditioning then. Each crew member found a comfortable spot, the softest plank to rest his head on, and that piece of wood became his. Years later, when the ship was decommissioned and dismantled, the men who had been aboard for years were given their planks as mementos."

"Well, I sure haven't been a crew member."

"That's okay. You're still a plank owner," he replied. "What happened was that later on, it became the practice to dedicate planks to participants in the history of the ship's voyages. Today, as you see, our oceangoing vessels are quite different. You sure couldn't sleep very comfortably on this steel deck! But we still consider you a special family member of the *Roosevelt*."

"Thanks," I replied. "And, although my dad was in the Navy, I'm not sure if he realized that I was born on Navy Day. Today's my birthday, too!"

That turned the day into magic, and as I said good-bye to the USS *Roosevelt,* the men put up their multicolored flags in a semaphore signal. Offering his help, my escort read their message: "Good-bye, Mr. Greenwood. Thank You."

Having survived a catapult off the *Kitty Hawk* and taken a look at the flight decks of the *Roosevelt* lined with those tough-looking helicopters and sleek jet fighters, I couldn't help wondering what it would be like to hit the air in a supersonic plane. The opportunity soon came my way, when our office received a call from Maj. Steve Salvatoriello, the aide to Commanding General Marcus Hurley of Nellis Air Force Base in Nevada.

"The 474th Fighter Wing and the precision flying team, the Thunderbirds, have chosen 'God Bless the U.S.A.' as their wing song," he told Jerry. "Would a visit to the base to perform the song be possible?"

"Lee will feel honored to know that these flying units have adopted his song," Jerry answered. "As a matter of fact, Lee and I will be at the Frontier in Las Vegas next month. Do you think we could have a chance to fly in one of your F-16s?"

"That would have to be cleared through the chain of command. I'll certainly try to obtain permissions. Please let me get back to you on that."

The reply came: "Your flights have been approved. Nellis Air Force Base is having an aeronautical competition during that week. We've got pilots and crews coming in from other bases, and they're going to be competing against each other. These will be like Olympic matches. There's a lot of rivalry, but the main purpose is to keep our readiness tuned to a fine edge. At the end of the week we'll be gathering everyone in one of our largest hangars to congratulate them on their efforts. Would Mr. Greenwood be willing to sing for us then?"

"That'll be fine," Jerry answered. "We'll be there . . . , ready to fly, too."

When Jerry and I arrived at Nellis AFB, General Hurley told us, "The F-16s are waiting. The major will take you to our VIP quarters, where you'll change into flight suits."

In the guest quarters, Jerry was pulling on the olive-drab flight coveralls. "Look at all these zippers and pockets. I've never seen so many in all my life. And then there's this jacket. I feel olive drab all over," he said, tightly lacing the standard black combat boots.

All suited up in military clothing, we were transported to the F-16 simulator, which was located inside a plain-looking office building. As two Air Force officers greeted us at the door, the first began, "You'll be spending about three hours here. This is a replica of the F-16 cockpit. We'll help you practice getting in and out, putting on the G suit and other gear that connects up to vital support systems, and fastening the harnesses. Also, you'll need to learn the emergency procedures, in case something goes wrong with the aircraft. You'll have to know what to do if you're still on the ground, and how to maneuver if you're airborne."

"Yeah. I see those parachutes hanging from the ceiling," I said. "Guess you'll be teaching us how to bail out."

"And also what to do if your lines are twisted. You'll have to be able to untangle the lines, or the chute won't open. We call it 'punch out,' " he added.

That didn't sound so wonderful. I was feeling the beginnings of apprehension creeping up: "Boy, what am I going to do if I have to punch out?" I glanced down at John Consolvo's name on my MIA bracelet with renewed respect.

"And you won't be actually jumping out," he continued. "If you press the ejection button, like the one up here on the simulator board, it will set off an explosive charge under your seat. The explosion will blow you out of the plane."

"That has to be some awful feeling . . . two, three, maybe four miles high, to be shot right out, not knowing if the parachute is going to open," I thought. By now, I was listening very, very carefully. This is a situation in which you'd better not make a mistake.

Jerry and I paid close attention to every detail. If something wasn't clear, we asked! Then after practicing everything over and over, we were given the last piece of advice: "Before pushing the ejection button, remember to pull your feet back. If you leave them down, going out, your knees could be left under the dash!"

"Now, let's practice," said the officer. "Your F-16 has a flameout. You've got to punch out. . . ."

After three hours in the simulator building, we headed to another location for a briefing on the flight. There we met the pilots. I was to fly with Maj. George Cella, but Jerry's plane had a mechanical problem.

"If you're not going, I really don't want to go," I said in a low voice.

"You're not getting off that easy!" Jerry whispered, giving me an amused look.

So we climbed into an Air Force van, which looked like a bread truck with two benches in back, and rode out to the flight house. Here, the pilot went through a "preflight" of the aircraft. First he walked up to the crew chief who was in charge of the F-16's maintenance and asked if there was anything about the aircraft's readiness that he should be aware of. Then he did a "walk around," slowly encircling the plane, looking for any type of damage, a leak or sign that looked suspicious. The pilot inspected the area underneath, where the wheels fold into their casements, and he looked into the engine itself. Finally he turned around to me and said, "Okay. Time to get in."

Climbing up into the F-16, I began to go through the preflight procedures, buckling the shoulder harness, seat belt, and parachute harness. I connected the pressure suit and oxygen hoses, before putting on the oxygen mask, which also protects you in case of fire. I pulled down my visor. It was like total wraparound sunglasses attached to the helmet. Finally I pulled on the flame-retardant gloves.

Major Cella climbed into the cockpit in front of me. He completed a five-minute checklist and programmed the on-board computer. Then we were cleared for takeoff. All the lights came on and I heard a buzzing noise from the engine. It sounded like a vacuum cleaner! Then the canopy was lowered. That's when it became very quiet. It also got unbelievably hot, with mounds of gear on and the bright sun burning down on our plane. The nauseous oxygen-mask smell was like liquid rubber.

"How are you doing back there, Lee?" Major Cella called out over the intercom.

I stiffened my shoulders against the harness. "Just fine," I answered, in my best military voice.

"Okay. After we go through our final inspection, we'll get this Fighting Falcon in the air," he said.

Soon we were taxiing up to a small building, and I saw three Air Force personnel run out. Major Cella called to me: "Hold your arms straight up, Lee, so they can see your hands. And keep them there. They're going to do the final check of the aircraft."

My hands flew up faster than if he'd said, "This is a holdup." A little on edge, I shouted back, "They're up!"

Calmly, he explained, "Keeping your hands up is just a procedure to let them know that you're not touching any instruments inside the aircraft. See, I have my hands up, too."

One of the men outside was holding his fists in a clenched position, indicating, "Don't move." Meanwhile, the other two were walking around, inspecting the plane. Then the one in front dropped his hands and saluted, giving us the "okay" sign.

"Ready for takeoff," Major Cella told the tower.

The jet taxied onto the active runway and I felt the first surge of its engine. The afterburner kicked in, slamming me back into the seat, and as it went through five different stages, the plane's nose lifted off the ground.

"We're airborne!" shouted Major Cella.

The landing gear was retracted, and the flight became smooth and silent. The sound was far behind the jet.

"Now we're going to do an inside loop," Major Cella told me. "Just let me know if you get uncomfortable."

The G suit is very tight around your stomach and lower torso, and pushes the blood into your upper body to prevent you from blacking out. But that can cause nausea, especially for the one behind the pilot. I was battling with that problem when my pilot asked, "Would you like to fly her a little bit?"

I looked down at the stick and throttle, then glanced at the instruments. Knowing that he would still have ready access to the controls, I said, "I'll give it a try."

Very cautiously I reached down for the stick, and I was flying it! After my few minutes he took over again: "Okay, we're heading up to 25,000 feet. We're going supersonic." Then, under the pilot's steady hand, the throttle fell all the way forward.

Surprisingly, things stayed calm. Only a slight buffeting makes you aware that you're moving faster than sound. But the feeling of being up there, making a white jet trail across the sky, is awesome. The earth below seems like just another planet as you streak toward its horizon. Having put his plane through its paces, Major Cella asked, "Ready to take her back?" And we were headed home.

Before I knew it, our plane made a fast loop and downward spiral in an earthward plunge and we were pulling about four G's. Then the wheels came down and we suddenly hit the runway. Of all the spine-tingling maneuvers we had been through in the air, that instantaneous jolt threw me the most overpowering queasy surge below my throat.

What a relief to feel the hard pavement under the wheels as our F-16 touched down! Climbing out of the cockpit, I must have been smiling from ear to ear. It was a thrilling flight. But in all honesty, I was thankful to be on solid ground. Pulling G's is too demanding for my body. I'll have to face the fact that I'm just not built for supersonic flight. Those machines are rockets that you sit on. It's incredible!

The antithesis of our one-hour flight in a macho Air Force F-16 was the around-the-world journey, completed a week later, of the imaginative airplane *Voyager*. The experimental creation carried five times its weight in 100-octane gasoline and looked like a trapeze of slender cylinders. It stayed in the sky for nine days, covering 25,000 miles on its way back to the U.S. and setting a record for mileage flown without refueling. This was also a record for endurance of its aviators. Tossed about like a leaf by typhoons and storms during its flight, with a near-empty fuel tank, the *Voyager* had only seven hours to go when its rear engine stalled, sending it plummeting 3,500 feet. Fortunately the forward engine saved it. Copilot Jeanna Yeager insisted, "I never really felt frightened."

After landing the craft at Edwards Air Force Base, pilot Richard G. Rutan called their achievement "the last major event of atmospheric flight." Above the sound of 23,000 cheering well-wishers, Rutan told reporters, "That we did it as private citizens says a lot about freedom in America."

As the *Voyager*'s pilot was expressing his appreciation of opportunities in our country, on the other side of the world, 50,000 Chinese students were beginning to gather in People's Square in Shanghai, demanding freedom of the press and other democratic reforms. Although their government reacted coldly to their cries for greater liberty, the students carried posters reading, "GIVE US DEMOCRACY" and "LONG LIVE FREEDOM."

Even the students admitted that a true American-style democracy was beyond their fondest dreams, but they felt that surely some democratic reforms were possible. One of the most ancient nations on Earth, and now the most populous, was reaching out for what we had won only 200 years ago.

CHAPTER XII

THE USO AND DEPARTMENT OF DEFENSE were setting up plans for our 1987 Mediterranean tour to entertain American troops. At the same time, our government was taking a strict stand on military readiness. In mid-January at Cape Canaveral, the Navy successfully tested a Trident II Intercontinental Ballistic Missile, which carried ten warheads. We were told that our nuclear submarines can be armed with twenty-four of them! In these precarious times of nuclear power, when the fate of the earth hangs in the balance, this seems like overkill. But those missiles and the other weapons that we've been testing for a number of years have kept us prepared to confront any aggressor.

Like most American citizens, I read the news and am always aware of the nuclear shadow, that cloud off in the distance that could blow us all away. Those of us who were raised under the threat of nuclear war sort of put it in the back of our minds. But we can't erase it. During times of meditation, we're cautiously looking to our left or right, wondering when the cloud might move directly over us. So I'm really concerned about international politics. Now, for two weeks in March we would have an introduction to nations beyond the Atlantic. Our band was headed for the Mediterranean.

"We've found sponsors for the tour," Chuck Hagel, the USO president, told me. "Pan Am and AT&T are going to underwrite some of our costs and donate the transportation for your whole troupe."

"That's great!" I answered. "We've got a new band, and these young guys are really excited about going on their first USO tour."

Marc was still on drums. He had been with the band since 1983, the first night we started touring with Barbara Mandrell. My good-looking son was a wonderful representative, drawing attention like a magnet with his flashy performances.

This was a good opportunity for some family togetherness. I picked up the phone and dialed. "Melanie, do you think you and Tedd could put together a dance troupe for our USO tour? What do you think of the name 'American Heat'?"

"I love that, Lee. And I'm sure Tedd will want to go, too."

So we began to choose other dancers to fill out the troupe, and for the first time four Greenwoods would be working on the same stage. The band now included Dave Watson, Steve Mandile, Kent Wells, and Tony Smith. Tony doubled as a backup singer, along with Laddie Cain.

After making the long flight to the Med, we played at bases in Italy, Spain, Turkey, and Greece. Our last stop was an unscheduled flight to the Navy nuclear aircraft carrier *Nimitz*. A large helicopter took us out to the vast carrier deck, where we felt the vibrations of the two most emotion-packed shows of our tour.

It was about this time that *The Atlanta Journal* repeated the concern that was coming to the fore in the careers of quite a few country recording artists. "Caught in the Crossover?" was its headline question. It's true that my songs were edging toward contemporary. By now I'd had seventeen Top 10 singles, and we were working on another album, *If There's Any Justice*.

The new Nashville president of MCA, Jimmy Bowen, was producing the album. In making the crucial change from Jerry Crutchfield, my management and I had been faced with a dilemma. We had the choice to retain him as producer even though our sales had begun to drop, and lose our position with the MCA label. Or we could say good-bye to the one who had helped us develop a successful career and stay with

MCA, using a new producer in hopes of regaining momentum. It was a difficult decision. If I had it to do over again, we would have kept Crutchfield and looked for another label.

It's true that Jimmy Bowen had produced for the Oak Ridge Boys, Hank Williams, Jr., Reba McEntire, George Strait, and Crystal Gayle, so his success was undeniable. And our album did have the country touch. But we took a lot of leeway in the selection of the songs, and several, such as "Touch and Go Crazy," were decidedly upbeat. Although I lean toward the more contemporary sound, there are some Nashville singers that I've admired for years, like George Jones, Tammy Wynette, and Anne Murray, with her especially beautiful song, "You Needed Me." I've always been impressed with Ronnie Milsap, who has a good all-around Southern style and was particularly great with his renditions of "What a Difference You Made in My Life" and the ballad "It Was Almost Like a Song." Along with "Lost in the Fifties," they have the contemporary frame that has been widely accepted as America's music.

Every song is a timepiece. It comes along at a certain point in history and affects the direction of music. It's like a little pebble that's thrown into the water, creating circles that float out like sound vibrations. Each song that I heard throughout the sixties, seventies, and eighties had an impact on me as a musician and as a songwriter. In those days, country music was still considered pop. Even into the early eighties, largely because of Mickey Gilley's *Urban Cowboy* craze, it was hip. Blending into it were some of Elvis Presley's songs, like "Love Me Tender." But "the King" had the rock market, too. Then there were acts like Bobby Darin, the Beatles, the Supremes, the Commodores, the Temptations, and Marilyn McCoo with the Fifth Dimension. These were among many who molded American music, and they affected my musical style.

I've always been fascinated by the intricate vocals of people like Donny Hathaway, Stevie Wonder, and Elton John. Dave Loggins inspires me, too. He's as good on the guitar as he is a singer and writer. Dave is the James Taylor of country, without any doubt. He wrote "Please Come to Boston," one of the songs I sang when I was playing piano bar in the Tropicana Hotel in Las Vegas and still sing today. It has the flavor of country; it's about "the number one fan of the man from Tennessee."

To say that music is always changing would be an understatement. Contemporary music is spreading out in many directions, and country music is staying in its own path. It may be swinging from contemporary to traditional, but it's running a steady course. Soul, rhythm and blues, and pop are also channeled, and now heavy metal has its own division. There are so many versions of what music is today. It's difficult to break out of a category, but that's an entertainer's ultimate goal.

That May, right in the middle of a performance in St. Louis, I had an experience that would make any artist completely forget about categories. The Judds, Roy Orbison, and I were appearing at the Fox Theater. Wanting to wear something innovative for the show, I had bought a stage outfit that had some fancy grey slacks with a row of buttonhook snaps at the fly. They were designed to slide through reinforced eyes, then snap down on the other side.

Well, many times I like to go out into the audience while I'm singing. On this particular night I didn't have a radio-controlled mike, just the hand-held kind with the wire trailing behind. Using this setup, you have to be careful not to trip over the wire or get it caught in any of the chair legs. Because people are accustomed to this happening, sometimes they will try to pull it for you if it gets tangled.

Walking past the first few rows, with the spotlight glaring straight into my eyes, I was facing the main section of the audience. I was looking into their faces, trying not to be blinded by the light, singing a song I had recently written:

"There's a strange vibration slowly rising that I know I've known before.
And it feels just like a heartbeat, but I really can't be sure.
It's an old familiar feeling and it's hard to recognize,
But it's always there when I look into my lover's eyes."

I was gently pulling the cord as I moved among the listeners, continuing to sing this soft tune:

"If I seem to lose my self-control, well I really can't explain.
It's an overwhelming reaction and it's driving me insane.
It's the thing I've gotten used to, and I've come to realize
That it's always there when I look into my lover's eyes."

The cord became hung up on something, and I gave it a sharp tug. When it didn't come loose, I pulled it across my body with a slightly harder jerk. Still I continued to maintain eye contact with my audience and began the bridge:

"Ooo, I've been lost in love before,
But I've never felt this magic in my soul.
Ooo, oh, like a drop of sweet perfume,
Your subtle fragrance lingers in my mind."

I was completely oblivious to the fact that the last pull on the cord had flipped up all the snaps on my fly, leaving it wide open. With the full spotlight shining straight into my eyes, I was partially blinded, except when I could blink and look away. But directly in front of me was a lady who suddenly began trying to tell me something.

Well, at a concert while I'm singing, people often try to talk to me. As they reach out to shake hands, they'll be asking, "Did you meet my sister when you were down in Houston last week? Remember her? She's tall and has blond hair. She wanted me to say hi and get an autograph. . . ." As I continue walking and singing, I have to ignore their words so as to maintain concentration. I'm listening to the band, trying to sing in meter, trying to sing in tune, and being careful not to trip on the cord. So I kept trying to concentrate, but this lady was insistent. She was pointing at me, saying something, and finally I couldn't ignore her anymore. During a break in the verse, I bent down to her and asked, "What is it?"

She said, "Your barn door is open!"

That was confusing. Leaning closer, I said, "What?"

She repeated it, this time louder: "Your barn door is open!"

Not hearing her too clearly, and thinking it must be the title to a song, I whispered, "I don't know that one," and continued singing:

"Looking in the mirror just to see what I can see.
Nothing but a fool in love, looking back at me."

Finally it occurred to me where she and the whole audience
were staring, and looking down I saw that I was standing
there, well . . . rather openly. I spun around, and with my
back to the spotlight as the crowd reveled in my embarrassment, went: "Snap, snap, snap, snap, snap, snap."

Everybody just howled!

You have to be a good sport, so it was "on with the show."

"I question my reflection, but the mirror never lies,
And I know it's so when I look into my lover's eyes."

A week later, my humiliating moment at the Fox Theater
was pushed completely from my mind. The morning headlines read: "IRAQI MISSILE HITS USS *STARK*." Thirty-
seven of our sailors were killed in the blast. It had been a
mistake on the part of Iraq's military, and it sent shock waves
throughout America. It was also a grim reminder that although our country was not at war, we continued to maintain
a military presence throughout the world.

And though it was peacetime for our country, we were still
trying to pick up the pieces after Vietnam. That August, U.S.
officials promised Hanoi that we would send humanitarian
aid in return for their help in resolving the fates of our
MIAs. All eyes were watching because this issue deals with the
living, not the dead. It's a tough situation, a subject that still
hovers in the news because the loyal families and friends will
never give up hope that some of our servicemen still survive.

All of us had compassion for one nineteen-year-old boy in
another part of the world when the Soviet courts sentenced
him to four years in their labor camps. Mathias Rust had

captured our imaginations when he single-handedly landed his light plane in the middle of Red Square. An idealistic amateur pilot from West Germany, Rust's hopes had been dashed at the failure of the Reykjavik peace talks. So he began planning his solo flight to the U.S.S.R. in hopes of reasoning with Mikhail Gorbachev or other high Soviet officials. He wanted to give them his own views!

Flying 500 miles across national borders, he did let them know that Soviet airspace could be penetrated, even by an unsophisticated airman. The accomplishment was mortifying for the Soviet political regime, and the incident pointed out that there was no impenetrable Iron Curtain. On rare occasions, people found ways to travel in or out, breaking through a closed society's shield.

Maybe Rust's brash act also showed that we are all interdependent nations on one planet. Anyway, he's a lucky young man. After he had served less than a year of his sentence, the Supreme Soviet decided to let him go.

Our hearts are touched by today's young people, so it was especially gratifying to be asked to give two consecutive concerts at Atlanta's Stone Mountain Park in September. "The Coors organization is putting on these benefits for college scholarships for veterans' dependents," a spokesman explained. "Would you be willing to take part in our efforts?"

"You bet!" I told him. "That's a great cause! The veterans deserve our support. And if more of our students get a good education, the U.S. will have a better chance to stay on top."

"Then you'll do both shows? he asked.

"Count me in!"

Another opportunity arose at that first Stone Mountain performance. I met Dana Walters.

Rain was pelting down in torrents. The guys in our band were basically drenched and more than a little discouraged. But not Dana. The nine-year-old was a real music fan and thrilled to be at a concert. Afterwards, her parents brought their daughter backstage to meet the musicians. While Dana was visiting with the others, her mother, Karen, quietly explained the little girl's swollen body and frail condition.

"Dana has cystic fibrosis," she said. "She's been going through one battle after another all her life. It seems like she falls prey to every illness. Dana's not strong. But she's going to pull through, no matter what it takes. I brought her here because your music has helped her through some painful times."

As she turned to me, Dana reached out and dropped a shiny medallion in my hand. "Here, Mr. Greenwood. This is for a necklace, and I want you to wear it. Will you, please?" she asked.

"Well, Dana, I will whenever I can, especially when I come to Atlanta," I promised, looking down at the prayer on the back. "I know it's really special to you. I'll put it on a chain. And I'm going to send you a bracelet to wear. Okay?"

"Okay!" And she flashed all of us an impish smile.

You can't help everybody, but you've got to reach out when you can. I've visited Dana in the hospital at times when she has needed surgery, and I call her to give some encouragement when she's at home, recuperating. We've had a lot of talks about life and the life after. But we don't talk on short terms. We speak of when she will be twenty-one, a grown-up. And she's looking forward to the goals she'll have then. That's the kind of spirit she has. So when she's under pressure, suffering a lot, that spirit will make the difference. Her courage touched me deeply, and in the hope of helping others like Dana, I made the cause to find a cure for cystic fibrosis a high priority.

Not long after those Stone Mountain concerts, I had the privilege of participating in a major national celebration. It was September 17, 1987, exactly 200 years since a group of delegates in Philadelphia gathered around the newly completed U.S. Constitution to sign it. For four months they had been working on it under the dignified guidance of George Washington, the Constitutional Convention's presiding officer. John Hancock, who had emblazoned his bold signature across the Declaration of Independence, stood ready to take the podium when the time came for the Constitution to be ratified. Benjamin Franklin, by now a distinguished figure at eighty-one, inspired his colleagues as they considered the strong arguments of the outspoken Alexander Hamilton. John Adams, who had written the Massachusetts Constitution seven years earlier, eloquently described the system of executive, legislative, and judicial powers, united into one political structure. But it was James Madison whose calm deliberations and leadership in compromise won for him the title, "Father of the Constitution."

These parliamentary scholars had researched historical documents all the way back to England's Magna Carta of 1215 and Jamestown's first representative assembly in 1619. On this day they approved a government that surpassed all other political systems in the world in its protection of individual freedom under the law.

So it was a good feeling for me to be with the group of governmental officials and public figures gathered in a Philadelphia theater on that bicentennial occasion to honor the original document and America's founders. The President had appeared the day before, and his speech was followed by "God Bless the U.S.A."

This program, "We the People," was being broadcast live on television. The stage with its "cast of thousands" was targeted by TV cameras stationed around the room, and there was a packed audience. Among the participants clustered in the Green Room backstage, watching the monitor while each of us waited for our turn to speak or perform, was Walter Cronkite. His eyes were as mellow as his well-known smile, and he was obviously enjoying the occasion.

"For as long as I can remember, Cronkite's been broadcasting the news before it turned into history," someone in the crowd said, in a stage whisper. "He seems like part of it himself!"

A native of Philadelphia, Patti LaBelle sang, and Sandy Patti, who has won countless gospel awards, stirred everyone with her incredibly impressive rendition of the national anthem. Then Marilyn McCoo, John Schneider, and I sang "We the People." It had been especially written for the occasion, and it's a beautiful tribute. America is a comparatively new nation, and like any other country we've made mistakes. But we had every reason, on this bicentennial, to be proud of her accomplishments in the name of freedom.

Freedom of passage in the Persian Gulf was getting a lot of attention in the news: "The U.S. Navy is providing protection for all commercial ships in international waters," a TV commentator explained. "The U.S. is maintaining shipping lanes in these vital areas. But Iranian gunboats have been attacking naval vessels and commercial tankers from Japan, Greece, and Pakistan."

But this warfare wasn't one-sided. Another newsman broke in with a startling report: "An Iraqi missile has accidentally hit an Australian shrimper in Iranian waters. Its skipper has been killed."

There was tremendous confusion in the Gulf, and America was placed in a frustrating position. How do you control a situation that has too many players?

It was this predicament America was faced with in Southeast Asia. We may have had the noble intention of helping the South Vietnamese remain independent, but it wasn't that simple. It involved North Vietnam, South Vietnam, Laos, and Cambodia, all embroiled in a confusing tangle of motives and goals. It was a complicated web of power struggles: a situation with too many players.

Well, the Iranians had placed mines in those Persian Gulf waters, but leave it to the Americans to come up with inventive countermeasures. The Navy brought in five trained bottle-nosed dolphins to do some underwater surveillance. These highly intelligent mammals were like bird dogs. They were adept in seeking out Iranian mines, which if left undetected would blow to bits the vessels of unsuspecting seamen.

Another approach to mine control made use of our outdated wooden craft, which had long ago been decommissioned and sent to ship graveyards. These were towed all the way from America to be used in the demining operations because wooden ships don't attract the magnetized mines as our modern, metal vessels do. If any mines happened to hit against their hulls, they didn't explode. They only bounced harmlessly along the sides of these old boats until they could be retrieved by the crew members. A little old-fashioned ingenuity goes a long way!

I soon had a chance to appreciate the meaning of freedom. Late in October, during one of my rare chances to be home in Nashville, I had some work to do at the office. So I slid into my Bronco and headed to town. As I was tooling down the freeway, getting ready to get off at the downtown exit, I noticed a police car parked in the median. The patrolman was giving me a hard look. To be friendly, I smiled at him and waved. He didn't wave back; he just continued to stare at me with a cold frown.

"That's strange," I thought, pulling off the freeway and heading toward the center of town.

Catching every green light as I sailed across the bridge, I was moving along right behind an entertainer's tour bus. The traffic flow was smooth. I was keeping up with its speed, probably doing 45 in a 25 MPH zone. Far behind me I heard sirens blaring in what sounded like a high-speed chase.

"What could the cops be after?" I wondered. "Well, I'll just ease over and let them pass."

A police car zoomed in behind me. So, I pulled over a little more. But in my rearview mirror I watched it edge farther in toward my Bronco. I looked again. There were three patrol cars back there, and the officer in the first car was motioning to me.

"Maybe the police at the Seventeenth Avenue substation have set up a radar trap," I thought. "I'll just be cool and find out why they're pulling me over."

As soon as my Bronco had come to a stop, I caught sight of a huge police officer striding up toward my car window. He must have been six-feet-six. "Sir, may I see your driver's license and registration please," he said, in a gruff tone.

"Of course. It's right here," I said, pulling out my wallet. It contained an honorary policeman's badge, an FBI clearance to carry a weapon in Nashville, and my driver's license, which was a temporary one due to my recent move. The interim license did look rather phony. It was a green piece of paper with confusing writing all over it.

Looking at my license, he said sternly, "Mr. Greenwood, are you aware of the speed limit through here, sir?"

"Yes, sir."

"Is there a reason why you're in such a hurry this morning?"

"No legal reason," I replied, trying to be polite.

"All right, I'll be back with you in a moment, sir." And he walked to his squad car.

In a minute he returned. "How about your registration?"

By this time I was rifling through my glove compartment. "Where is the damn registration? I know it's here. It has to be in here. I just put it there."

Frustration was building and I was getting plenty annoyed. Preoccupied with the immediate problem, I was oblivious to the fact that in the van now parked in front of my Bronco, cameras were rolling. My demeaning episode with the Nashville police was being filmed.

"I'm sorry, officer. I just put that registration in here. Now it's gone," was all I could say.

"Are you aware that Tennessee law requires you to have a registration with you at all times, sir?"

"I just don't have it at the moment. I think I can produce it," I said weakly.

He turned and walked back to consult with the other policemen waiting there. Then I saw him talking on his VHF radio. When he came back, he said in a firm voice, "Do you recall getting any citations out of state, sir? They have a warrant for your arrest in Wisconsin."

"What are you talking about? I've never driven in Wisconsin. I've never even been in Wisconsin!"

"Sorry, sir. That's what our records show. And you have no registration."

Then he said those six awful words: "Please step out of the vehicle."

I hated that. I'd never been arrested before, and I hadn't

ever been in front of a judge. At least not since my teenage years.

"I'm sorry, but we're going to take you downtown," he said as I climbed slowly out. "Stand up and place your hands on the hood of the cruiser." Then he frisked me.

"This is just a formality," he continued, snapping handcuffs around my wrists.

Sixteenth Avenue is a well-known country fan street, and I was cringing in embarrassment.

"Officer, can you drive my Bronco over to my office? It's right over there. You can see it from here," and I tried to point with my shackled hands.

"We're not allowed to drive the vehicle once you're under arrest."

"Couldn't I have someone from the office come and get it?"

"If you can get them up here before the tow truck comes . . ." As he was speaking the white tow truck, which had been waiting down the street, warmed up and ready, wheeled over to my Bronco.

Still trying to remain calm, I looked up at the tall officer. "Well, look," I said. "Before you tow my Bronco . . . I've got a firearm underneath the seat. It's a .22. Please get the gun out. I wouldn't want anybody to steal it."

With a sharp nod, he walked over to the car and reached under the driver's seat. Pulling out my gun, he glanced over at me with a dark scowl. Then he began emptying out the bullets on the hood of his patrol car, as if he'd confiscated the arsenal of the century's most wanted underworld character.

Without further ceremony, he put me in the squad car and headed for the Nashville police station. As we slid through the traffic, with me sitting in there handcuffed, there was no small talk. He continued to look straight ahead. As he pulled up to the station entrance, two other officers walked over. "We have a response to your inquiry about your suspect."

"What did you find?" he asked, in a low tone.

"We have a hit on the weapon."

"A hit?" I broke in. "What do you mean, 'a hit'?"

Giving me a sideward glance, one of them said, "Well, it appears that your weapon was used in a burglary in North Carolina. It's a stolen weapon."

"But it's not stolen!" I blurted out in a desperate, high voice.

"Do you have any proof?"

"Well, no. I've had it for years. . . ."

"Sir, it looks like you're up on four counts: speeding, evading arrest in Wisconsin, driving without a registration, and carrying a concealed and stolen weapon. Please come with us."

He grabbed my arm and led me, still handcuffed, into the building. Glancing around, I didn't see anyone who looked familiar, although I've been a strong supporter of the Nashville police and know many officials, including the police chief, Joe Casey, and Sheriff Fate Thomas. But all these guys were strangers. Vaguely puzzled, I wondered, "Where is everybody?"

The officers booked me, made me sit for mug shots, and asked for my statement. Then they took me in front of a bonding agent.

Finally the officer said, "Sir, we're ready to take you before the judge."

Flanked by six policemen, I was walking down the long corridor on the way to the judge's chambers when another officer sidled over to me. In a secretive, rasping whisper, he said, "You're going to see the hanging judge."

I gave him a bewildered stare as we moved into the police gymnasium, which was like an auditorium. Noting a camera crew there, I thought, "Oh, no! The evening news! Somebody's seen my arrest and called the TV station. My manager's going to kill me for getting arrested!"

All kinds of thoughts go through your mind when you're arrested. It's a real difficult situation and you can't reach out to anybody for help. They've got you, and they can do anything they want with you. I was feeling totally helpless, and it made me realize what it must be like to live in a country where dictators rule.

We passed the TV crew and turned a corner.

"Surprise!" There was everybody! Among those relishing the fact that I had been totally fooled were Larry Lee and Judy, Jerry, Ray Pillow and his son Daryl, our secretary, Debra McCloud, with her husband, Donald, and our accountant, Debbie Doebler, with her husband, Gary. My daughter Kelly, who by now had become a valuable member of my office staff but was obviously the leader of this plot, and her partner in crime, my secretary Debbie Byram, were consciously avoiding me until the shock wore off. The band members stood with a cluster of close friends, including Police Chief Casey, laughing at the descriptions of my ordeal. This was the day before my birthday, and I hadn't even thought about it. On the table was a cake with black icing, embossed with a huge vulture.

Almost weak with relief, I chatted with the policemen, including my arresting officer, Buford Tune. Shaking his hand, I told him, "You sure are a terrific actor!"

It was fun to enjoy a joke with my friends, even though I had been the target. However only two weeks later, Jerry and I flew to Washington, D.C. for a serious evening. Entitled "The Mission Continues," the gala event was a benefit initiated by Vice-President Bush for the Challenger Center for Space Science Education. The Center was being planned by the Challenger Committee, chaired by Dr. June Scobee. A family member of each of our *Challenger* astronauts was on the board of directors as well as some of America's most outstanding citizens.

It was a black-tie affair in a room packed with dignitaries, including Vice-President Bush. There were statements concerning our deep loss on the morning of the *Challenger* accident and an explanation of plans to overcome defeat. They were described this way: "Born out of tragedy, the Challenger Center for Space Science Education is a triumph of the human spirit . . . to point the way to tomorrow for an entire generation of young people. The Center will become our nation's leading educational adventure and create the twenty-first century classroom—here and now."

As the evening drew to a close, our host, Walter Cronkite, announced, "And now, the man who has written a beautiful tribute to his country, Lee Greenwood, is here to sing 'God Bless the U.S.A.' "

The musical introduction began and I started to sing. But I felt that the relatives of our fallen heroes should be included. The past year must have been heartbreaking for those striving to overcome their sorrow. As the first verse ended I paused and said, "Would all of you who are family members of our *Challenger* crew please come up and sing with me?"

With this, the mothers and fathers, spouses and children moved up to join me on the podium. There were even brothers and sisters who walked forward. With arms encircling each other, together we blended our voices in the second verse, ending with ". . . I love this land. God bless the U.S.A."

Throughout the room, emotions were strong as Cronkite, who has always reported our news as staunchly as the Rock of Gibraltar, stepped to the podium with tears rolling down his cheeks. "And that's the way it was," he said. "Ladies and gentlemen, what could you say after this? Thank you and good night."

The following Monday brought me the fulfillment of a lifetime wish. In Jacksonville, Florida, at the Seniors Convention made up of generals, I became a member of the U.S. military. On behalf of the Air National Guard, Air Force Gen. John Conaway presented me with the officer's stars, saying that as a citizen-soldier I had something to offer the country. So when I put those two stars on my lapel, it was a very proud moment. I thought, "What a wonderful thing! Somebody in the military actually said I could be a brevet major general! At last I can be a part of our armed forces team!"

That wasn't long before December 7, which is Pearl Harbor Day, of course. Maybe it was a coincidence, but on that date, Ronald Reagan and Mikhail Gorbachev met in Washington to sign an International Nuclear Forces treaty. It was another step toward an ultimate goal.

Two weeks later, Jerry was enjoying a Sunday in Alabama when he was called to the phone. It was Dick Howard, our agent in L.A. "Where's Lee? Can you find him? Do you think he wants to go with Bob Hope on his USO Christmas Tour?"

"Yes, Dick. I'm sure he would. He's been wanting, for a long time, to tour with Bob Hope. When do they leave?"

"Twelve hours from now."

There was a short pause. "Well, Dick, I'll get him on the phone and see what's possible."

When Jerry reached me in Atlanta, I had some quick questions: "Is this the tour to the Persian Gulf? How long will we be gone? When do we leave? In twelve hours . . . from California? You must be kidding!"

Then I shifted into high gear. "Jerry, I'll have to get up to Nashville first. My music and clothes are still on the tour bus. It must be back from Ohio by now. Can you meet me there? I don't even have any keys! And, Jerry, we don't have a cassette of the background music for 'God Bless the U.S.A.' Could you call Dennis and see if he can transfer it from the large reel? Gosh, Jerry, do you think I can make it?"

In a matter of hours I was on a 737 to Los Angeles. Dennis McCarthy, a well-known arranger in L.A., had quickly whipped up the tape, and my gear was rapidly assembled for an extremely impromptu around-the-world journey.

The Christmas Tour's cast and crew gathered in Burbank for our send-off. With Bob Hope as headliner, the other entertainers included Connie Stevens and her two daughters, Tricia and Joelyn Fisher, Barbara Eden, the reigning Miss U.S.A., Michelle Royer, and the L.A. Rams cheerleaders. The U.S. Navy Pacific Fleet Band would be joining us to provide musical backing for the tour.

Our large group flew out in two C-141s, courtesy of General Cassidy. When we arrived in the Philippines, thousands of people were waiting in the football stadium at Clark Air Force Base for a midnight performance. A huge American flag was draped over the goalposts, and the crowd was feeling a deep reverence for their distant homeland during this holiday season. They rose to their feet in the darkness. Many sang along with me as I closed the show with "God Bless the U.S.A." while spotlights found the enormous Stars and Stripes fluttering against the night sky.

The eight days whirled by in a flurry of helicopter flights to stadiums and ships. The choppers took our assortment of singers, dancers, musicians, and comedians out to entertain on the USS *Midway,* stationed in the Persian Gulf. Nearby, tucked up near Saudi Arabia, was the tiny island nation of Bahrain, and learning that Bob Hope's troupe was in the vicinity, Ambassador Zakhem invited us to perform at the American Embassy there. Our group headed for Bahrain at dusk, prepared for a unique evening. Playing the piano for our intimate show was fun, but getting to know Crown Prince al-Khalifa was a really neat experience. Although he was dressed in the formal robes and Arabic headgear of the region, this guy was really cool. He was in his early twenties, and had been educated at George Washington University in D.C. He even spoke "street English" with all our American slang, like, "So what do you do on a weekend? Hang out? Play a little ball?" In learning to communicate with Americans, he's preparing for his future as leader of Bahrain.

On Christmas Day, our band of base hoppers alighted on the deck of the USS *Iowa.* We recognized this as the ship that our President had been aboard during the Statue of Liberty dedication in New York Harbor. Although our assortment of troupers was far from home, all of us on the USO Christmas Tour did our best to bring the joy of the holidays to the Persian Gulf.

Around the world in only eight days calls for unbelievable energy. How has Bob Hope done it for so many years? He sure has earned his wings! When Jerry met me at New York's Kennedy International Airport, his first words were, "Lee, you look like death warmed over!"

But it had been a real adventure!

CHAPTER XIII

THE U.S. WAS DEALING with one of our most serious problems as 1988 moved in, tightening inspections of imports from Colombia. A Colombian judge had freed the top boss of the Medellin drug cartel, which was responsible for almost 80 percent of the cocaine coming into our country each year. Concerned about the situation, along with other entertainers I began speaking out about the dangers of mind-altering substances.

"A lot of the drugs come from Bolivia and other South American countries," a military officer told me. "Some of these people think that drug trafficking should be legalized because it's a strong portion of their economy."

"That's ludicrous! We've got to find a way to keep them out," I said. "'USA Today,' has even shown some of the routes the drug runners take. They'll use any way they can possibly find to get into the States."

"We've upscaled our border checks, but that hasn't even slowed it down," he said.

I nodded. "I guess as long as there's a user, there'll be a buyer. And as long as there's a buyer, there's going to be a seller. It's a hard battle to win."

I continued to fight that battle through the Drug Abuse Council, but remained focused on my singing career. In Nashville that year, I was invited to sing the national anthem at Vanderbilt for their basketball game against the University of Tennessee. It's a fierce in-state rivalry, so there was a capacity crowd.

"The Star-Spangled Banner" has a wide range. When you sing it in the middle of a football field, you have the added disadvantage of a large environment. But at an inside event like a basketball arena, the sound has startling clarity. Singing in such an enclosed area is like having on a set of headphones. You can hear your voice perfectly.

The stands were packed with students in their school colors and other sports fans revved up for the intense contest. The emcee stepped forward and after a brief introduction, handed me the mike. The pregame cheering stopped and the spacious room fell silent. As I began to sing and could hear so wonderfully, I became increasingly artistic with my phrasing and emphasis on each note. The more I listened, having a great time with the sound, the more I became mesmerized by my own voice. I came to the bridge, and suddenly heard myself singing, "O'er the ramparts we watched. . . ."

"Oh no!" I thought. "It should have been 'And the rockets' red glare!' "

At that moment I froze, knowing I had screwed up. My mind was frantically retracing my steps, trying to figure out where I was in the song. Completely lost, I was flushed and disoriented.

Even people who don't know the national anthem know when you've fouled up. So whispers started rippling through the audience. There was nothing else to do but make a clumsy recovery.

I've sung our nation's song so many times at major events, including New York's Shea Stadium, Busch Stadium in St. Louis, the Nashville Sounds Stadium, and Arlington Stadium, home of the Texas Rangers. At some of these places the sound is unbearable, but I've gotten through it fine. This was the first and only time I'd blown the national anthem. Now the cardinal rule is etched on my consciousness: "Don't listen to yourself!"

On the following day the media in Knoxville said something like, "Vanderbilt massacred U.T. and Lee Greenwood crucified the 'National Anthem'!"

How humiliating to have blown lines that are so meaningful! They're a perfect description of the situation Francis Scott Key was in, as a captive of the British fleet during the War of 1812. On board the admiral's flagship in Chesapeake Bay, he watched through the rocket-filled smoke all night while Fort McHenry was bombarded. Could his compatriots stand up to England's forces? Would the Stars and Stripes still wave above the American fort when morning came? With those fears and hopes flooding his mind, he wrote down the words of "The Star-Spangled Banner."

For me, like a cowboy who had fallen off a horse, the best thing to do was get up on it again. Two days later, I was scheduled to sing "God Bless the U.S.A." before the Tennessee Senate.

"Is it all right if I sing the national anthem?" I asked, still seared by my public blunder.

"That would be fine," they answered. And this time Francis Scott Key's stirring words resounded through the Senate chambers unscathed!

In early April I flew to Anchorage for two performances in our largest state. Alaska stretched out below our plane in endless miles of craggy blue mountains and ice-patched tundra. Waiting there after one of the shows were two surprises from my past.

"Goody! Goody Javier! It's wonderful to see you again!"

"Man, it's just so good to be here. Your show was terrific," he said, in his same Filipino accent. His face was still the fun-loving, round happy face that I remembered from our days with the Apollos.

Then, Mae Axton walked over to introduce some friends in the oil industry. She had brought the Apollos our first female singer, and later renewed our friendship in Nashville.

Gen. David L. Nichols, leader of the Alaskan Air Command attached to Elmendorf Air Force Base, was there too. In our casual conversation, I said, "I'm going to Fairbanks tomorrow."

"That's too bad," he replied. "We'll be having a luncheon and awards ceremony here. It's for the civilians and Air Force personnel who've donated their time to help with the renovations on our installation. We're responsible for the maintenance of the Ballistic Missile Early Warning System, which gives the U.S. first notice of an enemy attack over the North Pole. During the past few years we've been strengthening the entire perimeter of NORAD [North American Air Defense Command]. Anyway, we're honoring those volunteers tomorrow."

Although I'd already experienced Mach 1 flight, I couldn't pass up the chance to make my band and crew jealous one more time. For that, I was willing to confront the sound barrier in an F-15. I'm a glutton for punishment! Sensing the opportunity for another gut-wrenching flight, I said, "How would you like me to sing at the awards program?"

"Would you?"

"Sure, if you'll just get me to Fairbanks in time for my show. Any commercial flight that'll fit my tight time schedule will do. . . . Or do you have some little jet lying around?"

"Certainly that can be worked out. I think we have an F-15 available."

I smiled, trying to suppress a light laugh of anticipation.

The next day, after the luncheon, I put on all that flight gear again and climbed in behind my pilot for the thrill of my life, streaking up through glaciers—those huge ice mountains that reach down to the sea—up over the top of one, then down toward the water. As we pulled up, the afterburners blasted out over the ocean, sending sprays of mist behind the jet. It was gorgeous!

Zooming through the majestic peaks of Mt. McKinley, at speeds up to 700 miles an hour, I knew that my body wasn't made to go faster than the speed of sound and that I get very airsick: I was turning green. My mind wants to soar, but my stomach screams, "No way! This is going to make you sick!"

The hardware for an Alaskan flight is a lot heavier than normal gear in case you end up out in the freezing terrain. It includes all kinds of tools and subzero clothing. You've got a flight jacket, your helmet and parachute pack, oxygen—the whole bit. As we sailed over the barren and frozen ice cliffs, I shouted over the intercom to the pilot: "That ejection apparatus is one thing I hope we don't have to hit!" And a nervous laugh escaped as I stiffened to the incredible sensation of being propelled through the sky like a missile.

Back in Nashville, Jerry had just taken over the reins as my business manager. It was a friendly arrangement. Larry Lee had been my personal manager as well as handling the business side of our partnership. He was the one who had headed me toward a Nashville career. But since my directions had broadened, I had begun to make more of the music business decisions and decided to assume responsibility for seeking an audience beyond country music.

"It's still a friendship, Larry. We'll get together. I'll beat you on the racquetball court and you'll clobber me on the golf course."

"Well, no matter who wins, Brother, you'll owe me one," he said with a grin. "Don't forget you stole my laugh!"

On the phone to Alaska, Jerry was giving me a rundown of the following week. It sounded like the usual crushing schedule. "Lee, it's Valdosta, Oklahoma City, Fayetteville, Pittsburgh, Johnstown, Lexington. . . . Then you're flying up to Washington, D.C. for dinner with the American Veterans. The Amvets have planned a black-tie evening to present you with their Silver Helmet Award."

"What's that for, Jerry?"

"Well, they said it's especially for your song. They told me that 'God Bless the U.S.A.' has helped the morale and patriotic spirit of Americans serving at bases around the world, and even our civilians. To them, it's like a second national anthem."

It's a humbling experience to receive recognition like this because you accept it with the knowledge that there are many citizens who deserve it more. It's the same way with the American Legion and VFW awards. Because I didn't actually serve in the military, I'm grateful to have found a way of doing something for our country. I guess my feelings were expressed in the title of our album, which was released that month: *This Is My Country*.

It was mid-May, and some charitable citizens in Corpus Christi, Texas, had planned an early summer social occasion. They were having a gala benefit for the Cancer Fund, and our band had agreed to perform. It was a lavish black-tie affair. Champagne and candles were on the tables. Although the location was a warehouse, it wasn't a barn, but a beautifully constructed, well-lighted site. A raised stage abutted one wall, which had been taken out so that the patrons could sit inside. A gracefully festive atmosphere prevailed, with each detail completed to perfection. As the dinner drew to a close, the emcee stood up. "Ladies and gentlemen, may I present a true friend of our fight to overcome cancer, Lee Greenwood."

"Thank you," I smiled, giving him an appreciative wave.

After the opening music, I turned to the room full of elegantly dressed dinner guests, and said, "This morning we got back from Japan. It's a long trip, and we're glad to be back. Now we'd like to play for you our latest release, 'I Still Believe.' "

The band struck up the intro, and I began to sing. But as night fell, the June bugs began flying. Soon they were getting quite thick, almost as though they were a swarm of bees attacking us onstage. But these were large, heavy "bees."

The June bug is a smooth, hard-shelled flying bomber, we quickly learned. It's attracted to the light, and the spotlights were aimed directly at us. Dodging the bugs, the guys were finding them under the strings of their guitars. Before long, the shiny bugs were scrambling all around the drums. I was being extremely careful, hoping not to get one in my mouth while I was singing. They were crawling down our necks and over our backs, so we must have looked real fidgety as the performance continued.

Taking the mike from its stand, I said, "Ladies and gentlemen, at this point in the show I usually introduce the members of my band. Playing bass, a guy we've enjoyed working with in Nashville, Matt McKenzie." Glancing up at the wing-ing June bugs, Matt gave a slight bow.

As the polite applause diminished, I continued, "Tony Smith of Las Vegas is on keyboard. And my son Marc is our drummer. . . ." I looked back at Marc as he gave a wry smile from behind the bug-encrusted drum kit.

"On the guitars, we have Eric Horner from Paducah, Ken-tucky, and a musician coming from your home state . . . , Steve Mandile from San Angelo, Texas! Please give these guys a hand!"

The applause had increased at the mention of Texas, and June bugs slid off both instruments as Eric and Steve stepped forward to acknowledge the enthusiastic welcome.

Looking around, I noticed that the bugs had found count-less places to light. It seemed that they were everywhere. Well, the band members were anxious to get the heck off the stage, so they were delighted when it came time for them to leave during my piano solo. All of them hastily beat a retreat, shaking off insects as they went.

I remained, the June bugs' only target. As I walked care-fully across the floor to my keyboard, there were loud crunch-ing noises. It was very audible. "Surely the audience can hear this crispy, smashing sound," I thought as I crossed the stage. When I reached my piano, I saw that they were lying all over the keys.

I looked up at the guests. "While the band's taking a short break, I'd like to play a few tunes for you. Several years ago, a songwriter named Aaron Wilburn and I got together in Nashville and wrote this one." Then I began to sing:

"I've been the one you've talked to when things were on
    your mind.
I've tried to be a friend to you when friends were hard
    to find.
I've even been your lover and gave myself to you.
But now you're asking something I just don't want to do."

A June bug lit on my hand. "Oh, no. I've got to shake this

thing off," I thought. "It's almost impossible to keep brushing the bugs from the keys while I'm trying to play."

It's a major sin in the entertainment business ever to let the audience know you've got a problem. So I was straining to maintain the momentum of the show as I moved into the chorus:

"I don't want to be a memory,
Someone you just leave behind.
I've always tried to be everything you'd ever need,
But I don't want to be a memory."

As I kept playing, my motions became more frantic.

"I've given you the freedom when you felt the need
    to fly. . . ."

Gazing up, I felt a surge of relief. "Gosh, they've stopped flying! Maybe I can make it through this song," I said to myself. The bugs were now subdued, almost dazed, lying all over our equipment and on the floor.

"A shoulder you could lean on, a place where you could cry."

I was wearing knee-high riding boots, and my jeans flared over the outside. As I continued playing, a movement became apparent up near my knee, on the inside of my boot-cut jeans.

Before long, the invader had gotten up quite high, near my inner thigh. We're talking about a bug with a mission, because it didn't stop there. It continued its ascent until it got into dangerous territory. "It's nibbling on me! Or maybe that's just its claws," I thought. "Is there any way I can abort this number and run off stage for a minute? No, I'm not giving in to some June bug!"

"Our time has meant so much, it's more than I can face
To think that I could somehow be someone you'd replace."

"Can I smash it between my legs without taking my hands off the keyboard? I'm going crazy!" Then I invented three new dances, while playing the piano! Eventually, for survival's sake, I gave several quick shots with my hand to an area that no entertainer should ever touch during a show. Finally my tormentor was subdued, I decided: "I've knocked it out cold! Thank God!"

I hope that never happens again! The miniature enemy had almost gotten the best of me, but I still think it would have been a mistake to run off stage.

Unfortunately, a serious mistake occurred that summer, due to mounting hostilities between two nations. On July 3 our Navy was involved in a misjudgment. The crew of the USS *Vincennes,* stationed in the Persian Gulf, detected a plane from Iran heading into their airspace. Frantically, they tried to determine its mission. The jet appeared to be closing in on their ship. Time was short and tensions were high. Determined to protect the *Vincennes,* the crew launched a missile attack against the approaching aircraft.

It had been a terrible error. Their target turned out to be an Iranian jetliner with 290 passengers aboard. These innocent civilians died because their plane was falsely identified. I couldn't help thinking of the parallels between this tragedy and the downing of KAL 007 over the U.S.S.R.

But in this confusing world of ours, there are times when opposing nations work together. Early in October, long after California grey whales had migrated to the Baja California coast, scientists discovered three young whales trapped by an early freeze in an ice pack near the North Alaskan village of Barrow. These mammals need to surface for air at regular intervals, but they had no way to reach open water. The Alaskan National Guard and the U.S. National Oceanic and Atmospheric Administration began mapping out a plan to free the whales. But the U.S. didn't have an icebreaker large enough to crush the imposing ice barrier blocking their path to the Pacific. Russia did. The situation called for international cooperation.

When they learned about the problem the Soviets, who had just outlawed all their own commercial whaling, were anxious to help. Eskimos with chain saws were already creating a line of air holes toward the ocean. Driven to migrate by their instinct for freedom, the whales were following this path, surfacing at each breakthrough. One of the whales disappeared. But the other two, which their rescuers had affectionately named Crossbeak and Bonnet, seemed to sense that these humans were on their side.

Two Soviet icebreakers arrived, flying both Soviet and American flags, and began reducing to huge blocks of floating ice the massive ice ridge blocking the whales' path to freedom. Meanwhile American workers used enormous tractorlike machines to clear away the floating ice masses.

"We feel very good about it," Rear Adm. Sigmund Peterson of NOAA told reporters. "The cooperation has just been fantastic. The Soviets came in here with a very positive attitude and went to work immediately. And the whales seem to be doing fine. It's like they expected something to be happening."

First Mate Vladimir Moroz aboard the icebreaker *Admiral Makarov* said, "Our Moscow newspaper is receiving many calls about the whales. Our country is watching. We love animals, just as everyone."

After a week of monumental effort by rescuers working in five-degree weather, Crossbeak and Bonnet broke through. As Alaskan National Guard Lt. Mike Haller put it, "The whales are loose and in the channel, headed out. To look at them, you'd have thought they had their bags packed and were ready to head south."

If only in a small way, international cooperation had succeeded!

Throughout America the political climate was building in intensity as the presidential campaign moved into its final week. Vice-President Bush had asked me to appear with him on behalf of his candidacy. At a rally in Grand Rapids, Michigan, former president Gerald Ford joined us in singing "God Bless the U.S.A." Afterwards some of the campaigners drifted across the street to the hotel where Mr. Bush was staying. In the lobby, one of his secret servicemen walked up to me and said, "Mr. Bush would like to see you upstairs."

Following him to George Bush's suite, I was led into a drawing room. After a few minutes, the Vice-President walked in and said, "Thanks for coming, Lee. Would you like to sit down and have some lunch?" A plate of sandwiches had been prepared and placed on a table there, so I joined him for a light meal and conversation.

I accompanied the Vice-President several times during the campaign. "The Fisherman" was what I called him, in admiration for his personal way of reaching people. Whenever we were riding in his limo, we'd see spectators along each side of the street. Whether there were fifteen or a hundred, or even just one old man sitting on a bench, he'd pick out one and say, "Watch this. I'm going to get that man's attention."

He would wait for the right moment and then wave at him, and point and keep waving until they had made eye contact and the person waved back.

"Got him!" he'd say.

That gave me a personal glimpse into the nature of the man who would soon be our President. It was the individual, more than throngs of people, that he was concerned about and wanted to reach. To him, each person is important. And that's the same way I feel. In my shows I'll go from person to person, and try to make eye contact with everybody. If I see some of them sitting on their hands, it's a challenge to get them to respond to me in some way, to show real emotion. I have that need to feel as though I've really reached them.

Two days before the election, my group left on our Pacific Air Force Tour. Although the PACAF Tour was sponsored by the U.S. government rather than the USO, our mission was the same: to bring entertainment to our foreign-based servicemen and -women. This time we'd be gone a month, stopping at bases in Korea, Japan and Okinawa, the Philippines, and Hawaii. It was a substantial commitment.

Our first stop was Korea's DMZ. The Demilitarized Zone, which is two and a half miles wide, marks the battlefront at the war's end in the summer of '53. It divides the north from the south all the way across Korea, cutting through the 38th parallel. In the center is a neutral area with several stark official buildings. In this central portion, very few of the pines, oaks, and elms remain. Because they blocked the view for guards on each side, they were chopped down. The perimeter fences, which are barbed wire in most places, meet at posted gates, clearly marked in Korean and English. When the war was over, citizens had been allowed to cross this "Bridge of No Return" in either direction. Crowds of refugees poured into South Korea. A few traveled north. Then the gates were closed.

Since that time the DMZ has been visited by officials who oversee the cease-fire and negotiate differences between the two countries. I walked through their meeting place, a long, one-story building that has windows along both walls so that each side can observe the proceedings. There were guards posted at either end, representing the UN, North Korea, and South Korea. As a tension-breaking gesture, I posed for a photo with one of the North Korean guards in the background. He gave our group a suspicious stare. The atmosphere here is always strained. There is no pointing, and no overt hand gestures are allowed: "One false move and . . ." You have to be careful!

The beautiful paradox is that this high-strung human atmosphere has created a wildlife refuge beyond the guardhouse, where the wilderness remains. Since there has been no shooting within this strip of land, the animals have become aware that it's a safe place. So an abundance of wild creatures live there. They say that even a few tigers slink beyond the guard towers that unintentionally protect them. It's fascinating!

We found a contrasting irony as we flew into Japan. Over forty years ago, this was the final Axis nation threatening the free world. Now our military bases provide security for the Japanese. Of course, maintaining our presence in this area of the Pacific increases our global awareness. In our most northern base in Japan, an Air Force officer explained, "The listening station here is the one which picked up transmissions from KAL Flight 007. These provided evidence concerning what actually happened."

On to the Philippines. The crew from the Air Guard of West Virginia, which was transporting us, had one request: "Please play 'Take Me Home, Country Roads.'" John Denver's popular song was close to the hearts of these guys — "Take me home, country roads, to the place I belong, West Virginia, Mountain Momma. . . ." But it's not just about West Virginia. It's about every country boy and every city boy who ever wanted to be going down a country road.

They knew all the lyrics and everyone sang along. Then the words came true. Their request was answered, and our flight crew was transported back to West Virginia. Replacing them was an Alaska Air Guard crew. Somehow "Country Roads" didn't seem right for them. My mind flashed back to the breathlessly beautiful scenes of an Alaskan USO trip. A long time ago, taking in those frosty wonders, was an eighteen-year-old who had just stepped from his Air Force transport plane onto the runway and learned of the birth of his first child. My vision of Alaska was unforgettable.

Now, years later, it seemed as if I had come full circle. Here I was, still entertaining our troops, this time working with the Air Guard from Alaska. They were warmhearted guys, and I began secretly writing a song for them. Fooling around on the piano, trying to find the right chords, I had just discovered a couple that seemed perfect.

It was the final night of our South Pacific stay, the last time our Alaskan guard would be with us because in the morning they were flying our equipment to Hawaii. All of us gathered in the catering room of the Officers' Club for a small dinner. The warmth of new friends saying good-bye radiated through the room as one of our Alaskan Air Guard members stood up, his arms loaded with gifts. With emotion heavy in his voice, he said, "Lee, it's been great being with you and your band. These 'State of Alaska' shirts are for all of you. Don't forget us!"

Then Josie, the U.S. Military MWR representative, presented us with hand-carved nameplates. And since this had become gift-giving time, I decided that it was the moment for my present. I asked someone to bring my keyboard from the stage into the club. With this piano in place and my backup singers standing on each side, I turned toward the Alaskan Air Guard crew and said, "Tonight you guys will be leaving us and heading for Alaska. We've become good friends and I've been writing a song for you while you've been so far away from home."

Then with Tony and Steve, I began to sing:

"Way up north there's a mountaintop
That's protected from the snow.
And when I need some time alone
It's a place where I can go
'Cause I share my dreams with the caribou
And the whisper of the wind.
And I long to be in Glacier Bay again.

"I want to go home to Alaska
Where the eagles fly across the golden sky.
I want to go home to Alaska
'Cause the northern lights are in my woman's eyes.

"I've seen the giant grizzly
And the salmon as they run
And all of nature's wonders
In the seven months of sun.
I've seen the mighty Yukon
As it races to the sea
And heard the barking of the huskies calling me."

These were familiar scenes to our departing Alaskan Air Guard crew, and they were deeply moved as they listened to their special song. That moment of sharing it with them was the high point of our PACAF Tour.

It wasn't until our group reached Hawaii that I was able to finish the bridge. It seemed to me that many of us revel in the warm climates of the Caribbean or Hawaii. And we were just returning from the sunny Philippines. But for the man who has left his mate in Alaska, it's a different warmth that calls him:

> *And though the tropic sun can turn my skin to golden brown*
> *It's the ring that's on my hand that keeps me warm.*
> *I want to go home to Alaska,*
> *Where the eagles fly across the golden sky.*
> *I want to go home to Alaska,*
> *Where the northern lights are in my woman's eyes.*
> *'Cause the northern lights are in my woman's eyes.*

At the Commanders' Conference in Hawaii, I thanked the Audio Visual Squadron, our "GDFC," for their tireless editing. Mountains of film had come in from our tour and they stayed awake over forty-eight straight hours, getting it ready to be shown on Ralph Emery's "Nashville Now" cable TV show, which was to be filmed as soon as we got back to Tennessee. And we'd need some of it for the variety show emceed by Lorrie Crook and Charlie Chase.

While we were gone, the B-2 Stealth bomber had been put on display for the first time. Rolling out on the airstrip of Northrop's plant in Palmdale, California, it looked like a grey and black wing. It was tailless, with a sleek form that was supposed to be undetectable by enemy radar or heat sensors.

The Pentagon had also introduced the F-117A Stealth fighter, designed for air-to-air combat. This was a small black, single-seat delta wing, reminiscent of Batman's aircraft. So it was instantly labeled the "Bat Plane." In Okinawa, at Kadena, we had been allowed to see its earlier counterpart, the SR-71 Blackbird. Because of its streamlined design, some of the guys called it the "Habu," which means "snake."

Knowing that I had flown in their aircraft before, and that I deeply appreciated their American Spirit Award, Air Force officials invited me to fly in an F-4 Phantom.

The F-4 doesn't have quite the power of the F-15 or F-16. In order to break the sound barrier, it has to go into a dive. So I was headed in a downward plunge for my next Mach 1 experience. As soon as we pulled out of that, my Air Force pilot said, "This is what we do to avoid a pursuing missile." With that, he broke into a body-crushing nose dive, pouring on the G's. The farther he turned, the more my body rejected it. The centrifugal force was shoving me right down into the seat until I couldn't even move.

It's amazing to watch the Thunderbirds or Blue Angels fly. They perform all those acrobatics with precision. Then they bring their high-powered planes to a stop on the airstrip, climb out, and lift up their helmets. Pulling off their gloves, these cool jet jockeys saunter over to the crowd to start signing autographs, looking as though they just stepped out of the shower!

Our submarine crews are another cool group. In December, I was lucky enough to participate in the commissioning of the USS *Tennessee*, one of our newest Trident subs. These submerged cities have two alternating crews, which have to stay at sea, in close quarters, for months at a time. We flew up with officials from Tennessee, bringing memorabilia for our state's namesake, and it was Tennessee's Gov. Ned Ray McWherter who gave the most popular ceremonial speech to the large military audience shivering in the subzero weather. Wincing as the bitter wind whipped off the waves and across the icy deck where the crew stood virtually frozen at attention, he began, "In view of the cold, I have eliminated a lot of the adjectives and other elements of my talk. This will be short." He received a resounding ovation.

With the first of the year, the U.S. got a new President. During the campaign, George Bush had jokingly called me one of his "secret weapons." Now he asked me to sing at the Opening Ceremonies of his inauguration. Those of us who were there to participate stood on the steps of the Lincoln Memorial, looking out into a multitude of almost 200,000 people. Sandy Patti opened the event with the national anthem. Among the entertainers continuing the evening of music were the Gatlin Brothers and the singers from "Up with People." After I sang, President Bush took the podium. Giving me a nod, he said, "And a special thanks to my friend, Lee Greenwood. Lee, I've heard you perform many times, and it still gives me chills whenever you sing 'God Bless the U.S.A.' "

The American Presidential Pageant followed. Emceed by Buddy Ebsen, it featured the forty-piece U.S. Army Band and an all-Army cast, presenting nine scenes from America's history. They ranged from a stirring Civil War reenactment to a mock-up of our lunar module, which rose in the air, roaring through the sparks and smoke of a real lift-off. This was in Constitution Hall! There was a living statue of our Marines raising the flag on Iwo Jima and also a replica of the three young comrades-at-arms at the entrance of Washington's Vietnam Memorial. The young men were slicked down with oil, standing motionless, and they looked exactly like the true bronze figures. During the two days of celebration there were five of these dramatizations, each concluding with the entire cast singing "God Bless the U.S.A.," and then "God Bless America."

In March the Soviet Union surprised the world by taking a step toward a democratic government in their first nation-wide elections since 1917. The voter turnout was heavy. The Russians showed their desire for drastic change by throwing out many of their Communist leaders. But this shift in power was not totally unexpected. During the last few years, Mikhail Gorbachev had been carefully laying the groundwork for economic and political reform. The Soviet leader was dealing with a difficult economic situation, and he reinforced his policy of openness, stating, "Democratization of the atmosphere in society and social and economic changes are gaining momentum largely thanks to the development of glasnost."

President Gorbachev was also trying to lessen tensions with the Free World by contributing to the de-escalation of the cold war. Skyrocketing defense budgets can wipe out a nation's resources, so arms reduction was going to help America, too. And it was gratifying to see other countries moving toward our economic system. To me, it seems most practical.

Democratic capitalism, which encourages individuals to work hard for their own well-being, must be the best way to increase a nation's production.

While we watched in approval as the Soviet Union headed in the direction of freedom, Americans were spellbound by reports of the bald courage being exhibited by China's university students and intellectuals. By late April prodemocracy demonstrations were raging, especially in Beijing and Shanghai. Dismayed at the death of their hero Hu Yaobang, who had fought for greater citizen voice in government and broader freedoms, the students began marching toward Tiananmen Square, ten miles away. As they left the Beijing University campus, according to a *Newsweek* reporter, a voice rang out over the public address system: "If you go out and demonstrate, we can't say what the consequences will be."

But those defiant college kids kept marching. They were cheered from the roadsides by the children and the older people looking on. The students came from forty other colleges, and their numbers increased to 150,000 as they were joined by Chinese journalists waving a banner reading, "WE WANT TO TELL THE TRUTH." Foreign journalists were there, too, witnessing a revolution unfolding. One student shouted at Graham Hutchings of London's *Daily Telegraph*, "We are making history, aren't we? You must tell the world."

On the other side of the world life was more peaceful. Danny and Joanne had moved to Nashville, where he became the public relations manager of our office, and we were releasing a new album, *If Only For One Night*. Producing it in collaboration with James Stroud, I was pleased that we could include "Home to Alaska." Our first single off the album was a love song, but in my own home, the love had disappeared. Melanie and I were separating.

Throughout high school, I really didn't have a steady girlfriend, and I think that holds a clue to why my marriages haven't lasted. I had mixed emotions, wanting to have the solidity of a family that I didn't have while growing up, but also desiring to remain a free spirit, to be who I am. Eighteen was so young to become a married man. Then my career, which came a lot later, gave me an avenue for experiencing all those relationships that I should have gone through in my twenties. Instead, I encountered them in my late thirties and forties. I think that Melanie was robbed of a lot of happy years, because it took a while for me to settle down. By then, it was much too late to save our marriage.

So through all of my marriages, not being able to remain a steadfast husband has been my own failure. Melanie had been such a positive influence on my life that there was a cloud of remorse overshadowing the spring.

But during this springtime I was given an opportunity to reach out to some young Soviet athletes. As a follow-up to the Olympic Summer Games in Seoul, Korea, the USA-USSR Friendship Tour presented the gymnasts of the two countries in friendly competition. One of their exhibition sites was Cedar City, Utah. In order to make their Soviet guests feel welcome, the city's leaders had planned a parade and an evening show.

That night, about five or six thousand spectators and athletes crowded into a huge arena. All the gymnastic equipment was set up for the next day's exhibition and the athletes from both countries sat on the floor in front of the high stage. Halfway through my performance, just before the song "I.O.U.," a thirteen-year-old Soviet gymnast walked timidly up to me. In her arms were a dozen roses.

Looking up at me, she reached out to hand me the flowers. The language barrier was insignificant. She didn't need to speak. Without a single word, I could see the true gift of friendship in her eyes.

"Oh, thank you. Really, I wish I could say 'thank you' in Russian. This is a beautiful gesture."

Smiling shyly amid the audience's applause, she skipped lightly back to her place among her teammates.

The roses had been unexpected. But I had a little surprise for them too. As the show drew to a close, I was getting ready to sing "America" from the movie *Rocky IV*. It was about a boxing match between an American and a Soviet fighter. I turned around and, facing away from the spotlight, tore off my tuxedo shirt to reveal a sleeveless T-shirt with the hammer and sickle of the U.S.S.R. This was my friendship gesture to them, and everyone loved it. As I broke into the tones of "America," they all began to sing along, even the kids from the Soviet Union, who didn't really know the words. At the opening strains of "God Bless the U.S.A." that followed, they stood up and saluted, trying to sing with the rest of us in their classroom English. Finally I reciprocated by shouting out the only Russian words in my vocabulary: "Das vedanya—good-bye."

The show was over, but they were all still clapping and waving. I walked down a short stairway and underneath the stage to emerge upon the wooden court, where the gymnasts had been sitting. Now we were all shaking hands and hugging, while officers of the K.G.B. and the F.B.I. looked on from a distance. Then one young Soviet handed me a small gold medal. With deep pride, he pointed to the inscription. It was a Soviet World War II medal, minted and dated back during the time that our two countries fought the Nazis as allies. It must have been passed down to him by his father.

"This means a lot. Thank you," I said. "I will wear it to remember you and your teammates."

Later that day, I pinned the medal on my heavy denim jacket beside the tiny gold replica of the *Challenger* given to me by a lady who works with the NASA Center in Huntsville. With the several other pins that have been added, this has become a kind of international friendship jacket.

The Friendship Tours are a good way for us to share feelings. They're a chance to communicate on a nonpolitical level, which, in a small way, helps alleviate the problems diplomats have in dealing with each other.

But the struggle was intensifying back in Asia, where 3,000 young Chinese were daring to confront their country's powerful officials. Crowding into Tiananmen Square, the hundred-acre expanse dominated by an enormous portrait of Chairman Mao, they began a hunger strike, requesting a meeting with China's leaders. Unmoved, Communist Party

Leader Deng Xiaoping insisted, "We must crack down on these students, whatever the cost."

Before long, the students had defiantly erected their "Goddess of Democracy," a twenty-seven-foot tall sister to our Statue of Liberty. America had inspired the French to fight for their freedom. Now these Chinese youths acknowledged the same inspiration by enshrining the symbol, raising their Lady Liberty who clutched the torch of truth firmly in both hands.

It was a crusade by idealistic young people, but the Chinese government forcefully shut it down. On June 4, soldiers suddenly appeared from the Forbidden City and raced into the Square as a convoy of troop trucks streamed toward the students. Columns of soldiers armed with automatic weapons took aim. As the representatives of China's next generation stood their ground, the militia opened fire, gunning them down, then moved forward to bayonet those still standing.

One student yelled above the roar of the bullets to a *New York Times* reporter, "We appeal to your country. Our government is mad. There must be something that America can do!"

Immediately afterward, the Chinese government began expelling foreign journalists. It's the first thing that happens when people make a bid for freedom. The government gets rid of the writers so no one will learn of the repercussions. But people are designed to be free, so freedom is inevitable. Eventually it will come to every country on Earth. But there will be a lot of martyrs. Those young people in China paid the price. They gave their lives.

According to *Newsweek,* before the massacre one of the students said, "Without democracy, it would be better to be dead." Her words ring with the sound of Patrick Henry's proclamation, "Give me liberty or give me death!"

Americans were powerless to aid the Chinese students, but their outrage was expressed through the press. Our country had been opening the doors of communication with our former opponent, but this tragedy put a strain on our overtures of friendship.

At the same time, we were solidifying a different alliance fraught with irony. The Bush administration announced that our government would join with Japan to develop an FSX fighter similar to America's F-16. Some critics had doubts about a military endeavor in conjunction with our former World War II enemy.

Japan was not the only rival nation we were coordinating with. Plans were under way for a Concorde business jet with Mach 2 capability to be built by the U.S. and the U.S.S.R. With telecommunications, fax machines, and millions of computerized devices, we can reach around the world in a heartbeat. People need to be transported quickly, too. In today's world, speed is essential. To increase our capabilities, the U.S. has to work with other nations. As with the drug crisis, international cooperation is the key.

CHAPTER XIV

"THE MAGIC OF MUSIC," a CBS television special, was set for the spring of 1989. I flew to New York to work with an incredible assortment of vocalists. It was a cross section of artists representing pop, contemporary, R&B, and country music. Among them were Marilyn McCoo, Maureen McGovern, Crystal Gayle, Whitney Houston, Sissy Houston, Gary Morris, Michael Bolton, Freddie Jackson, K. T. Oslin, Jeffrey Osborne, and Lou Rawls. Everyone was outsinging everybody else. But Patti LaBelle outdid us all. What a stimulating environment for a singer!

While some of us gathered to talk backstage, Lou Rawls asked, "How would you like to appear on the 'Parade of Stars'? It's going to be a seven-hour telethon to raise money for the United Negro College Fund." A lot of us said, "That sounds terrific!" And it turned out to be another exhilarating time of musical sharing.

But the news was tragic from the scene of another entertainment project, a movie dealing with the fight against drugs. Chuck and Aaron Norris had asked me to sing the theme song, "Winds of Change," for their upcoming film, *Stranglehold: Delta Force II*. As a scene was being filmed in the Philippines for the riveting, fast-action movie, the French-made Dauphin helicopter that the cameras were focused on suddenly plunged into a forty-foot ravine and exploded. The Filipino pilot and three film crew members were killed. It was a shock to all of us associated with the movie, but Chuck and

Aaron said they were determined not to give up on making their film about the drug war.

That summer, "God Bless the U.S.A." was the finale for the fiftieth anniversary of the USO. In Dearborn, Michigan, the musical evening honored Pearl Bailey, who had been singing for U.S. troops since World War II. Pianist John Bunch, guitarist Remo Palmier, Major Holly on bass, trumpet player Joe Wilder, and Don Menza on the saxophone collaborated on their own brand of nostalgia with a collection of jazz classics, highlighted by the performance of the legendary drummer Louie Bellson. I sang the USO anniversary anthem, "Always Home," before closing the celebration with the song that had been echoing at the end of almost all of the shows sponsored by the USO.

In mid-June we were asked to take "God Bless the U.S.A." to Panama. Quite a few of the U.S. military families had already been sent back to the States or were confined to the base as our troops were moved to a higher state of readiness. A "PML" directive, limiting the movement of all personnel, was in effect. Our people needed a break from the stress. It was President Bush who asked us to go: "It will be a quick trip, Lee, but our servicemen and -women in Panama are working under tense circumstances, and they certainly could use a taste of home."

"We'll be glad to make the trip, Sir," I answered. Although I was aware that there was some trouble down there, I had no idea of the real situation with General Noriega's Panama Defense Force. It never occurred to me that before long, Panama was going to become a battleground.

The USO is financed solely by donations, and my mother was one of the Americans receiving a letter asking for support of my Panama tour.

"Lee," she told me on the phone, "they asked me to send twenty-five dollars, so I sat right down and wrote them a check. In my letter back to the USO, I said, 'I am enclosing the twenty-five dollars. But Lee Greenwood's my son. And I don't think he's safe down there!' "

"Thanks, Mom," I laughed. "But I can't believe you said that. Typical maternal protection!"

"Well, you're always going somewhere, stirring up patriotism with your song. Do you know what happened in my Costa Mesa grocery store? I was walking along, shopping in the market, when I noticed a little boy in a grocery cart. While his mother was pushing the cart along, he was tapping a stack of cans in the cart, hitting them in perfect rhythm. He was singing in tune, repeating over and over this one line: 'Proud to be an American. Proud to be an American. Proud to be an American.'

"I stopped and just stood there, watching him," she continued. "I couldn't believe it! He must have heard your song somewhere. That's the only way he could have learned that line."

The contact with our troops in Panama was worth all our office's rescheduling efforts. But it wasn't a jubilant tour. As one of the soldiers told us, "Our morale right now is really stretched."

We stopped at Fort Clayton and Fort Espinar to perform and then visited with groups of soldiers posted in outlying areas. These young men appreciated our music, but it was evident that deep inside they were not emotionally involved. They obviously had their minds on what was going to be happening soon.

Our last performance for the troops in Panama was televised, live, from Howard Air Force Base and was broadcast across the entire Canal Zone. It was an opportunity to make a personal statement to the local populace, so before closing the program with "God Bless the U.S.A.," I paused and began to speak from the heart: "I know this message is going out to the Panamanian people, and I want to address you personally. I was born a poor farm boy in California, in the western part of the United States. Today I am enjoying success. It took years of hard work, but democracy gave me the chance to reach my goals. Democracy works. It's worth fighting for. Freedom is worth it. Go for it!"

July marked twenty years since Americans became the first humans to go for a walk on the moon! All three of our original "Moonwalk" Flight crew, Neil Armstrong, Michael Collins, and Buzz Aldrin, attended a reception at the White House with their families. Along with the congratulations to our space heroes were words about the Astronaut Memorial Foundation's "Space Mirror" under construction at Spaceport USA. Only a few days before, I had sung my patriotic song there at NASA's Kennedy Space Center. They told us that the forty-two-foot-high memorial would be made of polished granite, tracking the sun throughout the day, reflecting the sky like a mirror. The names of our fourteen astronauts who have died would be etched on its surface, and a gold star representing each of them would be pressed into the cornerstone. It would read: "To those who gave their lives to bring the stars a little closer."

Near the Milky Way galaxy, a supernova exploded, leaving a cloud of dust and a spinning pulsar. This year we found it.

"A star is born!" At least that's what astronomer Carl Pennypacker of Lawrence Berkeley Laboratory in California told us. "The discovery of a new pulsar is like winning the triple crown in racing," he said.

Astronomers from the United States and Japan had been simultaneously tracking the supernova's progress. With the birth of the star, a team of astrophysicists from the U.S., Chile, and Canada measured its weight and speed. Are you ready for this? One teaspoon of the pulsar would weigh 300,000 tons on Earth. And it's spinning at a rate of 1,968 revolutions per second. That's what I call moving!

The more we learn about outer space, the better prepared we'll be to take care of the earth. To our credit, we're trying to clean up our act. The U.S. and the Soviet Union agreed to a chemical weapons ban and signed a treaty, marking another step toward a safer, more humane world. Two days later in Washington, D.C., citizens from the fifty states and our territories gathered to receive Pride In America awards, given to leaders in the nationwide environmental cleanup campaign. As presenter of the fifty-four awards, I was with the gathering of recipients and their friends assembled in chairs on the White House lawn. I felt formal and serious because it was my first time introducing President Bush. After he had entered to the sounds of "Ruffles and Flourishes," I walked to the front, unaware that I was in for an embarrassing moment.

The presidential podium is high because Mr. Bush is tall. But there's a pullout step for anyone else who might need it. Since the riser had been placed there for me, I stepped up on it and began: "Good afternoon, ladies and gentlemen. It's great to be here to honor some of our finest citizens. The President would like to recognize these environmentally concerned Americans. Will you please welcome President Bush."

While the crowd was applauding, I stepped down and moved aside for Mr. Bush. Walking up to take the microphone, he casually kicked the riser under the podium. The President gave a short talk recognizing the efforts made on behalf of the nation, then he turned the program over to me and headed back toward the Oval Office. I approached the podium and nonchalantly tried to slip the riser out from underneath with my foot. It wouldn't budge. Still looking into the expectant faces of those waiting for their awards, I tried again. No way! Finally, feeling like a real fool, I had to bend over and reach under the podium to pull it out with my hand. Of course, there were chuckles rippling across the White House lawn.

In Washington, a turn of events shed a different light upon the Boeing 747 airliner tragedy that had triggered the writing of "God Bless the U.S.A." On August 2, six years after the incident, a federal jury found the Korean Air Lines crew of Flight 007 guilty of "willful misconduct" by purposely flying into Soviet airspace, when they knew it was against international law. The pilots had knowingly given false reports to ground stations concerning their location, while they actually took a shortcut across Sakhalin Island on their way to Seoul.

So the Soviet shoot-down of KAL 007 was not an unjustified act after all. The Soviet pilots protecting their airspace over this sensitive area had no choice when their warnings to the intruder went unanswered. The mysterious plane might have been carrying surveillance equipment or a payload of bombs. As it turned out, it was the foolhardiness of the Korean pilots that brought death to themselves as well as all of their passengers.

It's ironic that the catalyst for the writing of "God Bless the U.S.A." was a misinterpreted event. But the patriotism behind it is real. Maybe the song can stand as a tribute to those innocent people who died, as well as to all who have lost their lives in the cause of freedom.

It's possible that the bid for freedom by China's youth had lighted sparks in neighboring Communist-held nations. Certainly President Gorbachev's policies of *perestroika* and *glasnost* were easing the heavy restraints felt by the powerless citizens of those countries. So many factors entered into the equation because political realities emerge from complex circumstances. But the time was right. Oppressed people throughout the East began increasing the pressure for individual rights within their national borders, and many of them were escaping to lands where they could finally live in freedom. Thousands of boat people were pouring out of Vietnam. At the same time, Budapest stated that policies restricting the movement of Eastern Bloc citizens were against its human rights commitments. Then they let over twelve thousand East Germans pass through Hungary to the West.

Two weeks later, Moscow announced that the Soviet parliament was considering a law to ban censorship and adopt a policy of freedom of the press.

It's hard for us to believe that in some countries every journal, magazine, and newspaper is censored by a government agency before publication. Access to information is one of America's most important rights, and the fact that all of us can receive a free education has helped to develop our strength.

Obviously, America's future is in the hands of our children. In August, I was lucky enough to see some of our most motivated youngsters in action, while participating in their 1989 Boy Scout Jamboree. It's hard to even picture in your mind, but 32,000 Scouts gathered near Fort A. P. Hill, Virginia, to spend an exciting week in ten square miles of countryside.

"Just getting here may have been an adventure for some of you," Ben Love, the Chief Scout Executive told them. "The theme for this jamboree is 'The Adventure Begins . . . With America's Youth.' That's you. Before you is a universe of knowledge, waiting to be explored. If you're lucky, you'll never outgrow the desire to plunge in and experience all you can."

"Plunge in" is exactly what those Scouts did! Forming twenty subcamps, they set up 15,000 tents. Like a miracle, an ephemeral city was born. It sported medical facilities, a post office to handle over 100,000 pieces of mail, and stores—all designed to remain for only one week.

Even a daily newspaper, called *Jamboree Today,* was established, and 350 Scouts volunteered to send reports back to their hometown newspapers. Some of these correspondents worked in a large air-conditioned trailer, which housed seven computers. Others knocked out their stories in the big yellow and white striped tent, which had a floor of straw spread over the bare dirt. The newsroom of these cub reporters was truly primitive. It was filled with long tables on which scores of electric typewriters waited for the halting efforts of a computer-trained generation. But the Scouts managed to adjust to the outmoded machines, and their articles were mailed or faxed to cities throughout America and overseas.

Steven Spielberg, the director of *E.T.* and *Raiders of the Lost Ark,* was scheduled for an interview with the budding journalists. They began gathering hours earlier, eagerly awaiting his arrival.

"I got my start in films while earning my merit badge in photography," Spielberg told the cluster of media enthusiasts when he arrived. "I produced a four-minute Western called 'Gun-smog.' "

The sound of muffled laughter came from a few of the boys at the mention of this parody title.

Spielberg's sophistication as a film-maker had increased from there. At this jamboree, a cinematography merit badge was initiated to encourage Scouts in the field of film. And Spielberg, who had earned membership in the Order of the Arrow as a Scout, was presented with the Distinguished Eagle Scout Award.

At the '89 Jamboree, Scouts were learning a lot more than journalism and film-making. "Space exploration is one of the most exciting adventures facing mankind," Ben Love told them. "And our symbol for this jamboree shows the space shuttle soaring away from Earth. The emblems for our sub-camps show actual U.S. space missions flown by former Scouts. Eagle Scout Neil Armstrong was the first man on the moon. Scout Buzz Aldrin was the second. In fact, over half of our astronauts are former Scouts. NASA is planning other missions in the years ahead, and it will need Scouts like you to man them. You may be too young to go up in the first U.S. space station in the late 1990s, but perhaps you'll help build a base on the moon early in the next century."

"Never be satisfied with what you've done so far—keep reaching," was the challenge to these young men.

Since writing "God Bless the U.S.A.," I have had opportunities to bring its message to groups of youngsters throughout the country. Often they send letters to our office, and we respond. One afternoon, a large envelope arrived. It contained a neatly written letter from each member of a second grade class at Crockham Elementary School in Winton, California. One little boy wrote, "Dear Mr. Greenwood, I will like if you will come here and sing with us. Why did you make the song? God Bless The USA? Did you make that song because you love are country, is that why?" It was signed, "Your friend, Jerry."

My thoughts turned to another young friend, Dana Walters, as I heard some terrific news. A research team from Toronto's Hospital for Sick Children and Howard Hughes Medical Institute at the University of Michigan had isolated the gene that causes cystic fibrosis. Doctors expressed a hope that the discovery will lead to a cure. But we've got to continue helping the ones like Dana, who are afflicted. The talented David Foster wrote a song for this cause, and he presented it to Canada's prime minister as a donation. It's entitled, "Don't Let Me Walk This Road Alone."

That summer in Huntsville, Alabama, at NASA's George C. Marshall Space Flight Center, I made an excursion through the Space and Rocket Center, climbing up into the Space Module mock-up for a preview of Space Station Freedom, which is a horseshoe-shaped construction that looks like scaffolding. In this Center, the Space Camp students plan simulated missions. The facility was developed by the Challenger Committee to honor our fallen astronauts and to encourage America's students to enter the field of space exploration.

"Wind Beneath My Wings," sung to the background of a beautiful NASA film about flight, opened the evening's forum, "Into Other Worlds." The distinguished Mr. Georg von Tiesenhausen, who began his career with Verner von Braun's rocket experts, explained the background of our space exploration program. Our second speaker, former chief engineer of the Galileo project Gentry Lee, combined his photographic memory with a tight grasp on reality, and the Space Camp kids in our audience warmed up to his approach. These young people represent America's next generation of explorers.

During the fall, the pace of the Freedom Movement in Central Europe began to quicken. Throughout the closing months of 1989, boldface headlines blazed with each startling turn of events in these Communist-dominated nations.

From East Germany came the news: "OPENING BORDERS MAY SIGNAL END OF IRON CURTAIN. JUBILANT CITIZENS DANCE ON TOP OF BERLIN WALL."

Near the Brandenburg Gate, East Germans rushed through powerful streams bursting from water cannons, the final attempts by police to prevent them from leaving. But the escapees were pulled up onto the wall by young West Germans who were clapping and shouting words of encouragement.

"It's like a dream!" shouted one young East Berliner.

All their lives they had lived behind the heavily guarded sinister wall, which was embedded in some places with razor-sharp wire. Many had tried to climb over it, but only the most fortunate succeeded. Almost two hundred had died and four thousand had been caught by East German police and thrown into prison.

Now, the border guards no longer had orders to open fire. Some even helped chip away at the concrete and wire barrier; others smiled as fleeing citizens handed them roses.

Most of the world was caught off guard by the sudden collapse of Communist control, and the fall of the Berlin Wall wasn't our only surprise. The Polish had just overcome their government's Communist majority. At the same time, Czechoslovakians were rocking their capital with demonstrations demanding the ouster of their own Communist government. Waving red, white, and blue national flags and shouting, "They must go!" and "Resign! Resign!" 150,000 Czechs called for free elections. The entire hard-line Communist party leadership resigned. Then in a move that amazed all of us, the U.S.S.R., East Germany, Poland, Hungary, and Bulgaria issued a statement formally apologizing for their 1968 Prague invasion, which had quashed Czechoslovakia's bid for freedom. The Soviets called their own former actions "illegal."

Soviet leader Gorbachev was preparing for his summit meeting with President Bush. On his way to Malta, he made an historic visit in Rome. In talks with Pope John Paul II, he stated that Moscow was ready to revise its policy: the Soviet people would be given freedom of religion.

What a perfect time for a meeting of the two superpowers! Although the initial discussions had to be moved to the huge Soviet cruise ship *Maxim Gorkey* because of high winds whipping the storm-tossed Mediterranean, the negotiations were unusually friendly. They emphasized arms agreements and the unfolding Eastern Bloc reforms.

But the revolutions in Communist-held nations kept raging. The Bulgarians ousted their old-line leadership and the situation of the Communist government in Hungary was almost humorous. After decades of mismanagement, Premier Miklos Nemeth stated that he would give up sole power in favor of participation by opposing parties. No one accepted!

"I don't blame them," he said, acknowledging that Hungary's economy was in shambles. Nevertheless, Hungary was preparing for its first free elections in forty years.

But it was violent in Romania. Hundred of demonstrators, mostly the country's youth, were being slaughtered by secret police and soldiers. It was a bloody battle that ended on Christmas Day with the executions of the cruel and grasping Ceausescus, who had dominated Romania for twenty-four years.

Like dominoes, Lithuania, Latvia, and Estonia began tilting toward multiparty systems. Freedom was on the move.

Uppermost in my mind, of course, was the clash in Panama. American troops had acted to enforce the Panamanian elections, which Gen. Manuel Noriega had refused to acknowledge. It took our military forces only five days to overcome his strong-arming PDF. The people were jubilant, banging pots and pans together and cheering. On December 25 Noriega surrendered to the Vatican embassy in Panama City. Soon he would be facing drug charges in the United States.

Meanwhile a new generation of entertainers was joining Bob Hope's tradition of bringing Christmas cheer to our troops. As one of those to follow in his footsteps, I was invited to take my band on a USO Christmas Tour to the North Atlantic. When the USO Tour manager Iona Sherman called me about the trip, I said, "Since it's the Christmas Tour, our troops will be expecting a variety group. Is it all right if I find some others to fill out the show?"

USO officials thought this was a good idea, so we contacted Miss USA Gretchen Polhemus, Miss Tennessee Kim Payne, and Miss Delaware Terry Spruill. To these beauties we added an athlete, former NBA All Star player from the Boston Celtics, Dave Cowens. Then to keep them laughing, we took comedienne June Boykins, "Just June."

Although we would miss spending Christmas at home, all of us were psyched as we took off from Nashville in our C-130, heading for frozen territory.

Bad weather closed in as our plane headed for Newfoundland, so the pilot had to turn back to Nova Scotia. But the following day found us winging north. Scheduled along our route were continual shows and basketball games to give our troops a break from their long tours of duty. The games, complete with referees and audiences, were fast and not too serious . . . at first. It was the guys on the bases against us. Everyone in the band played. The group, which we called Night Shift, included Steve Mandile, Steve Hornbeck, Eric Horner, John Howard, and Chuck Tilley. Also on our team were our audio engineer Mark Swift, sound engineer Mike Thamann, production coordinator Terry Whisner, and lighting director Mark Whisner. Of course my road manager Kip Ingle, Danny Bradley, and I played. We felt like an awesome team . . . as long as Dave Cowens was on the court! Of course, we had our three-girl cheering section, Kim, Terry, and Gretchen. With Dave, we were a winning combination at each base, but it was all in good-natured fun.

In Thule, Greenland, I can still remember being jolted from a sound sleep by a raucous, ear-piercing voice: "Listen up! Emergency conditions! Storm alert! Storm alert!"

This land, a barren stretch of almost uninhabited snow and ice near the North Pole, was under Storm 2 Alert when we arrived. There were storm warnings here all the time. The Air Force couldn't take the chance of having someone caught outside and frozen in his tracks, so an alert warning was deafening. It blared out over every loudspeaker, including the halls of the barracks where people were sleeping.

Between the Air Force base and the Ballistic Missile Early Warning Radar Site a highway stretched across the ice. About every quarter-mile there was a hangar equipped with cots, food and water, blankets, and a phone. In case the weather got bad really fast, someone could take refuge there.

"When the snow starts blowing around, you can get lost," one of the officers told me. "And a storm's velocity can get so ferocious, that two years ago Shack #7 registered 220 mile-per-hour winds before it was blown over. And it can come up instantly."

"That sounds like a little too much wind for hang gliding!" I joked.

"It gets dangerous," he answered. "One time we had a pilot land on the base, and he got lost walking from his plane to the terminal. Heavy winds blew the snow in circles so he couldn't see at all. Gusts of wind were sending flurries in all directions. He probably got vertigo and became confused. Out here, everything can become a blank wall of white.

"But we have an emergency command center," he continued, with a tone of urgency. "Whenever you leave the barracks, call in and tell them where you're going. As soon as you get there, you need to check in again with the command center."

Luckily the storm calmed down enough for our show and basketball game. Then it was on to the U.S. Naval Air Station in Keflavik, Iceland, where basketball stole the show. News of our winning team had preceded us, so the Navy was prepared to challenge us. They had even invited the local high school cheerleaders. Of course we had three beauties of our own. And we had Dave! Usually when he realized that there was not a lot of pressure, he'd just lie back and let all of us participate. But this time the game was close. Our team was three points down as the clock was counting out, but we had the ball.

"Nine seconds!" Danny yelled to Kip, watching him pull up to the three-point line.

Kip focused on the basket, gave the ball a careful push, and "whoosh!"—it slid right through, just as time ran out.

"The game's tied. What do you want to do?" I asked Admiral Haley, a good athlete who was serving as captain of the Navy team.

"Well, let's play three minutes," he answered.

Catching my breath and trying to hide the fact that I was quite winded—in fact all of us were panting—I suggested, "How about two minutes?"

"Okay," he laughed.

The game was on again, up and down the court. As the clock ticked down to the fifteen-second mark, our team was losing by one point. Dave Cowens came out from his normal defensive position to play on offense. The crowd was screaming for the Navy team, as they moved ahead, 45-44. This was getting serious!

With ten seconds left, the ball went out of bounds and the Navy passed it back in. Our team went into a full-court press. A towering six-feet-nine, Dave easily intercepted a pass as Navy was bringing the ball up court. He threw it to Kip, who snapped it up and dribbled at breakneck speed to the other end. Before all of the players could make it down there, Kip made a beautiful lay-up from under the basket. The scoreboard read 46-45 as the buzzer sounded.

"Yea, Kip! We win by one point!"

Our Navy opponents were polite, but they didn't like to lose. The Greenwood Tour team was now 3 and 0. The next day Admiral Haley put in a call to Scotland, where we were scheduled to play another Navy team. Speaking to the commanding officer, he made one thing clear: "Your men must not let these guys beat the Navy again."

And they didn't!

On Christmas Eve, a service brightened by traditional carols was held in the chapel. Afterwards we clustered in small groups to visit the 200 men and women on security duty in small command posts around the perimeter of the base. Kim and I climbed into one of the military vans, hoping to bring a feeling of special cheer to those who hadn't been able to come over to our show. Big fluffy snowflakes had begun to fall. Trudging down icy paths, we were carrying gifts.

"These are little mementos of thoughtfulness. The wives of airmen on the base baked these cookies especially for you," we explained to the on-duty soldiers in each hangar. Touched by the holiday gesture, their faces brimmed with emotion as they said, "Thanks. This makes it seem almost like home." It was a cold night, but a very warm way to spend a Christmas Eve.

On Christmas Day our entourage flew to Bentwaters, England, to perform for a huge crowd assembled in a hangar at the Royal Air Force Base. The British fliers assigned to duty in Bentwaters are excellent pilots and a very proud bunch. And the U.S. Air Force has a highly skilled Aggressor Force there, which flies against its own pilots in training. World leaders remember this base as the home of our F-111s that gave Libya's Colonel Qaddafi his wake-up call.

In England we were reminded of what was happening on the European Mainland. Some members of a British football team who came to our show had just returned from an excursion through Germany. They brought us some photos and several rocks from the Berlin Wall, which was rapidly becoming a nightmare of the past.

Near Holy Loch, Scotland, our group gave two performances, then visited the immense submarine tender in the area, which serves as a base for U.S. nuclear submarines. With its quaint beaches and rugged cliffs, Scotland is gorgeous, even in the wintertime. But we were headed for Glasgow, then Gatwick, and home to the United States. I had to be in Evansville, Indiana, for a New Year's Eve show, then on to Dallas and the game between the University of Tennessee and the University of Arkansas. On New Year's Day, during half time at the Cotton Bowl, "God Bless the U.S.A." would ring out once again.

CHAPTER XV

A MAGICAL EVENING WAS DRAWING to a close as a capacity crowd awaited the finale of my New Year's Eve concert in Evansville, Indiana. They were crowded together, sharing all those colorful party favors and throwing confetti. The convention hall started to grow quiet as I moved to center stage. Then standing in the spotlight's full intensity, I looked around, searching their faces. What I had to say was serious, and it must have shown in my eyes.

"Thank you!" I called out to those in the far corners of the room, beyond the stage lights. And again, "Thank you!" to bring a hush to the audience. Then I began to tell them what I felt.

"Ladies and gentlemen," I shouted. "Here we are, standing on a piece of free ground. Recognize it yet? It's called the United States of America!"

The crowd broke out in a cheer of agreement.

"We're here together at the start of a new year," I continued. "But tonight is special. The world is changing. Millions are demanding their freedom in countries all around the earth, from the Latin American countries to the Eastern Bloc nations, and even eventually into China. And we're going to keep on encouraging them until people everywhere are free!"

A series of shouts and shrill whistles rose throughout the room, and I broke into their applause to continue.

"Last summer we flew to Panama to help break the tension for our troops there. That was just before the invasion, and our men were under a lot of pressure. But they were whole-heartedly ready to complete their mission, whatever it took. They fought, and they won the government back for the Panamanian people. But victory doesn't come easy. We lost twenty-six good men in Panama.

"Every once in a while, we need to take time out and think about who we are as a nation. There are a lot of citizens out there who've made sacrifices. They may be standing beside you. Maybe they're in your own family. Most of them, you don't even know. Many are veterans of one of the wars, or in the active military. And it's sad, but some are POWs and MIAs.

"Please accept this song in memory of those we have lost and in appreciation of all our men and women serving in defense of the freedom that we're so fortunate to share.

"America is alive, and I'm proud to be an American. God bless the U.S.A.!"

Suddenly a deep stillness filled the room as the band's first silver-high strings announced the opening of this hymn to the nation. There was an almost breathless silence. Then the music increased in volume as the light, bell-like tones of the synthesizer chimed out the familiar intro, and I began to sing:

"If tomorrow all the things were gone I'd worked for all my
    life
And I had to start again with just my children and my wife
I'd thank my luck stars to be living here today,
'Cause the flag still stands for freedom,
And they can't take that away."

It seemed as though New Year's Eve almost blended into New Year's Day. In twelve hours' time I had been whisked across the country to Dallas and was standing in the center of the Cotton Bowl, looking up at the University of Tennessee and University of Arkansas fans. The air was electric with the fighting spirit that makes a team, or a nation, strong. The intercollegiate rivalry was dominating the scene, and in the U.T. stands, a frenzy was building.

It was almost overwhelming to be a participant in this final athletic competition of the season, with its packed grandstands and the added millions in the national TV audience. When I arrived, my heart beat faster as I picked up the spirit of the football fans. It had been a quick trip to Dallas, and I had barely made it. In the distance, I noticed the look of relief on the face of Professor Julian, who had arranged for my appearance here. Soon the action began. Quickly, I made my way out to center field. On the thick turf, the Army's Golden Knights were landing to the accompaniment of the U.S. Marine band.

"Great job!" I shouted to my Army paratrooper friends as they stood waiting for the pre-game activities to be completed.

Walking a little closer, I noticed that pinned on each of their black jump suits was a small green ribbon.

"The green ribbons are something new. Do they represent a special mission?" I asked the captain.

"Yes, in a sense that's true," he replied. "We're wearing the ribbons in memory of our men who were killed last week during the fighting in Panama." Motioning to the green ribbon, he added, "Would you like to wear this for those guys?"

As I nodded, he took off his ribbon and pinned it on my jacket.

Then we snapped to attention as the band opened up with the first chords of the national anthem, and Janie Fricke began with, "Oh, say can you see, by the dawn's early light?"

How many times had we heard this stirring melody? Remembering my one disaster while singing it, a slight smile crossed my face. Then I fixed my gaze on today's singer, confident that Janie's rendition would be excellent.

Now the game was on, and the crowd began shouting their partisan support for each team. Living in Tennessee, I cheered for their side. And it was the huge University of Tennessee "Pride of the Southland" Band that accompanied me to the field for the half-time performance. The musicians marched forward in single file and formed the shape of America's familiar symbol, an enormous eagle, completely surrounding me. Holding the mike, I began my song. The strong tones of the trumpet section joined in, and my thoughts returned to my red POW bracelet and the new green ribbon on my jacket as I reached the chorus:

"And I'm proud to be an American, where at least I know
     I'm free.
And I won't forget the men who died who gave that right
     to me.
And I'd gladly stand up next to you and defend her still
     today,
'Cause there ain't no doubt I love this land—
God bless the U.S.A."

Time and time again, I had sung this song, exposing my deepest emotions to friends and strangers, and they had responded with their hearts. By now, "God Bless the U.S.A." had become an integral part of my soul, and I could hardly imagine life without it.

With the new year, came some career changes. Because of a web of coincidences, Jerry Crutchfield and I were back together again, this time on a new label. Then Crutch moved from MCA to Capitol Records, and Jimmy Bowen had taken over for Jim Foglesong at MCA, but after Bowen became president of Capitol the three of us decided we could rekindle our earlier gold record success if we were back together. Lo and behold, the deal came down! Jerry Crutchfield became my producer once again, this time at Capitol.

"Looks like we've come full circle!" I said to Crutch.

"And *Holding a Good Hand* is going to be a great album for Capitol. It's got an optimistic, up-tempo title song, which *this time* is definitely going to be released first off the album!" he smiled, kidding me about that day when Irving Azoff had passed over our album's title song in favor of "God Bless the U.S.A."

It was fun to share a joke while our careers were again on the rise. We were settled in together for another round. Unfortunately, the world wasn't so lucky. Iraqi troops had invaded the oil-rich nation of Kuwait and were moving 100,000 of their soldiers south, near the Saudi Arabian border.

It didn't alarm me much at first because there hadn't been any bombs dropped. It was an uncomfortable feeling to see another little country being taken over, but I had seen it happen before.

President Bush made the terse statement: "This will not stand." Then he started the military buildup known as Operation Desert Shield. Determined that the Saudis would not be taken, he decided to send 2,300 men from the Army's 82nd Airborne, some Air Force F-15s and Navy planes, and a Marine amphibious brigade of 116,500 men. Then to make sure our ally in the Persian Gulf was defended, he said he was ready to commit 19,000 troops from our 101st Air Mobile Division and 12,000 from the 24th Heavy Armored Division.

Almost immediately, the President ordered economic sanctions against Baghdad and put a freeze on Iraqi and Kuwaiti assets. America applauded his moves. At least it put out a message, worldwide, that there was a big problem.

France and Great Britain followed suit, and the Soviets stated they were suspending all their arms deliveries to Iraq, which had been their client before the invasion. A trade embargo against Iraq was ordered.

The pressure increased, and in just a few weeks America achieved a modern miracle. Our airlift to the Persian Gulf was greater than anything accomplished at Normandy. Saudi Arabia was much farther away than the beaches of southern France. And the number of people, planes, and equipment was incredible: 100,000 tons of cargo, 72,000 service personnel, and planes of all types were transported 7,000 miles to the far side of the planet.

Further aggression was the President's first concern at this point. Sending troops to defend Saudi Arabia and its oil fields was primarily a protective measure. It was an understandable move, because although the Saudis had a rich country, their army wasn't very large. I don't think anybody felt that Iraq, a smaller country, would be able to take over Saudi Arabia, a much bigger area with all its wealth, and get away with it. But Iraq had an unbelievable stockpile of arms and the fourth largest army in the world, over a million men. And they were experienced. They'd been trying to conquer Iran for the past eight years. Unable to do that, they set their sights on Kuwait, with its oil fields, miles of coastline, and deepwater port. In fact, their leader, Saddam Hussein, came right out and said, "Kuwait is now part of Iraq."

There were a lot of people in the world ready to disagree with him. The United Nations' Security Council voted to declare his invasion illegal. Then they set up a blockade to back up their decision, hoping to force a withdrawal without resorting to war.

But Saddam began capturing foreigners and calling them "detainees." I was outraged when I heard him say they were his "guests." That made us all pretty angry because it was obvious that they were hostages.

Each new move by the United Nations allies brought no sign of retreat by Saddam's forces. I was beginning to think our steady pressure wasn't going to work. Then, three full months after the invasion of Kuwait, President Bush gave a stern announcement: "Four hundred thousand U.S. troops, along with our UN allies, will be in the Persian Gulf by early next year. Iraq must leave Kuwait, unconditionally."

It showed in the faces of the people at my concerts: the fear and anxiety. As our nightly performances continued, and I kept singing "God Bless the U.S.A.," I was getting stronger vibes from my audiences. They were worried about what was going to happen, afraid for the lives of their loved ones. When that many troops are gathered, you just know there's going to be a war. Those folks singing with me, "I'm proud to be an American," could feel it coming. There was the glint of pride in their country, but the apprehension was there. I could see it in their eyes.

About this time I had an unbelievable schedule, recording two albums at once. We were laying down the tracks for ten songs to be included on a solo album. In addition, we were cutting a second album, called *A Perfect Ten*. Capitol Records had asked me to record duets with ten females. We ended up with a wonderful group of duet partners. Years ago I had toured with Barbara Mandrell, a terrific entertainer and a good friend. Marie Osmond, with her vibrant personality, had recently crossed over to country. We were happy to get Tanya Tucker and Lacy J. Dalton, two of country music's well-known names. Carol Chase and Karen Staley were relatively unknown to the fans. Donna McElroy was a special choice because we wanted to record "If You Don't Know Me By Now," a magic R and B song of the past. Donna has that rich gospel sound, which none of the other women possessed. Adding to the diversity, Cee Cee Chapman's voice is similar to Cher's, and the Wild Rose group is extremely country. Suzy Bogguss, who sounds kind of like Emmy Lou Harris, has a purity of voice that blended perfectly. We recorded a waltz entitled "Hopelessly Yours," which turned out to be the first single release, rounding out *A Perfect Ten*.

Early in December I was at the White House as cochairman with Barbara Bush in the Salute to Veterans' Hospitals. It was the first time I'd seen the President troubled. George Bush looked weary and somber, but he wanted to address the veterans issue. Edward Derwinski, Secretary of Veterans Affairs, and Lee Iacocca were there, along with several others.

The President was cordial as he always is, but I sensed preoccupation with what was going on. He was obviously tired from the long hours he'd been spending at the Oval Office. Of course, he had been heavily involved in decisions about the air war and a potential ground war, and the weight was on his shoulders. He was very serious, deeply troubled. I could tell.

The holiday season was not joyful. I kept our band's schedule open so that we'd be available to bring an uplifting message to our troops, in case they needed us. But entertainment in the Persian Gulf was being kept to a minimum, partly due to a few faux pas that earlier shows had made. The word came down, unofficially: "The Arabs do not like us pushing our Western culture off on them. They are uncomfortable about our females in uniform, preparing for combat along with the men. They may be offended by the way our women are dressed and will be especially shocked by any bare skin showing."

We understood, of course, but stayed ready to go, just in case.

As the New Year arrived, Saddam remained stubborn, and the tension increased. I don't think that anyone even remotely believed that a man with that much war machinery and power would say, "Okay, I'll just get out of Kuwait." He was there to annex the country and take its enormous wealth, which centered upon a thousand oil wells dotting the tiny emirate.

The UN allies had set a deadline: "Saddam must withdraw his forces by January 15." The whole world waited with a feeling of dread. Iraq refused to budge.

Meanwhile, our troops were on a knife's edge of expectancy. Leading a display of support for these Americans at risk was XTRA-AM disk jockey Randy Miller, who arranged for "God Bless the U.S.A." to be played simultaneously by radio stations throughout the United States on the day before that UN deadline.

On January 17 the air war began. First, the allies sent a few F-117A Stealth fighter-bombers to wipe out Baghdad's telecommunications. Operation Desert Storm had begun. Other aircraft began obliterating Iraqi radar and anti-aircraft missile sites.

Iraq began firing Scud missiles at Israel, and the allies countered with Patriot missiles, taking them out with amazing accuracy.

Allied B-52s were hitting units of the legendary Republican Guard and their supply routes as Iraq embarked on an unconscionable tactic. They began setting fire to Kuwaiti wells, and even started pumping millions of gallons of oil into the Persian Gulf. They had literally become the enemy of their own environment. And Saddam was parading newly captured allied prisoners for all the world to see.

Back in the U.S., I watched the TV news reports with growing apprehension. There was no way to fully comprehend the hardships and danger that our people were going through over there. And there wasn't much they could look to, that would relieve the tension. A Disney representative called my office: "Would Lee be able to put on a show to be beamed, live, to our troops in the Persian Gulf?"

After checking with the Department of Defense, we agreed. AFRTS, the broadcast system for the military, would send the show not only to the Gulf, but also to 130 other countries. This would be a TV special, followed by a live radio broadcast. Both would include the packed crowds of visitors at Walt Disney World.

February 3 was hot in Orlando, Florida, although certainly not as hot as Saudi Arabia. The DOD had given Disney the rules of dress, so the Disney hosts insisted, "You must be covered from your neck, and your wrists, down to well below camera level."

Even our lively dancers on stage had to wear wrist-length khaki shirts and long slacks. No way were we going to offend the Arab nations!

Fireworks hitting the Florida sky closed out the television special. On screen, the song title appeared written in sand. A steady blast of the strong "Saudi" wind blew over the words, and when the wind died down, there was nothing left but "God Bless the U.S.A." Oh, man. That was awesome!

As darkness fell, we began broadcasting the radio show for anyone who might be listening so far away. One song I wanted to sing for them that had special significance was "Just Like Me." When I first recorded it, I had no idea it was about the troops. It sounded like a song about a woman who had left a guy. They may have been separated or divorced. Or she might have died. I really didn't know what the real scenario was. Then one day someone said to me, "Well, what if she's a woman serving in the military?"

The possibility started running though my mind, and I decided, "I'll just phone the writer and find out."

The lyricist was Debbie Hupp. Bob Morrison had written the music. I found Debbie's number in Louisville, Kentucky, and soon she was on the line: "I wrote 'Just Like Me' about my daughter-in-law. She had signed up for the reserves when there wasn't a war, but her unit was called up. Then my son was called to active duty. He came back first, so he was home with their little boy, missing her. That's when I wrote the song. Remember the second verse that says: 'I always keep your picture in our room by the bed,/ but every now and then it disappears./ I know I'm going to find it propped under Snoopy's lamp,/ and I know he's been pretending you're still here. . . ./ Just like me./ But we'll hang in there together./ We're both strong enough to weather this old storm 'til it goes by. . . .' My son's wife was in the service and they were missing her."

"Well, it should be dedicated to the women in the military."

An excited crowd had piled into Paradise Island for the evening broadcast from Walt Disney World. There were people galore, packed in like sardines. The lights made it magic, as I introduced the song: "When we do this radio show, we instantly think about past history when America has been at war. The American soldier has always been depicted as a man with his woman waiting at home. . . . The next song deals with loneliness, but instead of the man going out and doing the job, in this case it's the woman who's out there. Dedicated to the woman soldier out there in uniform, here is our brand new release on Capitol Records, 'Just Like Me.' "

After that, we dedicated "The Great Defenders" to all the troops. Danny Bradley had recently written it, and we had been singing it only to USO audiences.

The next song on the show list was "Wind Beneath My Wings." Trying to picture the situations that our listeners might be in, I started speaking: "Can you imagine what it feels like on an aircraft carrier, in the middle of the night when a plane starts to take off . . . the anticipation of what's to come, for that pilot, in the deserts of Saudi Arabia, where there have been weeks and weeks and weeks of waiting, and then all of a sudden a bomb blasts somewhere, and just totally unravels your nerves? . . . A fallen buddy . . . The time that you're out there alone by yourself . . ."

The first words of the song eased in: "It must have been cold there in my shadow. . . ." Then I started talking again: "The shadows . . . the shadows are scary. But for each one of those guys and gals, putting their lives on the line for a small country like Kuwait, it's not allowing somebody to take away their freedom. We love you."

As I was singing, the crew members would come by and say, in a stage whisper, "Twenty-two minutes . . . sixteen minutes . . ."

And while I was singing, thoughts were racing through my mind. I was wondering, "How much time am I going to have left to sing another song or two, and then say some things that I want to get said? Because I'm talking to the troops in the Persian Gulf, who are there putting their lives on the line. And they're real close to going into battle, or they're already in battle. And they may be listening to this while they're sitting in a tank, or when something happens. . . . If they have their radio, they're going to hear it."

So I broke away from the show list, and crew members were scrambling around like crazy, wondering what I was going to do next. I wanted to make sure that I got the message out to the troops. And I knew I had to say it just right, from all the people in America—not just those in attendance, but from all the people in Iowa, and California, and New York, who wished they could be there with us to speak to someone special over there.

The concert was under my control, and when I got down to the end, I cut out two songs to give myself an extra four minutes to talk. Where do you get four minutes of vocabulary that would make sense? But somehow I did. I've never seen, in my lifetime, such support of our country behind its military. I wanted to make sure they knew that. And then I wanted to say the word "unwavering." Because it was something constant. It wasn't as if we were swayed by CNN and what it said today, and then were not as supportive tomorrow. So I wanted to say, "unwavering support," so they'd know.

And they'd know they were getting this message from a farm kid—that's what I am—who's not controlled by the media. That they were getting an honest message from me. So, as I was counting down the time and trying to give them my true feelings, I came up with, "All of us here at home send our unwavering support for all of our troops, and our hope for your safe return home.

"For each one of you who has suffered through the hardship of many, many days in the hot sun and many, many nights of loneliness . . . we salute you.

"For each one of you who has been there and waited in anticipation of the possibility of being shot at, and having to shoot back . . . we send you our hearts.

"For each one of you who's putting your life on the line for your country . . . we are humbled by your attitude.

"Please come home soon. And by the way, when you do, bring that guy next to you with you!"

Those last words echoed one of the messages in the Disney World video. Radio and TV stations around the country had taped amateur messages from the families, like, "Hi, Dad! We're here in Detroit and want you to come home safe. Now, here's your little girl. . . . Say something, Andrea."

These weren't eloquent, but they were real and from the heart. One of them came from a black couple. The man was standing beside his wife, who was seated. And he said, "Come home soon, son." Then after a short pause, he added, "Oh, by the way, bring that guy next to you with you." I was watching, and thought it was *so cool* when he said that! So I included it in the show.

Then, along with the whole group of Disney singers, I signed off with a truly heartfelt performance of "God Bless the U.S.A." Deep inside, I was hoping my words had, in some way, helped our men and women who were enduring the danger.

The next week, on Valentine's Day, Barbara Bush was in Washington, D.C. and I was in Tuscaloosa, Alabama, for the Salute to Veterans' Hospitals. Visiting these hospitals, I met a lot of fine people. Whenever I do that, I try to get their life stories, to find out what they're about and then give them something that's of value to them, for the price they've paid. There was one proud Marine, a famous coach from Tuscaloosa, who had been admitted to the hospital with a life-threatening disease. But he was as stoic as ever, very exemplary of his past. When I asked, "Are you feeling any better today?" he straightened up as tall as he could and snapped out in a proud voice, "Yes, sir!"

What a wonderful old guy! And I relive these incidents with our veterans again and again. I visit whenever I can, but it's emotionally draining. You have to give a part of your mind and soul to help somebody.

The Indians have a saying: "If you take my picture, you are stealing my spirit." Well, when you meet people, they are looking for a personal connection, an uplifting feeling from you. And I think you only have the ability to give so much. If you continually give of yourself, pretty soon it pours out like blood. It's as though your life juices are going away, because you give so much. There's a limit to how much you can give ... because it takes energy, and you can't just give unemotionally. You have to give with a true spirit, with inner strength. And when you do that, it's exhausting.

At this same time, back at the bases in the Persian Gulf, our troops were hearing both the Saudi anthem and "The Star-Spangled Banner" every night and "God Bless The U.S.A." each day at noon. On the "McNeil-Lehrer News Hour," the program director for the Desert Shield Network, Army Sgt. Maj. Bob Nelson, called me "the poet laureate of the military," adding that my song was being repeated throughout the day over there.

Then after six weeks of air sorties over Iraq's military targets, the time was right. The deadline for Iraqi troops to leave Kuwait was noon, February 23. But there were no signs of withdrawal. President Bush announced: "The liberation of Kuwait has begun." Along with UN troops, he launched our nation's largest offensive since World War II. The first Tomahawk cruise missile blasted upward, heading from a U.S. battleship to Baghdad, 400 miles away. Invisible to radar scanners, Air Force Stealth fighters were in the air, moving to blast out Iraqi communications. They were joined, in the sky, by F-15E Strike Eagles, F-16s, F-111s, Navy F-6s, and Britain's Tornadoes. Scout Birds, Chinooks and Apache helicopters, and even B-52s, reminiscent of Vietnam, were partners in this air armada.

Operation Desert Storm moved across the desert. The ground battle surprised everyone with its speed. Our Army's 101st Airborne was airlifted far into Iraq to set up a base for fuel and supplies and to fly into the Euphrates Valley below Baghdad. Meanwhile, allied tanks moved in, the French 6th Armored and the 82nd Airborne, to the far west of the 101st. Then the 3rd Armored Cavalry and 24th Mechanized Infantry rolled. Toward the center came the 1st and 3rd Armored and 2nd Armored Cavalry, the British 1st Armored, and U.S. 1st Infantry and 1st Cavalry. Egyptian and Syrian forces moved through eastern Kuwait, alongside their Saudi brothers, flanked to the west by America's Army Tiger Brigade and 1st and 2nd Marine Divisions. Simultaneously, the Saudi task force pushed up the Kuwaiti coastline.

After every Army artillery strike, the allies would move forward, take the position, and then call in another strike. The outmaneuvered and hungry Iraqi soldiers started surrendering by the thousands. United Nations forces moved in so fast that there were Iraqi troops walking along the dusty desert paths trying their best to surrender to somebody—anybody! But the allies were rushing past them, heading for the next established front. These Iraqis with their hands raised were actually pleading, "Take me! Take me!"

Nobody had time. So they had to keep on walking south, waiting 'til other allied troops caught up and could actually take them into custody as prisoners of war.

These Iraqi soldiers were caught between a rock and a hard place! They couldn't be sure if they would be beaten, or worse, when they became captives. But the Republican Guard, which would probably kill them, was at their backs. It took a great deal of courage to surrender, knowing that if they ever went home, they might be branded cowards and be executed. I think maybe we should have given guns to all of those guys who returned, to defend themselves against the Republican Guard!

It was basically a 100-hour ground war—over in a flash. In just a few days, the allies were holding over 60,000 Iraqi POWs and had obliterated eight divisions of the Republican Guard. They had freed Kuwait and protected its oil-producing neighbors. I loved seeing the colorful flags raised over Kuwait City! Actually, our Special Forces had parachuted in, by chopper, the night before to secure the embassy. So they were waiting there when the Kuwaitis came home, along with a group of UN forces.

Americans watched the victory as it happened. I don't think ever before in history has a nation been so well informed about current events the moment they took place. The news coverage of the Persian Gulf was immediate, especially the continuous live coverage by CNN. Even the ongoing boxing match between Saddam Hussein and President Bush was shared with the television audience. The President did a very good Muhammad Ali act of ducking the punches. And he pulled a fast one himself, creating the impression that the allies were planning an amphibious landing on the coast of Kuwait. General Schwarzkopf had thought up this surprise. Later he said, "Go back and remember the battle of El Alamein . . . a deception operation that caused the Germans to think the main attack was going to come somewhere else. . . . I remembered the fact that in desert warfare you can deceive your enemy as to the point of the main attack, and said, 'That's it! That's the key!' "

By leading Iraqi officials as well as the media and the general public to expect this landing, our military leaders achieved the repositioning of the Iraqi forces. Meanwhile, the allied ground troops were actually encircling the Iraqis from their southern border.

News reporters didn't like being used as a ploy. But they had set themselves up for it by saying, "We want every bit of information we can get."

The American people look at television, and that's their communication from coast to coast. They can pick up the telephone and call around the world, but basically they like to watch TV to find out what's going on right now, and what is the truth, and how it makes us feel as a nation. But because the American news services are heard around the world, there's a possibility of the reporters being so persistent and then so honest that our position would be endangered. The military people could say, "You're being so honest that I could get taken out!" It's an obvious negative that calls for extreme sensitivity by reporters.

While all of this was going on, I was giving a performance in Fairfield, Illinois. During a quick break, Kip ran up to me. He had just phoned home and talked with his wife, Kathy, and now there was a glint of triumph in his eye as he grinned and said, "Guess who just said that he requested to hear 'God Bless the U.S.A.' before they went into battle . . . Norman Schwarzkopf!"

"You're kidding me!"

"He was on the Barbara Walters' '20/20' show . . . ," Kip continued.

"All right!" I split the air with a triumphant fist. It really felt good, and I could hardly keep from sharing my excitement with the audience right then. I finished our show with the emotion-filled words of "God Bless the U.S.A.," eager to find out what General Schwarzkopf had said about my song.

It seems as though sometimes bad news closes in right after the good. The blow that hit our Nashville community was the plane crash that killed eight members of Reba McEntire's band and both pilots. It had a big impact on all of us in the entertainment field, and we responded. Reba had been booked that next weekend in Chicago, so we volunteered to fill in for her. Sawyer Brown was there as the opening act for all three days. Then Merle Haggard took Friday night, we played Saturday, and Charlie Daniels performed on Sunday, along with Kathy Mattea. These were benefit concerts that raised $176,000 for the band members' and pilots' families.

Another benefit took place the following month in Nashville. I hosted "Nashville Now," for the usual host, Ralph Emery, so that he could appear with Kenny Rogers, the Oak Ridge Boys, T. Graham Brown, Patty Loveless, and a variety of others to add to the fund set up by the Third National Bank in Nashville. Reba had lost a talented group of very artistic players. And while she was starting over, rebuilding her band, the nation was saddened by another death. Lee Atwater, the young political genius who had directed George Bush's presidential campaign, died after a long battle with cancer. Lee had become a close friend as my guest of "Lifestyles of the Rich and Famous Runaway," so it was tough to hear that he was gone.

In April, Geraldo Rivera's topic for his Good Friday show was "Peace and Patriotism." Tony Orlando, who's responsible for all those yellow ribbons, told him, "I've been watching the war every minute, and seeing the ribbons become a symbol of love for the people fighting this war." Then a young Israeli singer/songwriter told about being in the U.S. while she viewed the TV coverage of her neighborhood in Haza, Israel, destroyed by a Scud from Iraq. She was grateful for the defense of her nation by our Patriot missiles. In agreement with her, I spoke in support of our efforts to halt Iraqi aggression.

But most of Geraldo's guests were trapped in the sixties, insisting that we shouldn't be in this war. The father of the Peace Movement, Pete Seeger, along with his grandson, sang his classic, "Where Have All the Flowers Gone?" And P. F. Sloan was there with his foreboding song, "Eve of Destruction." The folk singer Richie Havens presented "Lives in the Balance," and kept insisting, "The people are not informed. They're not listening."

"Richie Havens is a great artist," I replied. "But, Richie, I don't agree with you. I think the nation is most informed by both TV and radio, and that the nation *is* listening."

I believed that these protesters were on the wrong side of the fence on this issue. We, along with other UN troops, were there to liberate a little country and protect the others in that region. I think that it was necessary to prevent the entire oil-rich Persian Gulf from falling under the control of a dictator. It was imperative that Saddam Hussein be prevented from putting the finishing touches on his nuclear warfare capabilities. Utmost care was taken to keep losses to a minimum, even among the enemy troops, and all of them who surrendered were promised humane treatment.

Not long after that Geraldo Rivera segment, we gave a Welcome Home to the Troops show in San Angelo, Texas. After the concert a solid, Hispanic-looking man walked up to our bus. Reaching inside his shirt pocket, he handed me some dollar-size slips of paper.

"These are surrender leaflets," he said, holding out the strange paper bills. "They're from the Persian Gulf." Tanned and rugged beside his delicate wife, he looked like a seasoned soldier.

"I'm Army: First Cavalry. Fort Hood, Texas," he went on. "I was patrolling along the Kuwaiti border. It was 3:00 A.M., and I had on my headphones, listening to my Walkman. Your show from Disney came on, and it felt like being at home, just hearing music from the States. Then all at once, these little white leaflets started coming down. They were being pitched out of an allied helicopter. They were blowing around, and I was picking them up."

Looking down at one of his unusual gifts, I saw that it was covered with lines of curiously embellished Arabic writing. At least I guess that was the language! Anyway, on the other side were two pictures. The first showed an Iraqi soldier on the desert, handing over a piece of paper like one of these to an allied soldier. The second was a happy setting: three Iraqi prisoners beside a tent, overseen by their friendly guard. They were sitting around trays of fruit, bread, pitchers and cups, presumably enjoying their first meal in a long time.

"I've never seen one of these," I told him. "Thanks for bringing them." Folding them carefully, I slid the bills down into my pocket, resolving to place them in my collections of memorabilia at home in Nashville. Along with the patriotic treasures and keepsakes that had found their way to me during a multitude of shows, these represented the pride of Americans all over the world.

That same concert brought another surprise. Kip came backstage to tell me, "Hey, Lee. Look what someone just gave me. The guy looked like he had been in Saudi, and he just walked up and handed them to me. I hardly finished saying, 'Thank you very much,' when he disappeared."

"Well, look at this!" I carefully turned over the three bronze bracelets. One was engraved with the words, "Operation Desert Storm, and the second said, "God Bless the U.S.A.—Lee Greenwood." But my face darkened as I read the inscription on the third: "Major Thomas F. Koritz, USAF—Illinois. Missing—January 16, 1991. IRAQ."

This was an MIA bracelet. Kip reached over and slowly put it on his wrist. America had moved from the two World Wars, through Korea and others, to Vietnam . . . and now to another war—with more POWs and MIAs for families to agonize over. There's no way we'll forget them. Glancing down at the red band of steel on my own arm, I thought of John Consolvo, Jr. Realizing that he was only two years younger, I wished that we could have been buddies. If I had known him, I would have called him "Jack." That's what his family and friends always called him.

Jack was born into the service. When he arrived at the beginning of 1944, his father was an Army captain, serving with Gen. George Patton's infantry. They were getting ready to back up the Normandy Invasion to set Europe free from Hitler's troops. So it was only natural for Jack to follow his father's path in a military career. On the day he graduated from the United States Naval Academy, he was commissioned as a Marine, to be trained at Pensacola as a jet pilot.

Jack came home from his first tour in Vietnam with the Distinguished Flying Cross for heroism in combat, the Bronze Star for nineteen air support missions under hostile fire, and many other medals. But the year of shore duty quickly passed, and not long after his twenty-eighth birthday, Marine Capt. John Consolvo, Jr., returned to Southeast Asia for his second tour. His Fighter Wing had been in Da Nang only a few weeks. It was before sunrise on May 7 that the first pilots and their navigators, or Radar Intercept Officers, gathered for intelligence briefings on the day's missions. They flew the F-4J, a small, highly maneuverable two-seater. Drawing midafternoon flights, Jack and his RIO, Chief Warrant Officer Jim Castongua, and the crew of a second F-4J, Capt. George Mayer and 1st Lt. Richard Stearns, were dressed in full flight gear as they listened to their final instructions.

"You are designated as Bootleg 5-1 and 5-2," the four Marines were told. "The target is in the lower panhandle of North Vietnam. It's a suspected Surface to Air Missile storage depot, ten miles north of the DMZ. We'll have your Air Force Strike Leader mark it with white phosphorous smoke rockets just before you come in. He's Maj. Paul Robinson, your Tiger Forward Air Controller, and he'll be flying an F-4E, with the designation Seafox 01. Major Robinson will be providing an on-site assessment.

"You'll be making two runs per aircraft," the briefing officer continued. "On the first run, drop your MK-82s. Come back with the rock eyes. Then head for home."

"Bootleg 5-2 is off the runway before us," Jack said to Jim, as they left the briefing room and headed for their plane. "We'll be in the air at 1445 hours." In the casual tone of his voice there wasn't even a hint of the perilous mission they were facing.

As always, the pilot and RIO went through the final "walk around." With that completed, Jim climbed into the second seat, attached his oxygen hose, and fastened his seat harnesses as Jack secured himself in the front seat. They finished their preflight checklist, then closed the canopy. Soon the F-4J rolled down the airstrip and took to the sky.

"We're airborne," Jim radioed to ground control. "Heading for flight level twenty," he said, indicating they were going to an altitude of 20,000 feet. "Will rendezvous with Seafox One east of Quang Tri City."

"Roger, Bootleg One. Da Nang AB out."

Soon the radio crackled, "Bootleg One, this is Seafox One.

Proceed inbound. The target is in a high threat area," Major Robinson called. "Here goes a pass by the target," he added.

As Robinson's plane swooped down, releasing its first phosphorous rockets above the slender enemy SAMs, it became obvious that the missiles were mounted on transporters, so they could be easily moved to zero in on American planes.

"This is Seafox. Your targets are loaded on trailers and some tractors down there, Bootleg One. I'm going in for one more smoke run. Then it's all yours."

Again the white-hot phosphorous lit up the ragged terrain, pinpointing the scattered vehicles with their missile loads. The F-4E swooped past the cluster of war machinery at minimum altitude, then shot up into the western sky.

"No ground fire encountered, Bootleg," came the report. "Roll in on an east-to-west heading. Your safest bailout area is to the west, in the karst."

"Roger, Seafox," Jack replied. "Closing in on target." The F-4J made its pass and swooped up toward the midafternoon sun.

"Jim, I think our ordnance failed to release. Did you see the impact?" Jack asked his RIO.

"No. But our wingman is ready to unload his MK-82s, and we're set for our second pass," came the answer.

"Off-dry, Bootleg One," called Major Robinson.

"Roger, Seafox," Jack replied.

"Bootleg Two. All clear," radioed the FAC.

"Coming in, Seafox," called out George, as he nosed his plane down toward the target, releasing six bombs, then zoomed up to 14,000 feet.

"Second load armed," reported Jack, confirming that all switches were recycled. "We're ready to go," he said, as he rolled his plane in from the north.

All at once, thirty rounds of 37 MM anti-aircraft artillery burst from the area east of the target. The flak hit the plane, sending a violent shudder through the cockpit.

As Jack pulled up from the target, his left engine fire-warning light flashed on. "We've been hit! Our left engine light is on!" he shouted. "We're on afterburners in the right engine. Still showing 500 knots."

"Bootleg!" shouted Seafox, who was accelerating to a distance of two miles behind. "Shut down that left engine! The exhaust is flaming! It's coming apart! Head southwest for bailout, in the karst!"

"Roger, we're shutting it down." Jack had already pulled the fire-wall shutoff handle, waited the required few seconds, and hit the firebottle switch. But suddenly the jet made two violent yaws to the right.

Then in a firm, low voice, Jack said to his RIO, "Jim, I'm having trouble controlling her. But we're staying as long as I can hold her up here."

A mile and a half behind, from a 25-degree angle, their wingmen, George and Richard, were following Bootleg One out of the target area. They could see fuel streaming from under the left side of the plane.

"Is that right engine holding, Jack?" asked Jim.

"So far. I'm climbing. I'll try to hold her steady 'til we're over a safe area."

But immediately the plane's nose pitched downward. It was still at 13,000 feet, as it began a rapid roll to the right, burning in flight. As this slowed its forward motion, the F-4E overshot the stricken aircraft. Robinson pulled his plane into a tight left turn to keep it in sight. "Bootleg! Bail out!" he yelled.

"Jim! Get out! Get out!" came Jack's simultaneous call.

Jim grabbed the ejection handle and pulled. An automatic explosion was set off beneath his seat. First the canopy blew away. Then he was shot violently upward. As the ejection sequence was completed, Jim felt the wrenching jolt of his chute opening.

Throughout this process, he had lost sight of the plane. Now he could see it headed downward, beyond him. By this time, it was engulfed in flames. Then he saw the flame-crested fireball of the impact, as the falling plane smashed violently into the terrain below.

Searching the sky for another chute, Jim thought, "I'm sure Jack ejected. I just know he got out of that plane!"

"Seafox. This is Bootleg Two," came the wingman's urgent call. "Can we help?" But there was no answer. "King twenty-six! King twenty-six! This is Bootleg Five-two. Five-one is down. Take note of her position. We'll remain in orbit, feet-wet, awaiting SAR instructions," George Mayer said, signaling to a plane arriving on the scene, and reporting that his craft was in danger of ditching in the ocean if its fuel got much lower. Neither he nor his RIO had seen any sign of ejections from the flaming aircraft. Now they saw only a tower of smoke rising from the spot where their sister plane had crashed, south of the DMZ. Although it was in South Vietnam, there were Vietcong troops throughout this region. They hoped the Search and Rescue planes could come in quickly.

While he was attempting to follow the incapacitated aircraft, from his position in the F-4E, Major Robinson had watched the canopy fly off and had seen Jim's chute floating downward as the still level plane lost altitude. Then it became inverted, in a nose-low position, as it dropped for impact.

Almost immediately a second FAC appeared on the scene.

"Seafox One, this is Seafox Six. Over."

"Roger, Seafox Six," Major Robinson answered. "Bootleg One impacted. I observed one chute. I had to jettison some of my stores to increase loiter time, but I've got to depart the area now. I'm running out of fuel."

"Ready to assume on-scene command, Seafox One. We observed set-down of the first chute. We'll look for the other pilot."

With that, the new team began Search and Rescue efforts for the downed crew. Before long, they had radio contact with Jim. A team of American aircraft searched the entire area again and again for the missing jet pilot, but found nothing. Jack Consolvo's name was placed on the long list of our servicemen in the category of limbo: Missing in Action.

> *From the lakes of Minnesota, to the hills of Tennessee,*
> *Across the plains of Texas, from sea to shining sea,*
> *From Detroit down to Houston, and New York to L.A.,*
> *Well, there's pride in every American heart,*
> *And it's time we stand and say—*
> *That I'm proud to be an American, where at least I know I'm*
> *   free.*

The men and women in uniform were from cities far across the country. And all of them had just returned from the Persian Gulf. Filling the huge coliseum in Los Angeles, they were there for the ABC special, "Welcome Home, America." Among them were former POWs and their families. The grateful Kuwaiti government had financed their trip to California.

Tom Selleck walked out on the star-spangled stage, and looking across the vast room to acknowledge the assemblage of America's Army, Navy, Air Force, Marines, and Coast Guard, he said, "If ever there was an audience that embodied the best in America, this is it!" Then he said, "I see two architects of the plan to get our troops overseas and back with a minimum of loss and maximum of support, Secretary of Defense Cheyney and Chairman of the Joint Chiefs of Staff Gen. Colin Powell."

As these two men nodded to accept the applause, Selleck continued, "And I see two presidents who are famous for their patriotism, Gerald R. Ford and Ronald Reagan. . . . And now, another President who has made America stand tall, the President of the United States, George Bush and Mrs. Bush!" With that, the President and his wife walked into the theater, to the strains of "Hail to the Chief."

The President brought a personal message to those who served in the Persian Gulf: "Where *did* we find such men and women? From the heart of America. You *are* the heart of America."

One of our country's outstanding vocalists, Frank Sinatra, was introduced by his longtime title, "Chairman of the Board," to sing "That's America to Me." Comedian Steve Martin gave the stand-up routine that he had brought to our troops in the Persian Gulf, and the Pointer Sisters presented a medley reminiscent of World War II. We watched the "Star Search" acrobat/breakdancers Four Boys and a Babe, and were surprised to see Tony Danza actually tap-dance! Then the atmosphere became more serious when Roger Moore presented heartwarming scenes of the USS *Saratoga* arriving home in Jacksonville, with hordes of families giving way to their deepest emotions.

It was a night overflowing with feelings, ranging from deep understanding of the tragedies of war to the exhilaration of a victory celebration. There were jokes from Martin Russell, and Tony Orlando led everyone in "Tie a Yellow Ribbon." Sandy Patti sang "I Want the Peace, I Want the Love," and Bob Hope smiled and waved at the expressions of thanks for his fifty years of service with our USO. Even the macho form of Arnold Schwarzenegger was subdued, almost mellow. When John Forsythe walked forward to center stage, he began, "On a recent interview on '20/20,' Barbara Walters asked General Schwarzkopf what he did the night of our invasion. This is what he said. . . ."

On the giant screen behind Forsythe, a video of Gen. Norman Schwarzkopf appeared. In response to Ms. Walters' question, the general paused, and then he answered, "The chaplain was there. I had the chaplain say a little prayer for the protection of our servicemen and-women. And then we played Lee Greenwood's 'God Bless the U.S.A.' We did. Everybody who knows me, knows I love that song. And then we said, 'Okay. Now let's get to work!' "

John Forsythe broke through the cheers from the crowd to say, "No entertainer has ever had a better introduction than that. Here's the man who wrote and first performed 'God Bless the U.S.A. . . .' "

It was time for me to come forward and sing, with the newly revised video of "God Bless the U.S.A." flickering on the enormous screen behind me. Medals commemorating our space heroes and the men we've lost in battle had been pinned on my white jacket, which has *USA* emblazoned down each sleeve. My red bracelet, with its inscription, *John Consolvo, Jr.,* caught the reflection of the spotlights. I glanced out into the vast expanse of upturned faces.

Out there among the sea of military notables was a remarkable lady. Maj. Rhonda Leah Cornum, an Army flight surgeon, had been released with the other POWs early in March. She had walked down the plane's ramp with both arms in slings, evidence of the grinding crash that she had been lucky to survive. Major Cornum had served with the

229th Battalion out of Fort Rucker. In Saudi Arabia, they were attached to the 101st Aviation Brigade, and she was always eager to volunteer for any duty whenever it came up. The airmen she worked with respected her courage and ability, considering her one of their own. Among themselves, they called her "Doc Cornum," and there were times when they were plenty worried about her safety.

Then one night an F-16 was shot down by anti-aircraft guns over Iraqi territory. The pilot was reporting his position as his plane headed in. Suddenly an explosion told the listening pilots that he was down.

"There's a chance that he got out," they hoped. A Search and Rescue crew was needed in case the pilot was alive. As usual, the major was quick to volunteer. So she climbed aboard the Black Hawk, a lift helicopter that transports personnel and equipment, and headed with the SAR team for the downed aviator.

As the Black Hawk reached deep behind enemy lines, volleys of shots flew up from the dark sand drifts below.

"We're taking heavy fire!" the chopper's pilot called out.

There was a short silence, then a deafening *boom!*

The helicopter had careened headfirst into the rock-strewn desert sand. Its fuselage crumbled, cracking almost completely in half.

"We've got a Hawk down!" shouted one of the pilots who was monitoring the ongoing battle.

Information was sketchy, as the word filtered back to the 229th and the 101st. Her comrades were concerned about the whole crew, but mostly they worried about the major.

"Doc's down! Doc Cornum's down in Iraq!"

"Man! She's got no business being behind enemy lines!"

"She shouldn't be out there. But she's the type that'd do anything . . . so gung ho." It was spoken almost like a rebuke from a friend who felt especially protective.

"Doc volunteers for everything!" her buddies agreed, afraid that this was one dangerous mission too many for their friend.

Then a report came back: "Looks like nobody made it."

"Oh, God! SAR better get out there!"

When rescue planes did get to the crash site, they found an appalling sight. The bodies of five crew members were strewn near the remnants of their crushed Black Hawk. But there was no sign of the other three.

The SAR team started searching through the wreckage.

"Their flight gear's here!" yelled one of them. "It's intact! And there's no blood! They've *got* to be alive!"

After rummaging through the debris, he said, "And someone's gone through the first aid kit! They must have been taken by the Iraqis, but we can't be sure."

After identifying the bodies of those who were KIA, military officials listed Major Cornum as one of the three who had vanished, an MIA. Americans who had been shocked with the capture of our first female POW, Army Specialist Melissa Rathbun-Nealy, felt the uneasiness of knowing that Saddam's forces were, in all probability, holding another of our military women.

With the abrupt end of the war, it was a relief to see our POWs set free, and we were overjoyed to learn that Major Cornum and the other two crew members from the Black Hawk were among them. The returning POWs were in better condition than we had feared. When a reporter asked the Army doctor, "How did you hold up during your ordeal?" she answered, "I held up fine until we were coming home on the plane. I had heard about the video for the troops, and I was worried that when they played 'God Bless the U.S.A.,' I wouldn't be able to keep it together."

That night in our "Welcome Home, America" audience, Maj. Rhonda Cornum's head tilted forward as the words of the song floated out into the hall and ABC's cameras caught her lightly brushing aside those tears.

"And I won't forget the men who died who gave that right to me."

Over 140 allied personnel were killed in the Persian Gulf.

In comparison to other wars, the number is small. But, on a personal level, just one casualty is a very great sacrifice.

"And I'd gladly stand up next to you and defend her still
   today . . ."

The cymbals clashed, and with the words "stand up," it seemed as though everyone in the whole audience rose to their feet. I looked out on a sea of faces and, by the reflected glow of the stage lights, saw thousands of forms tightly holding hands, their arms raised high above their heads.

" 'Cause there ain't no doubt I love this land—"

My clenched fist hit my chest, then struck the air above my head.

"God bless the U.S.A."

Then I called out to the standing, cheering crowd, "Do you feel the pride?!"
Shrill whistles and shouts of "Yea!" answered my question.
Then, walking across the stage, I continued, "Our servicemen and -women are here tonight—and are out there at home along with the rest of the nation, watching this tribute to our champions of freedom. And I want them to see some of the faces in tonight's audience.
"Sing it with me, one more time!" Then glancing back at the band I asked, "Guys, would you help me?"

"And I'm proud to be an American, where at least I know
   I'm free."

As this final chorus rang out again, taking over the evening, everyone rose to their feet again, searching for the words, their arms still reaching upwards. The moment glowed with their exhilaration to be cheering an American triumph. I jumped down from the stage and began walking through the aisle, out into the midst of the singing military men and women, while they swayed to the drum's strong cadence.

"Come on, y'all!" I urged.

One after another, voices joined in, singing with soft timidity at first, then increasing in volume until they sounded out with conviction and pride.

"And I won't forget the men who died who gave that right
   to me."

Because of sacrifices in the past and the people in the emerging democracies who are demanding their individual freedom, this world is changing fast. The will to be free persists. America has founded a legacy that will be victorious, bringing all of us together.

Here, in Los Angeles, flags were waving and the responding voices grew louder, unlocking emotions usually held tightly inside.

Like a scene viewed through a wide-angle lens, the song took over, its volume increasing in a steady crescendo. Then I was completing the final words. As they pounded down in a majestically deliberate beat, the patriotic strength of America reverberated through the night, celebrating a landmark victory in defense of freedom.

"And I'd gladly stand up next to you and defend her still
   today,
'Cause there ain't no doubt I love this land—
God bless the U.S.A."